◈ YAMAHA

これまでのドアの平均身長を30cm以上うわまわる2,335㎜。幅も894㎜と大きく広がりました。ヤマハのビックドア。その圧倒的な存在感は、住まいの第一印象を大きく変えるはず。次のシーンを語るヤマハの、満を持した解答です。従来のモノサシにとらわれない勇気ある家づくりへ。ヤマハビックドアなら、設計が生きます。設計で生かせます。═══ 新製品

あたらしいホームドラマが始まった。
ヤマハ ビッグドア

発想の間口をひろげる、2,335㎜/m。

D0925412

写真のドアはBU-523M-R(L)(南洋杉)

閉ざされたプライベートスペースから、開かれたリラックススペースへ。増築や改築の際にも、バスルームの考え方は確実に見直されはじめています。新しいライフスタイルにマッチした、新しいくつろぎのカタチ。たとえば、大自然のふところに抱かれて、ゆったりとひたる露天風呂の解放感。そんなおおらかさこそ、これからのバスルームの身上であるべきだとヤマハは考えます。そのためにも、ヤマハは思いきった製品開発に取り組んでいます。ヤマハバスなら、設計が生きます。設計で生かせます。

あたらしいホームドラマが始まった。
ヤマハ バス

バスの終点は、露天風呂かもしれない。

●ヤマハドア/ヤマハバスの
お問い合わせは、お近くのヤ
マハホーム用品営業所へ。
北海道営業所011-512-6111
仙台営業所0222-97-0101
東京事務所 03-375-2031
横浜事務所045-212-4841
越ヶ谷事務所0489-64-7731
関東事務所0273-27-3327
新潟事務所0252-41-2180
浜松営業所0534-73-8018
名古屋事務所052-782-6161
北陸事務所0762-43-6355

大阪事業所 06-647-1611
四国事務所0878-33-2233
岡山事務所0862-32-8651
広島営業所0822-73-3883
九州事務所092-472-2151
北九州事務所093-592-5874
南九州事務所0992-23-9769

●カタログ請求は、ハガキで
〒104 東京都中央区銀座
7-9-18日本楽器製造株式
会社広告課(ドア=HD-ON
係/バス=HB-ON)係へ。

'81ヤマハホームショウ
8/5(水)・6(木)大阪OMM
写真は新製品SDC-1481(寸法:幅1,476×奥行1,476×高さ625㎜ 容量:400ℓ 色:ルビー)

SPORTY & ELEGANCE

BORGO

菱屋 ◇ HISHIYA

【ボルゴ】：ダンディズムの仕上げに気の利いた皮製品をと、ヒシヤ・オリジナルのボルゴは、極上の材質と入念な縫製技術、洗練のデザインが自慢のレザー・コレクション。リッチなアダルトたちにこそふさわしい贈物といえよう。

JAPAN: CLIMATE, SPACE, AND CONCEPT

日本の風土と建築空間

PROCESS
: Architecture

1981年 8月 1日 発行　第25号

発行者＝宝谷文治

担当編集者＝八木幸二
編集主幹＝一ノ渡勝彦
編集監理＝栄 美智子

アドヴァイザー＝
ナディル・アルダラン（テヘラン）
ジョナサン・バーネット（ニューヨーク）
クレイグ・エルウッド（ロサンゼルス）
R・バックミンスター・フラー（フィラデルフィア）
ビル・N・レイシイ（ニューヨーク）
ディヴィッド・ルイス（ピッツバーグ）
槇文彦（東京）
イサム・ノグチ（ニューヨーク）
シーザー・ペリ（ニューヘヴン）
バーナード・ルドフスキー（マラガ）
ピーター・スミスソン（ロンドン）

発行所＝
株式会社 プロセス アーキテクチュア
東京都文京区小石川3-1-3
電話　東京(03)816-1695・1696
振替　東京6-57446　郵便番号112

印刷・製本＝
共同印刷株式会社
取次店＝
東販　日販　大阪屋　栗田出版販売　誠光堂

表紙デザイン＝丸茂喬司＋芳賀寿一
ロゴタイプ・デザイン＝脇田愛二郎

翻訳＝日野水 信
　　　伊藤真一
　　　小堀 徹

定価＝2,900円　送料＝350円

禁無断転載

CONTENTS ●目次

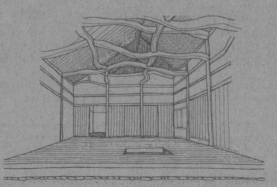

Front Cover: Hirose House (see pp.65-82).
Photo: Haruo Hirota
表紙：旧廣瀬家住宅．　写真：廣田治雄
Back Cover: House with an Architecturalized Ying-Yan Symbol by Monta Mozuna
裏表紙：住川邸．設計：毛綱モン太

PROCESS
: Architecture

Number 25

Publisher
Bunji Murotani

Editor in Charge
Koji Yagi

Editorial Director
Katsuhiko Ichinowatari

Managing Editor
Michiko Sakae

Advisors
Nader Ardalan, Teheran
Jonathan Barnett, New York
Craig Ellwood, Los Angeles
R. Buckminster Fuller, Philadelphia
Bill N. Lacy, New York
David Lewis, Pittsburgh
Fumihiko Maki, Tokyo
Isamu Noguchi, New York
Cesar Pelli, New Haven
Bernard Rudofsky, Malaga
Peter Smithson, London

Process : Architecture is published by
Process Architecture Publishing Co.,
Ltd., Tokyo, and Printed in Japan by
Kyodo Printing Co., Ltd., Tokyo.

Executive and Editorial
3-1-3 Koishikawa, Bunkyo-ku, Tokyo,
Japan.
Tel : (03)816-1695·1696

Copyright © August 1981 by Process
Architecture Publishing Co., Ltd.,
Tokyo, Japan.
All right reserved.

Distribution in U.S.A. and Canada
Eastview Editions, Inc.
Box 783
Westfield, New Jersey 07091, U.S.A.
Tel : (201)233-0474

Cover Design
Takashi Marumo
Toshikazu Haga

Logotype Design
Aijiro Wakita

Translater
Melissa Mukai

ISBN 0-89860-058-8

編集言

明治以来100余年，鎖国を解いた日本の近代化は急激に進んできた．

初期には西洋文化一辺倒となって煉瓦の建物をつくり，部屋の中でも靴をはこうとした人々も，次第に日本個有の伝統，習慣を再認識するようになってきた．組積造が地震に弱く，雨の多い国で靴をはいたまま室内に入ると泥土を持ち込むから，という理由からだけではない．もっと根源的な生活習慣や空間概念の違いがあり，異質な文化と同化出来る面もあるが，どうしても異なる点もあるからだ．

日本に来る外国人が，現実の日本を見て，本や写真から得た知識との相異に驚くことが多い．東京のような大都会でまず目につくのは西洋的建築群であり，それもおもちゃ箱をひっくり返したような大混乱である．これは必ずしも建築や庭園に関してだけでなく，衣，食，住，全般にわたっている．きものを着て，すしやテンプラを食べ，美しい日本庭園のある家に住んでいるはずの日本人が，洋服を着てハンバーグを食べ，コンクリートの箱に住んでいるのだから観光案内書に騙されたと感じるのも無理はない．

こうした初期のショックに耐え，日本に長く住み，日本建築の一側面を研究している外国人が次第に増えてきた．外国語で得られる資料は乏しく，むずかしい日本語を学んでも文献を沢山読みこなすのは大変なことである．従って彼等の見解は時として歴史的事実に反することもあるが，大変ユニークな意見であり，私達が見過ごしているような点を示唆していることが多い．

私はかねがね，こうした若い外国人研究者がその研究成果を発表する機会に恵まれていないのは残念だと思っていた．また，日本建築に関する資料が外国語で出版される場合，その多くが正統な歴史書であったり，現代建築に関するものであり，もっと，部分的でもよいからユニークな論があってもよいと考えていた．

丁度このプロセス・アーキテクチュアは，単行本でもなく，月刊雑誌でもない，その中間的性格を備えた出版であり，一つのテーマのもとに何人かが集まって一冊を作ることができるので，旧知の外国人5人に参加してもらい，その仲間の日本人も数人加わって本書を作った．

序文を書いて下さった清家清先生はかつて東京工業大学，現在は東京芸術大学の教授であり，私達全員がどちらかの大学で教えて頂いた師であります．いつも暖かく見守り適切な助言をして下さり，私達全員感謝の念に耐えません．

（八木幸二）

NOTE FROM THE EDITOR

Japan has modernized with exceeding rapidity in the over one hundred years since its opening from seclusion in the Meiji era.

During the first infatuation with Western ideas, some urged the building of brick buildings, others recommended wearing shoes inside the house, and so on, until now the pendulum has swung the other way. Gradually Japan's individual traditions and customs have come to be re-evaluated. It is not just because masonry construction is weak in earthquakes and wearing shoes inside the house in a rainy country like Japan simply tracks in mud. There are more fundamental differences in notions of space and lifestyle, and while there are elements of a foreign culture which can be assimilated, there are also many elements which will always differ.

Foreigners coming to Japan and seeing its true condition are often surprised at how much it differs from what they have read. The first thing that strikes one in viewing metropolises like Tokyo is that, although the buildings are largely western by type, the order is so confused as to look like an upset box of toys. This is not due solely to architecture and landscape, but to clothes, food, and housing as well. It's no wonder that tourists may feel cheated by travel lures touting a land of kimono, sushi, tempura and homes with beautiful traditional gardens, only to find upon arrival a populace that wears western clothes, eats hamburgers, and lives in concrete boxes.

The number of visitors to Japan who have not only survived this initial shock but have stayed to live a long time in Japan and study traditional architecture has gradually increased. Sources in other languages are scarce and it is a formidable task to learn Japanese and digest reference material here. The interpretations of these foreigners, though at times going against the facts of history, are unique, and they bring to our attention some things which we ourselves may have little noticed.

I have long thought it regrettable that there has not been an opportunity to publish the results of the research of these young scholars. Of the materials in other languages published about Japanese architecture, the majority are orthodox histories, or restrict themselves to contemporary architecture only, and for the most part seem content with only parts of the whole and heedless of authors' perhaps too-individual opinions.

PROCESS: ARCHITECTURE is a publication which holds a position somewhere between book and monthly magazine and can bring together the work of a number of people on a single theme. This issue contains the work of five foreigners and some Japanese associates.

We have tried to be neither too academic nor simply to present a collection of photographs, but rather to present a selection of informative, readable papers. Among them may be some items which, strictly speaking, are not accurate, but we beg the reader's indulgence in recognizing our aim.

Professor Kiyosi Seike, who wrote the Introduction, was formerly a professor at Tokyo Institute of Technology and is now a professor at Tokyo University of Fine Arts and has instructed each of us at one time or another at both of these universities. He has always given us warm and appropriate counsel, for which we are deeply indebted to him. (Koji Yagi)

CLIMATE AND NATURE OF JAPAN
photos by Haruo Hirota

日本の風土
撮影：廣田治雄

旧野原家住宅（日本民家園）Nohara House, Open-air Museum of Traditional Houses.

↑石川県白山麓　The foot of Mt. Hakusan.

↓石川県能登半島福浦　Fukura, Noto, Ishikawa Prefecture.

↑石川県能登半島高屋　Takaya, Noto, Ishikawa Prefecture.

↓長野県姫川地方　Himekawa, Nagano Prefecture.

奈良県飛鳥地方　Asuka, Nara Prefecture.

↑石川県能登半島甲　Kabuto, Noto, Ishikawa Prefecture.

↓富山県滑川市　Namerikawa, Toyama Prefecture.

↑石川県尾口村　Oguchi, Ishikawa Prefecture.

↙↓石川県能登半島宇出津　Ushitsu, Noto, Ishikawa Prefecture.

石川県能登半島富来　Togi, Noto, Ishikawa Prefecture

↑石川県白山麓　The foot of Mt. Hakusan.

↓長崎県天草　Amakusa, Nagasaki Prefecture.

↑↓奈良県今井町　Imai-cho, Nara Prefecture.

奈良県明日香村　Asuka, Nara Prefecture.→
↑↓奈良県今井町　Imai-cho, Nara Prefecture.

京都市祇園　Gion, Kyoto.

A CULTURE OF WOOD
by Kiyosi Seike

木の文化
清家 清

わが国は国土が森林に恵まれていたことから，ほとんどが木造建築で，わが国ほど木造建築の技巧の発達した国はない．古代仏教などとともに大陸から輸入された建築技術の成果は法隆寺，唐招提寺，薬師寺，新薬師寺などとして現存している．これ等は現存する世界最古の木造建築群である．当時すでに倭人は独自のすぐれた技術をもっていた．出雲大社は現存するものでさえ高さは30メートルに近いが，史前はそれをはるかに上まわる巨大なものであったという．

このように倭人が優れた技術を生み出し，また海外から伝来した技術をこなすことができたのはひとつにはわが国が美しい森林国であったことがあげられる．その辺の事象までは現存する古建築とか記録文献に頼ることが可能であって，誰しもが認めるところである．東大寺の大仏殿は現在でも世界最大の木造建築である

Japan is favored with many forests and most of her architecture has been of wood; there is almost no other country where the architecture of wood is so advanced. The oldest group of wood buildings in the world, the temples of Horyu-ji, Toshodai-ji, Yakushi-ji and Shinyakushi-ji, are evidence of the building skills that came to Japan with Buddhism in the sixth century and the excellence of the native Japanese craft of the time. The Izumo Taisha Shrine is reputed to have been by far the largest building before written records, and just what remains of it today measures nearly thirty meters in height.

It is generally accepted, and verified by ancient buildings and written documents, that one reason the Japanese were able to create so skillfully and to assimilate techniques from abroad was the existence in Japan of beautiful forests. The Great Buddha

東大寺南大門．South gate of Todai-ji Temple.

が，当初は現在のものの1.5倍も大きかったというから当時の壮大さが偲ばれよう．その巨大な建築物をたてるための木材が供給できたということは，大仏殿が創建された8世紀頃のヤマト帝国の森林資源は勿論，再度の炎上とその再建の資材を調達し得た森林について考えてみるだけでもわが国には美林が多かった．現在のものは3度目の建築で宝永6年（1709）落慶供養が行われた．
　（大仏殿は751年に第1回の大仏殿が完成した．1180年戦火で焼失．第2回の大仏殿は1195年．1567年再び内戦で焼失．現在のものは1708年に竣工．翌年落慶法要が行われた．創建当時のものは屋根の大きさは間口が100メートル以上，高さは60メートル近くあった．法隆寺の金堂や五重の塔は prehistoric で建立年代が正確に判らぬほど古い）．
　現在でもわが国の建築用材は主として松・杉・檜などの針葉樹

が主力で，国産以外にも米材とか北洋材と称している針葉樹も多く輸入されている．古い建築も主として針葉樹で，本当の木材という意味の真木（マキ）というのは現在の檜とも杉ともいわれている．スギはマッスグな木という意味で直木（スキ）と漢字を当てているが，檜やアスナロなど針葉樹を総称していた．
　また木は日本釈名によれば「木は生（イキ）るである．イを略してキという．また，気の生い出でる意」とある．古来，木はキともケとも発音した．少しく駄洒落めくが円珠庵雑記によると，「むかしはけという素盞嗚尊は身の毛を抜きて投げ給えるがさまざまの木となる故なり」とある．木と毛が同じ発音ということで牽強附会のきらいもあってあまり信用できないが，気晴しの間奏にもうひとつ．

Hall of Todai-ji temple is the largest wooden structure in the world today and the original structure was half again the size of the current building. The forests of eight-century Kingdum of Yamato must have been impressive to provide the resources to build something as large as the Great Buddha Hall and then to rebuild it each time it burned. The current Hall is actually the second reconstruction, dedicated in 1709.

Common Ancestry of Japanese and South American Indians

The other day I received a poster proclaiming "Brothers are All People", and parody of the popular commercial, "People are All Brothers". When we see the great physical differences among races, though, we may wonder how close the relationship is.

Japanese may, however, find among Pacific Islanders and South American Indians, all classed as Mongoloid races, those whom they may easily feel are truly relations.

It is accepted theory that the American Indians are descendents of Mongoloid peoples who crossed the Bering Straits tens of thousands of years ago, and recently among photographs of naked tribes of the Amazon, I saw one woman who looked so much like my sister that I had to laugh. All indians, at any rate, are brothers.

Next, I'd like to offer one of my own hypotheses

Foot prints, some several thousand years old, have been found

神明社，長野. Typical shrine in forest.

山と平野と住宅. Hill, field and house, designed by k. seike

インディオと日本人は同祖

先日，「兄弟は皆人類」という標語のポスターをもらった．例の「人類は皆兄弟」というテレビのコマーシャルをモヂったパロディのポスターである．兄弟というからには遺伝の法則に従ってもっと似てほしいと思うが，同じ人類でも白人や黒人を兄弟と言うには少しく抵抗がある．

しかし，東アジアから太平洋の島々，アメリカ大陸の原住民はモンゴロイドと総称されているだけあって，これ等の地を旅行していると兄弟といってもおかしくない原住民に遭うことがある．

定説では，アメリカインディアンは数万年前にベーリング海峡を渡ってアメリカに移り住んだモンゴロイドということになっている．アマゾンの裸族の写真を見せてもらったなかに，私の妹そ

っくりのオバさんがいて，大笑いをした．インディオは皆兄弟である．

ところで，ついでに憶説を開陳してお笑い種にしてみたい．というのは，最近日本列島にも何万年も前の人跡が発見されている．そうだとすると，私の妹そっくりのアマゾンの裸族のオバサンのルーツと，私のルーツが蒙古のどこかで一緒になって不思議でない．インディオと日本人は同祖であるという憶説である．

例えば，インディオの都邑はインカにしてもマヤにしても，すべて山の中にあった．日本の古都もヤマト，あるいはヤマシロにあった．

on the Japanese archipelago. When I read that, I though it not impossible to imagine my roots and those of that Amazonian woman who looked so much like my sister crossing somewhere in Mongolia. Japanese and South American Indians have a common ancestry.

For example, many Indian cities and villages from the Incas to the Mayas, are found in the mountains. The ancient cities of Japan were all in Yamato or Yamashiro, province names incorporating the word for "mountain", *yama.*

A Culture Born in Mountains

Although it is called an island nation, perhaps Japan should really be called a mountain nation. The country is actually 80% mountains and covered by forests. I haven't made a study of this so the following may all be simply conjecture. My wife is from the Tokyo area and uses the Tokyo dialect, and she tells me that even though it is a plain, forests are called *yama,* which also means "mountain", here. Perhaps, then, in ancient Japan *yama* had little to do with mountains or plains but with the presence of woods. Looking at it in this light, there is the feeling that Yamato and Yamashiro were closely connected with forests. The beliefs of the Japanese and those of the Indians would appear to date back thousands of years to a common ancestry.

Japan is a land of much rain with four distinct seasons and temperate-zone forests, and the beautifully grained wood grown here is probably partly responsible for the primacy of wood architecture in Japan. Whether Yamato or Yamashiro, this im-

桂離宮. Katsura Detached Palace.

ヤマに生まれた文化

海国日本というものの，本当は山国日本ではなかろうか．実際に国土の80％は山地で森林に覆われている．詳しく調査もしていないので共通語ではないかも知れぬが，愚妻は関東平野の産で，関東平野の方言を使う．彼女に言わせると平野にあっても林はヤマである．古来日本語でヤマというのは山地とか平地にかかわらず，森林をヤマと言ったのではなかろうか．そういうことから考えてみると，ヤマトにしろ，ヤマシロにしろ古来森林と深い関係にあったような気がしてくる．

そういうことで，日本人の信仰はインディオのそれと何万年もの昔に溯って同祖のように思えてくる．

特に我が国は雨の多い温帯樹林で，四季がはっきりしているから，木理の美しい建築用材を得やすかったことも我が国に木造建築を定着させる原因となったと考えてよかろう．ヤマトにしてもヤマシロにしても，その帝国の基盤はヤマであった．

神々もヤマに棲み，恋の願いをこめて歌う「伊勢に七度，熊野に三度，愛宕山には月参り」というのは今も唱えられていて，ヤマト，ヤマシロの森林地帯である．伊勢・熊野をテリトリーとしている尾鷲測候所（34°04' N，139°39' E）の月降水量，気温は次表の通りである（伊勢神宮には太陽の女神．熊野神宮は夜と愛の神神．愛宕神社は火神と，火神の母である女神が祭祀されている）．

		1月	2月	3月	4月	5月	6月	7月	8月	9月	10月	11月	12月	総量
雨量	mm	101	120	215	367	358	531	458	559	631	482	218	117	4158
気温	℃	5.5	5.9	8.7	13.5	17.4	20.9	24.8	26.7	22.7	17.3	12.5	7.8	—

perial nation was based on *yama*.

Japan's gods lived in the mountains, or *yama*, too, and the plea for love expressed in the refrain, "Seven times to Ise, three times to Kumano and every month to Atago-san," refers to shrines in the Yamato, or Yamashiro, forest belt.

The following table shows the average monthly temperature and rainfall at the Oase Weather Station which observes an area including the Ise and Kumano shrines at 34°04′ N and 139°39′ E.

As can be gathered from the above table, trees favored with summer temperatures and rainfall appropriate to the Amazon grow every quickly, and trees that grow in the upper altitudes with snow and hard winters have a lovely grain, like the trees of northern Europe.

The cedar forests of Yoshino are still famous for their beautiful wood. Ise and Kumano are in the Nankaido area with its abundant rainfall, sunshine and mild temperatures, and have lovely trees. The province called Ki-no-kuni, next to Yamato, means Land of Trees.

The Japanese belief in tree, spirits, persisting from the Yamato times, dates back at least as far as the myths of the common ancestors of the Amazon tribes and is a continuation of the belief in the various gods at the Ise, Kumano, and Atago shrines

	JAN	FEB	MAR	APR	MAY	JUN	JUL	AUG	SEP	OCT	NOV	DEC	TOTAL
rain mm	101	120	215	367	358	531	458	559	631	482	218	117	4158
temp °C	5.5	5.9	8.7	13.5	17.4	20.9	24.8	26.7	22.7	17.3	12.5	7.8	

美しい杢目，桂の月見台．Grain, Katsura Detached Palace.

この数表で見る通り，アマゾンに匹敵する雨量と夏の気温に恵まれて樹々はスクスクと伸び，きびしい冬には高地は雪となって，北欧の森林の樹々のように美しい杢目をつくることになる．

いまでも吉野の杉と称する美林．伊勢・熊野はこの豊富な雨量と日照と気温の南海道にあって，美林を育成してきた．ヤマトに隣接して紀の国というのは木の国という意である．

このようにヤマトの昔は勿論，日本人の木に対する信仰はアマゾンの裸族と同祖の神話に溯って，伊勢・熊野・愛宕の諸神に連なるわけで，何万年もの昔から神々の降臨する森や山に深く関係していたにちがいない．

わが国のどこへ行っても木魂についての民話が残されている．日本語の木魂というのは木の精霊という意味であって，樹木が信仰の対象になっている．なかには御神木と言って，神として祭祀

されている樹木さえある．

樹木と一緒に育った文化

わが国の住宅，特に農村などでは屋敷林といって，いろいろな面での防護＝むかしは軍事的な意味を含めて，風雪などの気象環境からの防護，最近では騒音公害などに対しても屋敷林の効果が知られている．これなども日本人の生活が屋敷林などの樹木と一緒に育ってきたことがわかる．しかもこれ等の樹木はすべて人工的な植林であって，多くは樹齢100年を超す巨木である．歴代の家長の植林への熱意が子孫のために残されている．

かつてレバノンはレバノンの杉という極めて良質な杉林を産出し，フェニキア人はそれを使って地中海を征覇する艦隊をもって

and certainly has a very deep relationship with the forests and mountains to which the gods of thousands of years ago descended. Folk songs about wood spirits are heard in every corner of Japan; some have been the object of worship, and of those, some were called "god-trees" and worshipped as gods.

A Culture Nurtured among Trees

Japanese homes, especially those in rural villages, used nearby groves of trees for various types of protection — at one time this included military protection, but also included protection from the climate, wind and snow, and recently they have proved effective in blocking noise pollution as well. The Japanese way of life has developed among residential groves of trees. However,

these trees were all planted by man; some are now over 100 years old and quite large. Through the generations patriarchs have tended these groves with great care, thinking of posterity.

The Phoenicians used the extremely good Lebanese cedars to build their fleets and dominate the Mediterranean area. The caskets of the Egyptian Pharaohs were also carved from single Lebanese cedars. The shrine of Solomon must also have been built of these trees. Now, however, the hills of Lebanon are bare and only few Lebanese cedars remain as natural monuments. No one thought to replant the cedars of Lebanon as they were cut and carted off. Or perhaps they were replanted but in the political instability and wars the management of the forests was interrupted and the mountains all denuded.

The Japanese forebears, on the other hand, loved and revered

いた．またエジプトの歴代王朝の棺もこのレバノンの巨杉を一本でくりぬいてこしらえられた．ソロモンの神殿の建設にも使われたにちがいない．それが今，レバノンの山々はハゲ山と化し，わずかに3本のレバノン杉が天然記念物として残っているだけという．

人びとはレバノンの杉を伐り出したあとに何も植えておかなかった．あるいはだれかが植えたかもしれないが，政治の不安定や戦争で森林の管理が行き届かなくなってハゲ山と化してしまったのだろう．

それに比べ，私たちの祖先は森や山を信仰し愛した．現在われわれが使わせて頂いていると言ったほうがよい材木．例えば，秋田杉にしても尾州の檜にしてもその殆んどは江戸時代に植林されたもので，封建時代からずっと政情も治安も安定していた証である．国民の木魂への信仰，森や山を神域として保護・保存してきた賜である．

木材はまた他の無機の建築材料や近頃の高分子の合成の新建材とはちがって，オルガニックなアニミズム的な信仰の対象になっていた．たとえば，「三十三間堂棟木の由来」という伝説は熊野の森林にあった柳の精が武士の妻となって，子＝緑丸を生み，終末としては三十三間堂（京都の寺院）の棟木となる説話とか，炎上している堂宇の木魂が昇天するという話など，芸術にまで高められた木の神性を木造建築の中に感じることができる．

これは私の神学が幼稚なせいもあろうが，森に棲むインディアンや北欧の森にいる妖精たちと祖を同じくする日本人の森への信仰に由来すると思えてならない．

Japan's forests. Perhaps we should say that we today have been permitted to use these forests: both Akita cedars and Bishu cypress were planted in the Edo period and stand as proof of the continuity of political and social stability from the feudal age to the present. They are the result of the whole nation's protection and preservation of these forests and mountains as the dwellings of gods and the folk beliefs in tree spirits.

Trees were the objects of worship in an organic animism, their wood quite unlike new composite materials appearing recently or other non-organic building materials. Legend has it that the spirit of a tree in a forest in Kumano became the wife of a samurai, had a child, and later became the roof ridge of the Sanjusangendo, a temple in Kyoto; another belief is that the spirits of trees used in temple buildings ascend to heaven when that building is destroyed in fire; the godly nature of trees has been raised to an art which can be felt in the architecture of wood.

My theology may be simplistic, but I feel certain that the origins of the Japanese' belief in forests and her ancestors are the same as those of the forest dwelling Indians and the sprites of the forests of northern Europe.

The Post — the Essence of the Gods

Japanese gods make their descent to earth in the body of trees, in forests, in response to prayer. In Japanese, the counterword for counting gods is "post." The god-nature of trees has more than speculative foundation, then.

大切に運ばれる log. Carrying log.

神々の単位は柱

そういうわけで，日本の神々は樹々に降臨する．人びとが呼ぶと神々は森に降臨することになっている．この国で神々を計数する単位は柱である．これとて木の神性と無縁ではあるまい．

だいたい，木造建築の日本建築は，柱と梁を組立てて建築するシステムで，煉瓦造や石造や，木造でも 2″×4″ や logcabin の壁式構造の西洋建築とは本質的に異なったシステムの工法である．（日本建築では柱が主役であって，西洋建築でいえばギリシャ神殿とかゴシックのカテドラルに似たところがある）．

このように日本では伝統的に木の本質を神性にまで高めていた．例えば，現代語では唯物的に木材産業というが，伝統的には木材商である．日本語の漢字による造語法によれば，形容的な語が頭初となり，主体になる意味のことばは最後にくることになっている．

木材という語が木と材という文字から成りたっていても，材木と木材は根本的に異なったアイデンティティをもった同義語（？）ということになる．

考えてみると，木材ということばのほうが現代的な感じがして，前述したように材木店というのは伝統的な老舗である．面白いことに，木材商は西洋風に木材を横たえてストックしているが，材木商は材木を立ててストックしている．この辺にも伝統的な日本人の木に対する信仰があるようだ．木は生きている．

大工が家を建てるときには，製材された角材でさえ その 元末（根元と梢）を生えていたときの方向に合せる習慣がある．丸太とか押角はともかく正確に長方体に製材されて元末も判らぬ材で

The Japanese architectural system is largely post and beam, essentially different from brick, masonry, or even other Wood systems, such as the Western two-by-four and logcabin constructions.

Through such traditions the Japanese elevated the character of trees to that of gods. For example, current language reduces the old "timber merchant" to merely a part of the "lumber industry." In the Japanese language, using Chinese characters, modifiers appear first and the word-parts of greatest meaning come last. For instance, a cow which gives milk is a "milk-cow;" reversing the characters gives "cow's milk."

The characters for the building material wood can be read both "wood-material" and "material-wood" but, according to the above discussion, the ideas behind the two words are basically different. The word "wood-material" ("wood, among all the other materials available") has a more modern ring, while the older "material-wood-store" ("store of building materials, i.e., wood") conveys the image of the traditional lumber yard. Interestingly, lumber yards in Western countries stack lumber horizontally, while in Japan it is stacked on end, standing; this too betrays the feeling for wood in Japan, where the tree is a living thing.

It is custom for carpenters, when building a house, to install the milled lumber in the direction in which it grew, root end down. In any case, logs are milled the long way such that the original orientation of the wood cannot even be guessed, and the traditional attitude of carpenters that they would like to build with the wood in its original orientation is disappearing in this

Logs.

さえ，そのもとの姿勢で建築したいという大工の伝統的な姿勢も現代的な工業化社会では失われつつある．輸入材が主流の現代的な木材の流通やランバー・インダストリといわれる業界では，そのような因襲的な伝承に依っていては商売にならぬということでもある．集成材や合板で元末を云々することは土台ムリな話ということである．パーティクル材では元末がどうなっているのか皆目わからないではないかということもあろう．しかし，伝承の家相術では，柱の元末を逆にして建てるのは逆さ柱として凶相と信じられている．

　現在，この国で絶対多数を占めている伝統的な和風住宅は，今でもむかしながらの材木店で大工が材木を選んでくる．職人気質の大工は杢目を間取りに合せて，杢目が美しく見える面を居間のほうに向け，美しくない面は背面や真壁のほうに向けるよう目論む．しかし，その職人気質も失われつつあり，材木よりも木材が増えているのは残念なことだ．

清家　清
東京工業大学名誉教授・工学博士．
東京芸術大学教授・美術学部長．
日本建築学会会長．

industrialized society. With imported lumber being the major constituent of the materials currently in use and in the world of the lumber industry, businesses cannot compete with such traditional conventions. And the original orientation of composite materials and plywood cannot be determined. Who can tell which way is up with particle board? Yet to have a post in a traditional house installed upside down is believed to be bad luck.

Even today, in this country where the absolute majority of houses built are of the traditional type, the carpenters still choose their materials from the old lumber yards. Carpenters with a feel for their craft match the grain of the wood with the particular room in which it is put, with the most appealing grain facing the living space, and the least attractive side of the wood member to the back or plastered to a certain depth in the wall *(shin-kabe)*. However, such craftsmanship is being lost, and it is regrettable that *zaimoku* 木材 , "the building material, wood", is being replaced by *mokuzai* 材木 , "wood, as opposed to other materials."

Kiyosi Seike
Professor emeritus, Tokyo Institute of Technology
Dean, Shool of Fine Arts, Tokyo Geijutsu Daigaku.
President, Architectural Institute of Japan.
An author of "Japanese Joinary".

CLIMATE AND THE JAPANESE WAY OF LIFE
by Koji Yagi

日本の風土と住様式
八木幸二

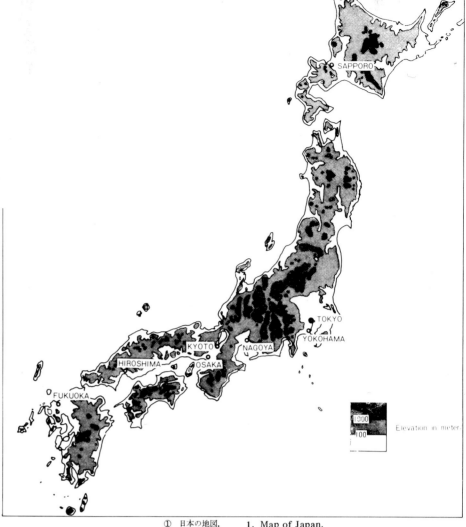

① 日本の地図.　　1. Map of Japan.

風土

アジア大陸の東端に，海をへだてて弓状に細長く連続する島嶼群である日本は，北緯24度〜46度あたりに位置する．これは，北米大陸ならフロリダ半島の先端からモントリオールまで，また，ヨーロッパ（アフリカ）ではサハラ沙漠からリヨンあたりである①②．

このように南北に細長い日本列島は，夏には太平洋高気圧，冬にはシベリア高気圧の影響を強くうけるモンスーン地域であり，亜熱帯から温帯へと四季とりどりの変化に富む．冬は比較的温暖で，乾燥しており，3月から4月にかけて南から北へ咲き進む桜の花が日本中に春の到来を告げる．春の終り，6〜7月にかけてしとしとと降り続く梅雨は2〜3週間続く，南から北へ徐々に梅雨があけると，カンカン照りの夏，

Japan lies between the 24th and 46th parallels in the northern hemisphere, a bow-shaped chain of islands strung through the sea at the eastern edge of the Asian continent. A comparable distance on the American continent would be from the Florida Keys to Montreal or, on the other side of the Atlantic, from the Saharan desert to around Lyon, France (figs. 1, 2).

Japan's narrow archipelago, then, is in a monsoon belt, subject to high pressure systems from the Pacific in summer and from Siberia in winter; as it extends from the sub-tropical to temperate zones, it is rich in seasonal changes. Winters are relatively mild and dry, and in March and April, the cherries bloom, from south to north, announcing Spring. Then in June or July a rainy season follows of two to three weeks. After that passes, again from south to north, comes the hot summer, with a mugginess derived from a temperate zone controlled by hot clind humid Pacific high pressure systems. Late summer and early fall is also the typhoon season, with yearly damage due to local driving rains and strong winds. Real fall begins after the typhoons, when rice fields are harvested,

the leaves on the mountainsides have turned, and festivals celebrating fall are held all throughout Japan.

These seasonal changes have a great influence on a people's way of life, their homes and way of thinking. Looking at the seasons in Japan, there are the four temperate seasons plus the rainy and typhoon seasons, making a rhythm of six seasons affecting lifestyle (fig. 3). There is a saying from *Tsurezuregusa*, or Essays in Idleness, written around 1330, that a house should be designed for summer aside from spring and fall, three of the remaining four seasons are really summer. If a house is designed to bear the demands of rain and humid heat, the body can bear the discomfort of the remaining season, winter.

Openness and Seclusion

Well-ventilated spaces are desired to cope with muggy heat, while closed spaces handle the cold of winter better. There were two main house types in Japanese tradition — the northern continental, pit dwelling (fig. 4) and the southern, high-floored house. The pit dwelling had enclosed spaces while the raised-floor type was relatively open (fig. 5). The

raised floor type was originally used primarily for rice storage, and its use as a house indicated a high social status. Eventually the common house evolved gradually from the pit dwelling to a ground-level building. Then, an enclosed space was devised in the open type by enclosing a room with plastered walls to form a storage room or vault within the open rooms (fig. 6). Movable partitions were then developed to divide the open spaces.

Partitions

The Japanese word for partition, *majikiri*, embodies the characteristics of Japanese architectural space. The first syllable, *ma*, refers to the interval between posts, as well as the space created beneath the roof supported by those posts. *Jikiri* or *shikiri*, the division of space, characteristically occurs in a timber-framed building after the roof is raised, unlike the Western method of building in stone, where the walls separating each room are built first and the roof put in place afterward, making a whole of separate spatial units. This is confirmed by the derivation of the word "partition" from the Latin, pars, or part.

高温で多湿な太平洋高気圧に支配され熱帯的な
蒸し暑さである．夏の後半から初秋にかけて台
風シーズン，局部的大雨と強風による災害は毎
年くり返されている．台風が去ると本格的な秋，
畑では稲穂が稔り，山は紅葉し，日本各地で秋
祭りが行われる．

　このような季節的変化は，人の生活様式，住
居，思考方法などに強い影響を与えていると思
われる．日本に適した季節区分を考えると，い
わゆる寒暖による四季区分にモンスーンの雨季
を加えて，春，梅雨，夏，台風季，秋，冬，の
六季に区分すると生活実感にあう③．「家は夏を
旨とすべし」という徒然草の考え方も，この六
季から快適な春と秋を除いた残りの四季につい
て考えてみれば，その内3季がいわゆる夏であ
り，住まいは雨と蒸し暑さに対処するように作
り，冬は耐えしのべばよいという考えである．

開放性，閉鎖性
蒸し暑さに対処するには風通しのよい開放的空
間がよい．しかし，冬の寒さをしのぐには閉鎖
的な空間の方がよい．日本の住居の源流には，
大陸的，北方的と言われる堅穴住居④と，南方
的と言われる高床住居があったと考えられてい
る．堅穴は閉鎖的空間であり，高床は基本的に
開放的であると言えよう⑤．高床はもともと米

The difference in construction method
and spatial intent is apparent in the
Chinese character and ancient Egyptian
hieroglyph for "house." As shown in
figure 7, the character for house takes the
shape of a section through a roof, with
the symbol below indicating the building's character, while the hieroglyph
takes the shape of a wall seen in plan,
indicating the defined space enclosed by
the walls.

The special characteristic of Japan's
architecture has been the module, based
on the standard size and interval between
posts. This enabled the development of
open space in wood frame construction
with its free plan (fig. 8). The module
was originally intended to accomodate
the construction method, but the movable partitions between the roof supports and the provisional fixtures developed for use within the room were
also designed according to the same
module.

Fittings: Flexible Infill
As the homes of the aristocracy grew in
scale, the open interior spaces grew in
proportion to the enclosed clay-walled
spaces they surrounded, but in the early

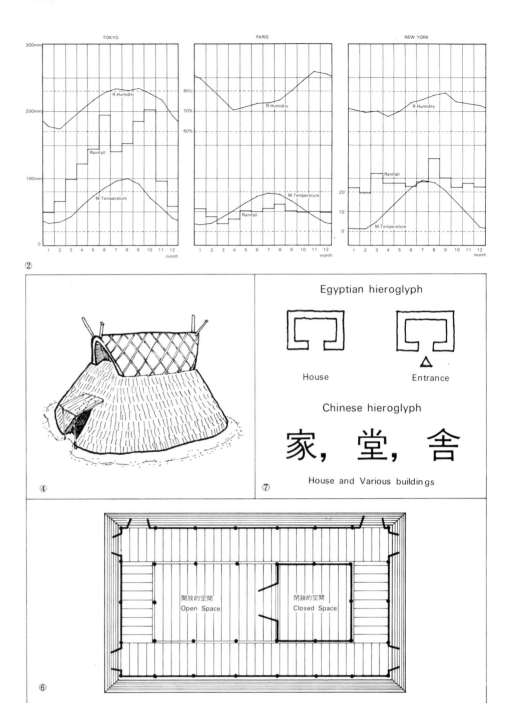

② TOKYO　PARIS　NEW YORK

④

Egyptian hieroglyph

House　Entrance

Chinese hieroglyph

家，堂，舎

House and Various buildings

⑦

開放的空間
Open Space　　閉鎖的空間
Closed Space

⑥

⑤

③

倉が主で，住居としては一部の高貴な人々のものだったと推定され，一般の住居は堅穴から次第に平地住居に移行していった．そして，開放的空間の一部に閉鎖的空間を設ける工夫がなされた⑥．その手法として，開放的な空間の内に塗籠（ぬりごめ）や納戸のような土壁に囲まれた閉鎖的空間を設けた．そして，開放的空間を間仕切るのには，可動な間仕切り類を発展させていった．

間仕切り，パーティション

間仕切りという言葉に日本建築の空間的特性がよく表われている．間は柱と柱の間であり，その柱により架構されている屋根の下の空間でもある．その空間を仕切るということは，木造架構の特徴として，先に屋根を建てあげるからできることであり，西洋建築の源流である組石造建築では逆に各室の壁を構築した後で屋根を架けるのであるから，単位空間の集合によって全体の空間ができあがる．パーティションがラテン語の部分 pars に由来するのも首肯できる．

架構方法，空間概念の違いは，漢字と古代エジプト象形文字における「家」のシンボルにもはっきりと表われている．図⑦に示すように漢字は屋根の立面を象形し，その下にあるシンボルの意味によって建物の特性を示しており，ヒエログリフでは壁の平面を象形し，壁によって閉ざされた空間単位を示している．

このように，開放的で平面計画の自由な木造柱梁構造の空間に規則性を与えるべく発展してきたのが，柱の寸法，柱の間隔を基準とするモジュールであり⑧，日本建築の特質である．これは元来建物を構築するための便宜であったが，その架構の中に鋪設（しつらえ）る可動間仕切りや仮設的な備品にも同じモジュールが用いられるようになった．

鋪設（しつらえ）

貴族の住宅規模が拡大していくにつれて，閉鎖的な塗籠に対して周囲の開放的な空間が拡大したが，初期（平安時代）にはまだ間仕切壁もなく，板の間に列柱があり外周には蔀戸（しとみど）を釣っていた．そこで生活するためには多くの仮設的な設備類を鋪設（しつらえ）ていた．日常生活だけでなく公的儀式，祭祀にも対応する鋪設方（しつらえかた）があり，季節，儀式の種類，客の身分などに応じた細かい約束事ができ，大貴族の家ではそのための専門家，蔵人（くろうど）がいた．

このように季節の変化や状況の変化に応じて空間の大きさや，装飾，備品を変えることができる仮設性は現在まで生きている日本の伝統であり，その原型はすでに中世に発生しているので，ここに当時の鋪設を概観してみる．

② 東京，パリ，ニューヨークの気候．
③ 傘で雨と太陽をさける．
④ 閉鎖的空間．堅穴住居復元（登呂，静岡県）．
⑤ 開放的な柱間．神宮熊野神社の長床（福島県）．
⑥ 閉鎖＋開放的空間
⑦ 家の象形文字．

2. Climate of Tokyo, Paris, and New York.
3. An umbrella (parasol) protects from rain and sun.
4. Enclosed space. Restoration of a pit dwelling. (Toro, Shizuoka Prefecture)
5. Open space between columns. *Nagayuka* of Kumano Shrine, Fukushima Prefecture.
6. Enclosed and open spaces.
7. Hieroglyphic character for "house."

days (the Heian period, 800–1180), there were still no partitioning walls, and the board-floored area was surrounded by posts between which were hung *shitomido,* or halfdoors hinged at the top corners to swing up under the eaves. Life in such buildings was further ordered by the use of accessory equipment. Appropriate fixtures were provided for public functions and festive events as well as daily life, and differentiated by season, nature of the event, status of the guest, etc., and the homes of the greatest of the aristocracy employed a professional, called a *kuroudo,* for coordinating such accessories.

The size and ornamentation of a space could be altered by the use of such fixtures, to respond to changes in the seasons or other conditions. This sense of the provisional, or temporary expedient, is a living tradition in Japan. Since it was already a part of daily life in the middle ages, it may be instructive to survey such fixtures as found today.

1. Floor furnishings: Items laid on the floor for use in sitting or sleeping on board floors, such as reed mats, constructed *tatami* mats, and cushions. Today, rooms are commonly floored wall-to-wall with *tatami,* but originally they were used individually on the wood floor only where needed for sitting or sleeping (fig. 9).
2. Panel partitions: Fixtures attached to or placed within the structure, such as *noren,* ungathered cloth or rope curtains, and independent pieces such as large folding screens, single-panel screens, and mosquito netting (figs. 10, 11).
3. Utensils: Various items such as utilitarian and decorative shelves, chairs, lamps, dishes and license burners; wood, lacquer, and ceramic techniques became progressively more refined (fig. 12).

The building, its partitions, and furnishings were all thus coordinated with the same module and therefore very flexible, and are similar to the current ideas of systems furniture and office landscapes.

Reception Spaces

As the samurai class rose to power after the Kamakura and Muromachi eras (1180 to 1570), rooms in which to receive guests became very important, and the rules governing them according to status became more complex. Spatially, the rules were concerned with the placement of people and things, who should sit where, and where what should be placed.

Concerning the placement of people, persons of high status sat on movable *tatami* or reed mats placed on the wood floors, where those of low rank sat on round straw cushions or on the floor. Later when rooms were fitted wall-to-wall with *tatami,* and became partitioned and fixed, the floor level itself was raised in one part (fig. 13). In some cases, platforms were built out into the garden for the viewing of dances, somewhat like Noh stages.

Objects were to be arranged for display on certain fixed elements, such as alcoves, particular types of shelving and desk arrangements. Along with the formalization of place, ornaments themselves came to have fixed meanings, and scrolls, flowers, and paintings adopted motifs of the seasons. By changing these decorative elements, the space could be made responsive to the garden and surrounding area (figs. 14, 15).

Looked upon in this way, the tea ceremony room put the least restriction on people, things, and space, and the

1 敷物類：板の間に座ったり寝たりする場合
に敷くもの．ござ，畳，茵など．畳は現在床全
体に敷き込んでいるが当初は必要に応じて持ち
運び，座る場所や寝る場所に置いた⑨．

2 仮設間仕切：可動の間仕切りで，建具，す
だれ，のれん，のように建物に取りつけるもの
と，衝立，屏風，几帳などのように独立したも
のがある⑩⑪．

3 調度類：収納台，棚，椅子，灯台，食器類，
香壺など多種あり，木工，うるし，陶器の技術
が次第に精緻さを極めてゆく⑫．

　このように，建物，間仕切り，家具に到る一
貫したモジュールと，それにより得られるフレ
キシビリティーは，現在のシステム・ファニチ
ャーやオフィス・ランドスケープの考え方と基
本的に同じである．

接客空間

鎌倉，室町時代以降の武士階級の台頭にともな
い，住宅の中で接客空間が重要となり，身分に
応じた饗応作法が次第に複雑になっていった．
作法を空間的に把えれば，結局，どこに誰が座
り，どこに何を置くか，であり，人と物の場の
問題である．

　まず，人についてみると，床が板敷の場合に
は身分の高い人が移動式の畳や茵を敷き，低い

greatest emphasis on spiritual communication between individuals (fig. 16).

Between Interior and Exterior

Another great characteristic in the composition of Japanese living space is the interface between interior and exterior. In masonry construction, a thick wall separates inside and out and is structurally important, so that few openings are permitted. Wood frame construction, on the other hand, requires no enclosure between the supporting posts and, with the use of movable partitions it was possible at any time to open interior and exterior spaces to each other.

These circumstances in wood construction led to a step-like hierarchy of spaces. Again, with the thick walls of masonry construction one room is much like another as far as separation goes, but with *shoji* and *fusuma*, paper-covered sliding doors, the degree of separation increases with the number of partitioning doors. In the deepest recesses of the house is the thick plastered wall, along which are arranged the sleeping rooms. Beyond those are more open and functionally free spaces, divided into any number of rooms by *shoji* and *fusuma*, and sur-

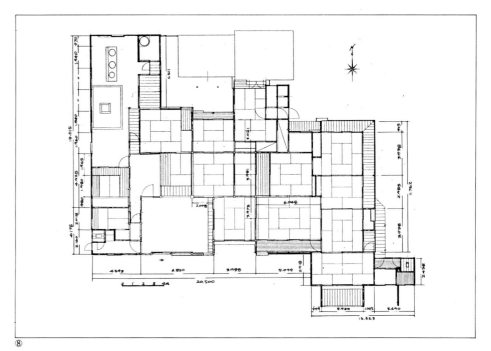

⑧

⑨

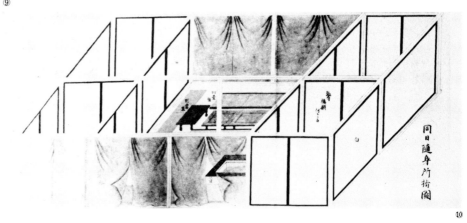

⑩

⑧ 畳によるモジュール平面例．
⑨ 急な客のため畳を舗設している．
⑩ 可動間仕切り．のれんによる舗設（平安時代）．
⑪ 間仕切り，調度類などによる舗設（江戸時代の遊里）．
⑫ お茶席の舗設（笹川邸，新潟）．
⑬ 上段の間，修学院離宮窮邃軒（京都）．

8. Example of a plan using the module of *tatami*.

9. *Tatami* mats arranged for guests arriving suddenly. *Tatami* floor mats were originally a portable element.
10. Possible partitions: partitioning with *noren* in the Heian age.
11. Partitioning with movable fixtures: red light district of the Edo period.
12. Arrangement of a tea ceremony room. (Sasagawa-tei, Niigata).
13. Room with a raised floor, Shugakuin Detached Palace, Kyusui-an, Kyoto.

28

⑪

者は円座や板座に座った．畳が敷詰になり部屋の間仕切が固定化してくると，次第に上座，下座の位置関係が固定化し，床が一段高くなった上段の間が発生してきた⑬．また，能の舞台のように人の舞を見せる空間として，庭に突き出した舞台も発生した．

一方，物についてみると，床，違い棚，付書院などのような物のディスプレイ，収納の場が固定化してきた．場の様式化とともに物にも一定の法則ができ，掛軸，花，障屏画などに季節感をとり込み，取り替えることによって庭や周辺の自然環境に対応する空間を作り出した⑭⑮．

このような観点から見れば，茶室は人，物，空間を最少限にすることによって，人と人との心の交流を最大限にせんとしている空間であると言えよう⑯．

内外の境界

日本の住空間構成の大きな特徴として，この他に，内部と外部の境界空間がある．組積造の場合には内外の境界には厚い壁があり，その壁は構造的に重要であるから窓のような開口しかない．しかし，木造架構では柱と柱の間が開いているので内外を隔てる壁はなくてもよく，可動建具の発達によりいつでも内外空間を連続させ

⑫

⑬

rounding these is a wide corridor bounded at the outside by heavy wooden doors which offer protection from rain and the cold night air. The eaves extend far beyond these doors creating a buffer space appropriate to Japan's rainly climate. Sometimes special verandas or moon-viewing platforms of various types of board construction extend far beyond the eaves, giving the space the attributes of both interior and exterior (figs. 17–21).

The Garden

What of the garden beyond? In comparing photographs of Western gardens and Japanese gardens, one notices that in many Western gardens the garden is viewed from outside and the building placed against that background, while Japanese gardens are intended to be viewed from an interior space against the background of a wall or fence.

This is because Japanese gardens are designed in concert with the room interiors, giving full consideration to sight lines from the rooms, the corridor, or a special platform (figs. 22, 23). The line of sight is from the interior to the exterior, and stopped by a wall or fence.

ることが可能である．

そこで生まれたのが段階的な空間のヒエラルキーである．組石造のように壁が厚い場合隣りの部屋も，そのまた向うの部屋も，隔離されている点ではあまり変わりがない．しかし，障子や襖のように紙が間仕切りの場合には，仕切りの数が多ければ隔離がよくなる．一番奥に，塗籠を原型とする壁面の多い寝室があり，その周囲の開放的な空間は障子，襖により幾部屋にも間仕切り，その外に広縁を設け，その外側に雨戸を通す．そして，その外は軒下空間であるから雨の多い日本に適している．また，濡れ縁や月見台などのように軒下や，その外にまで延長した板床が設けられることもあり，内と外の間に，その両方の特性を併ね備えた空間がある ⑰→㉑．

庭

その外にある庭はどうであろうか．西洋と日本の庭園に関する写真集を見比べると，西洋のは庭を外から眺めて建物が背景に写っていることが多く，日本のは庭を室内側から撮って塀や垣根が背景となっていることが多いのに気づく．

これは，日本庭園が，室内，広縁，月見台などからの視線を十分考慮して設計されているためであり，庭と室内を一体的に計画していると

考えてよい㉒㉓．即ち，視線は室内から外に向っているのであり，その視線を止める背景として塀や垣根がある．従って，石庭のようにその部分で完結している庭の背景には，土塀のように視線を完全に止める塀を作り，借景のように視線を庭の外まで延長させる場合には低い生垣にする．そして，外から内部に向かう視線を遮るためには，一般的に庭木，生垣，竹垣，塀，を適宜併用する㉔→㉗．

すなわち，視覚的には日本のインテリアは塀まで広がっていき，外の空気と一体となっている．

文化の相違

視覚的に内と外が一体となっているとは言っても，やはり建築とはある空間を外部環境から守るためにある．外部環境には視覚の他に風雨，寒暑，日射，音，匂い，よごれ，動物，人間などがある．それらの侵入をどの程度許し，どの程度遮るか，国，人種，文化などによって異なっている．日本ではその境界の処理が変化に富み，色々な手法が発達してきた．

紙の障子で仕切られた部屋に西洋人が住めば，きっとプライバシーの不足に悩むことになり，障子越しに聞こえる雨の音が風流だ，などとは思えないだろう．やきとり屋など，いくら視覚

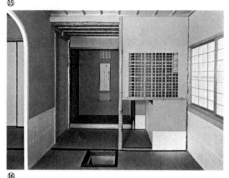

⑭ 住吉の仮設舞台（住吉）．
⑮ 床の間ディスプレイ空間（北方文化博物館，新津）．
⑯ 茶室内部．
⑰ 庭から屋内へ，障子による開放的仕切り（清水園．新発田）．
⑱ 屋内の部屋相互，襖による閉鎖的仕切り（市島邸，新発田）．
⑲ 格子，内から外はよく見えるが外から内は見難い（笹川邸，新潟）．
⑳ 縁側，内外の境界（北方文化博物館，新津）．
㉑ 月見台，縁側から庭へ突き出ている（桂離宮，京都）．
㉒ 江戸時代の作庭図．室内から庭を眺めるように考えている．

14. Temporary stage at Sumiyoshi.
15. *Tokonoma*, display alcove. North Culture Museum, Niizu.
16. Interior of a tea ceremony room.
17. Open partition of *shoji* paper doors, looking from garden to interior. (Shimizu-en, Shibata)
18. Mutuality of interior rooms, enclosing partition of *fusuma*, heavy paper doors. (Ichijima-tei, Shibata)
19. Lattice door. The outside may be clearly seen from the room, but it is difficult to see inside. (Sasagawa-tei, Niigata)
20. *Engawa*, veranda, boundary of in and out.
21. Moon-viewing platform, extending out from the veranda. (Katsura Detached Palace)
22. Edo period landscape, designed to be seen from an interior space.

Accordingly, in the case of a rock garden for instance, the view is fixed against the background of a mud wall which completely stops the line of sight; with *shakkei* or "borrowed scenery", a short hedge is placed at the boundary of the garden, blocking the view of its immediate surroundings but letting the line of sight extend to a framed view in the distance. To block the view of the interior from the outside, trees, hedges and bamboo fences are used as appropriate (figs. 24—27).

Cultural Differences

Although we speak of visually joining interior and exterior, buildings are meant, after all, to protect a certain space from the outside environment. Aside from visual elements, the outside environment includes wind and rain, cold and heat, sun and shadow, sounds, smells, and dirt, animals and people. To what degree such are allowed and to what degree pass through differs by country, race and culture. In Japan the management of these boundaries, the interface, is full of changes and various methods have been developed to deal with them. A Westerner would most likely bemoan the lack of

privacy afforded by rooms with paper walls and might not consider the sound of rain through those paper walls particularly poetic. And there are those who would think the smell of soy sauce floating from behind the *noren* of food stalls unpleasant no matter how visually isolated they may be.

It is not just homes that have been, by tradition, imperfectly compartmentalized; human relations as well have shared the same fate. The general vagueness of interface, or meeting, is felt by Westerners when, in talking, the Japanese smile profusely while their actual intent still cannot be divined.

In building or in human relations, this vagueness of interface might be attributable to Japan's island status and cultural homogeneity. For a people with a certain degree of common basic sensibility within a defined area, there is the easy assurance that somewhere along the line things will be understood without clearly stating them in black and white.

Housing Types
Figure 28 shows how these cultural differences are expressed in housing forms. The Arabian courtyard house

focusses on an inner courtyard with thick walls built to the edge of the site; the courtyard is necessary to create the proper environment for family life, in particular, that of the women. The typical American suburban home, on the other hand, marks the bounds of the site in no way, with a lawn and sidewalk in front. However, it is not unusual to

⑰

⑳

⑱

㉑

⑲

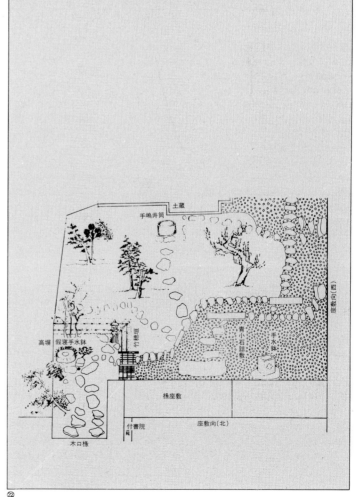

㉒

㉕

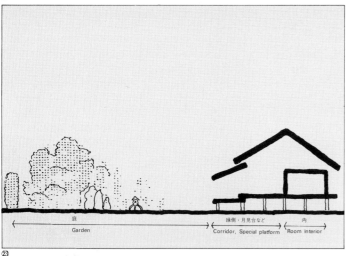

㉓

庭
Garden
縁側・月見台など
Corridor, Special platform
内
Room interior

㉖

㉔

㉗

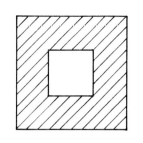
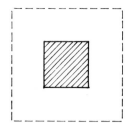
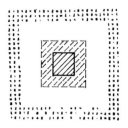

アラブの中庭住居
Arab court house

アメリカの郊外住居
American house

日本の住居
Japanese house

㉘

㉙

㉚

㉛

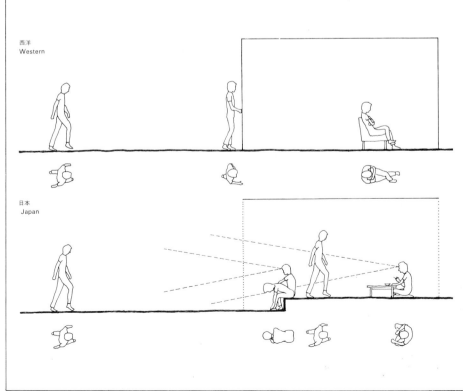

西洋
Western

日本
Japan

㉜

的に遮断されているとは言え，のれん越しに漂う醬油の匂いに不快感を感じる人々もあるだろう．

完全に遮断することが少なかったのは単に住居においてだけでなく，人間関係においてもそうである．西洋人にとって，日本人はいつもニコニコしているが実際は何を考えているのだろう，と考え込ませるのは，この境界のあいまいさにある．

住居にしても，人間関係にしても，この境界のあいまいさは，島国，単一民族，が主たる原因であろう．即ち，限定された場において，ある程度の共通した認識基盤を持っている人達にとっては，物事が完全に対立することはなく，白黒をはっきりさせなくてもいつの間にか解決するという安心感がある．

住居タイプ

このような，文化背景の相異が住居型にどのように現われているかを図㉘に示す．アラブの中庭住居は敷地の境界に厚い壁を設け，家族，とりわけ女性の生活の場として中庭が重要である．アメリカの郊外住宅の典型は，敷地境界に塀などを設けず前庭の芝生と歩道の芝生が連続している．しかし，建物の扉，窓は二重三重に鍵をかけ，内部には自己防衛と称するピストルやラ

㉓　日本の住居と庭の関係．
㉔　庭の背景として塀がある（報国寺，鎌倉）．
㉕　借景．庭の外の景観を背景として借りる（慈光院，奈良）．
㉖　竹垣，石垣．
㉗　竹垣．
㉘　住居タイプ．
㉙　アラブの中庭住居（ダマスカス）．
㉚　アメリカの郊外住居（ニューヘヴン）．
㉛　生垣，竹垣などによる敷地境界．
㉜　日本では家へ入る時に視界の転換がある．

23. Relationship of the Japanese house and garden.
24. A fence as the background of a garden. (Hokoku-ji temple, Kamakura)
25. Borrowed scenery: borrowing distant scenery outside the garden as backdrop. (Jiko-in temple, Nara)
26. Bamboo fence, stone fence.
27. Bamboo fence.
28. Housing types.
29. Arabian courtyard house. (Damascus)
30. American suburban house. (New Haven)
31. Visual boundaries: hedge, bamboo fence.
32. Revolution of the visual world when entering a Japanese house.

履物をぬぐ，床に座る

しかし日本人は心理的に内と外を明確に区別し
ている．それは，外から内へ入る時に履物をぬ
ぐという行為により，厳然と守られている．西
洋化が進んだ今日でも，この習慣が残っている
ことに疑問を感じたさる建築家が土足で家の中
に入るように設計したことがある．雨の多い日

㉞

㉝ 縁側に座って外を眺めている．ここではき物をぬぐ時，必
　ず一度外を見るので内外の接点として重要な位置である．
㉞ ロシア特使プチャーチンとの会談，1853年．
㉟ 日本駐在米領事ハリスの江戸城参内，1857年．

find two and three locks on doors and
windows and perhaps a pistol or rifle for
self defense kept within the house. In
contrast to these two examples, the
Japanese house has a hedge around not
just the edge of the lot but the perimeter
of the building as well, not isolating it but
neither making arms for defense of the
home necessary either; it is a soft enclosure (figs. 29–31).

Removing Shoes, Sitting on the Floor
Japanese do, however, differentiate between inside and outside psychologically.
The custom of removing footwear when
entering an interior is strictly adhered
to. For example, in this day of incleasing
Westernization, some architects doubted
the persistence of this habit and designed
homes to be entered with the shoes on.
The water and mud of rainy Japan that
came in with the shoes was a problem,
but the worst trouble was caused by
guests who dropped their cigarette ashes
on the floor. Apparently, they felt that
if the shoes were not removed, the space
is "outside," and it is permissable to drop
ashes outside.
　Shoes are removed in Japan because
the floor is raised from ground level;

33. Sitting on the veranda, looking out. When
removing shoes, one must turn to look outside,
making this an important point in the meeting
of outside and in.
34. Meeting with the Russian special envoy
Putyatin, 1853.
35. On the occasion of the visit of the American
representative to Japan, Townsend Harris, to
Tokyo Castle, 1857.

本では履物と一緒に土や水が入ってくることも問題ではあったが，一番困ったのは，客が来てタバコの灰や吸い殻を床に捨てることだったという．即ち，履物をぬがなければ外，外ならぬタバコの灰を落としてもよい，という意識の問題である．

履物をぬぐのは，日本の住宅の床が地面より高くなっているからで，床下にも通風があると蒸し暑い夏に適しており，室内を清潔に保つのにもよい．

日本の住居におけるもう一つの独特な習慣は，床の上に座ることである．靴をぬぐ習慣が現在でもほぼ100%存続しているのに比して，床に座る習慣は非常に減少し，通常の生活はほとんど椅子に座る習慣に変わった．

視界の変換
靴をぬぎ，床に座る習慣は，意識の上で内外を明瞭に区分するのに役立っている．その他，外から内へ人が移動する場合の視覚のシークエンスに重要な効果をもたらしている．

すなわち，図32に示すように，西洋の家では入る人の視線は常に一方向である．ところが日本では，外から内へ入る境界で靴をぬぐために体を回転するので一度外を見て，そしてまた，内に向って進むことになり，視界が180度転換するのである．そしてまた，部屋の中で床に座る時に，客の座は庭を正面か横に見るように座るので，視界が庭の方に転換すると同時に立居から座居になるので視界が下がる33．

このような視覚のシークエンスがあるために，玄関や縁側にアプローチする飛び石の配列や，玄関や縁側に腰掛けた時の庭の景観などが重要であり，室内では，床に座って見るスケール感が大切である．

SHOGUN
靴をぬぐかぬがないか，床に座るか座らないか，が日米外交の過程で重要な問題であったことがある．江戸時代末，1853年日本に開国をせまってきたペリーから，大統領書翰を受け取る時は，海辺に建てた仮小屋で行ったために，日本側も室内の作法に固執せず床几に座った．しかし，その2ヶ月後に訪れたロシア特使プチャーチンとの会談は，室内で行われたため着座か椅子かで何日も論争をくり返し，ついに書翰の受渡しは双方が立ったままで，その後の会談では日本側が畳を重ねて台を作りその上に座り，ロシア側は椅子を使用した34．

これ等は将軍自身との会見ではなく奉行が出席したのだが，1857年に日本駐在米領事ハリスが将軍に謁見することになった．それまで謁見を許されていたオランダ領事は，日本式に靴をぬぎ，土下座して将軍の前に進んでいた．しかしハリスの要求は室内の畳の上においても，完全にアメリカ式に振る舞おうというものであった35．すなわち，靴をはいたままあがり，椅子に座り，将軍に直接国書を手渡すことを望んだ．近代的武力を背景とするハリスに，幕府は大いに悩まされ，結局はハリスの要求がかなり通った．すなわち，玄関で新しい靴にはき替えれば靴のまま室内に入ってもよい．着座，土下座はしなくてもよいが椅子は使わず立ったまま国書を手渡す．将軍が直接物を受け取る習慣はないので外務大臣が受けとるというものであった．

その時将軍は畳を7枚重ねた台の上に座ったという．

---

drafts can pass beneath the floor this way and keep the rooms cooler and fresher in the muggy heat of summer.

Sitting on the floor is another custom particular to Japan. But while the custom of removing shoes is still observed today, that of sitting on the floor is rapidly diminishing, and chairs are employed in most aspects of daily life.

Transformation of the Visual World
The customs of removing the shoes and sitting on the floor are helpful in consciously differentiating inside and out. Further, it gives an important sequence to the act of moving from the outside in. As shown in figure 32, the line of sight usually remains stable when entering a Western house; in Japan, in order to enter a house it is necessary to remove the shoes at the boundary of in and out, turn the body and face the outside while removing shoes, then turn back to the interior and proceed; the visual world revolves 180°. Then, when about to sit on the floor in a room, as the guest is positioned to face the garden or view it laterally, the visual world turns toward the garden, and as the body is lowered to assume its seat on the floor, the visual world also declines (fig. 33).

This visual sequence makes the approach over stepping stones to the entry or veranda under the eaves and the view of the garden while sitting on the veranda very important; the sense of scale while sitting on the floor is also of great consequence.

The Shogun
Whether to remove the shoes or not, whether to sit on the floor or not were once great problems in Japan's diplomatic history. At the end of the Edo period, when Admiral Perry forced the opening of Japan in 1853, reception of the letters from the U.S. president was held in a temporary house by the sea and even the Japanese ignored the etiquette of the interior and sat on camp stools. Two months later, however, a meeting was held with the special Russian envoy, Puchachin. As the meeting was to take place indoors, arguments flew back and forth for several days over whether to sit on the floor or in chairs. It was eventually decided to receive the letters with both sides standing; for the following discussion, the Japanese sat on *tatami* which had been stacked to a sufficient height, while the Russians sat on chairs (fig. 34).

These were occasions when the Shogun himself did not appear, being attended by a magistrate. In 1857, however, the American representative in Japan, Townsend Harris, had an audience with the Shogun. In previous audiences permitted to the Dutch representative, Japanese custom had been followed with shoes removed and the representative prostrating himself before the Shogun. Harris requested that the meeting be held on *tatami* but in a completely American style (fig. 35). He wanted them all to step up to the *tatami* in their boots, sit on chairs, and hand the letters directly to the Shogun. With modern military might behind him, the *bakufu*, or feudal government, struggled but largely acceded to Harris' demands. If all changed to new shoes in the entry they could proceed to the *tatami* with shoes on; Harris need not bow but would remain standing when he delivered the letters; and as the Shogun was not accustomed to receiving things directly, the foreign minister would receive the papers.

It is said the Shogun sat on a platform of seven layers of *tatami*.

ORIENTATION
by Simon J. Gale

建築における方位学
サイモン・J・ゲイル

東の野にかぎろひのたつ見えて　月は東に　日は西に
柿本人麿

方位の規則以前の時代

日本においては，最初期の遺構の時から気候即ち方位への対応が読みとれる．今日の基準的な方位の法則はその当時は知られていず，これらに影響を与えたとは考えられない．このため，これら初期の住居の配置は現にある気候的条件と入手可能な材料に対する機能的・合理的回答であった．以下はこの点を明らかにする初期の日本の文化史と建築史から選んだ例である．

1. 日本における最初期の住居形態は縄文期のものである．これらは基本的には，竪穴住居であった．床は地面に約400ミリメートル程掘り込まれ，円形上屋の直経は4～6メートルの間であった．泥とわらと枝でできていた上屋は自然の脅威に対してほとんど役立たなかっただろうが，開口の位置は冬の寒風を避け，暖かい夏の風を取り込もうとする試みを示している①②．

2. 同様のことが，北海道のアイヌ住居にも見られる．ここではさらに，人体の表象が付加されている．即ち，北の壁面は背中，南の壁面は前，西の壁面は足，そして東の壁面は顔とされていた．南は暖かさと善，北は寒さを意味していたのがこのような配列の動機であった．東面の窓は「カミマド」と呼ばれ，日の出の方向に住むとされた神がこの窓より住居に入ると信じられていた．神が守ってくれるとされたので，貴重品は全てこの窓の外に収納された．南面の東寄りの窓は人間の目と鼻を形どっていた．この例は，迷信，気候および配置図に明らかなように，地勢への対応を示している③④．

3. 古墳時代は弥生から平安にかけての日本の歴史の初期にわたっている．この時代は当時の天皇や豪族の墳墓から名をとっている．これらの墳墓の多くは，「鍵穴型」であり，ほとんどは堀に囲まれており，一説によればそれは死後の世界での二つの体の合体を表わしているといわれる⑤⑥．これら古墳は現在は知られていない．従って我々の目には見えない一定の方位の型式に従っていると思われる．後期の古墳，特に6，7世紀のものは東西軸に片寄る傾向がある．このことは安閑（531～535）と欽明（539～571）天皇の古墳については確かであるが，あまり多くの不整合があるので，方位に関して正確な結論に到るのは難しい．

4. 建物としての神社ができる以前は人々は自然を拝んだ．そのため地勢との係わりにおける

Higashi no no ni kagirohi no tatsumiete
Tsuki wa higashi ni hi wa nishi ni

Kakinomoto no Hitomaro
c. 10th century.

There appeared a mirage in the field to the east
The moon was in the east and the sun in the west

Translation by the author.

Before the Rules of Orientation

From the earliest structures in Japan, a response to climate and therefore orientation is perceivable. The present standard laws of orientation had no influence on such edifices since they were at that time unknown. The arrangement of these early dwellings were therefore a functional and rational solution to existing climatic conditions and available material. The following are examples from early Japanese cultural and architectural history serve to illustrate this point.

1. One of the first dwelling types in Japan were those of the Jōmon Period. These were basically pit dwellings. The floor was dug into the earth to a depth of approx. 400 mm and the diameter of the circular structure was between 4–6 metres. Although the mud, reed and branch structure provided little resistance to natural forces, the positioning of the opening indicates an attempt to both exclude the winter wind and embrace the warm summer breeze (figs. 1, 2).

2. The same phenomena is seen in the Ainu dwellings in Hokkaido, added to this a representation of the human body in the built form. The North wall — the back of the human; the South wall — the front; the West wall — the feet, and the East — the head. The South being representative of warmth and good, the North of cold, was the motivation for such an arrangement. The window at the East end of the house was termed the 'Kamimado' or 'window of the God' who was believed to dwell in that direction — the direction of the rising sun — and was believed to enter the house through this window. All valuable items were stored outside this window because the God would offer security. The window at the east end of the South wall formed the eyes and nose of the human. This example demonstrates a response to superstition, climate and topography, the latter of which is evident from the diagram (figs. 3, 4).

3. The Kofun Period spanned the early periods of Japanese history from the Yayoi to the Heian. It took its name from the characteristic burial tombs of the Emperors and head clansmen of the period. These tombs were often 'key shaped' in form and were invariably surrounded by water and one theory states that they represent the union of two bodies in after life (figs. 5, 6). They would appear to obey also some form of unknown and thus invisible orientation pattern. The later Kofun, in particular those of the 6th & 7th centuries tend towards an East/West directional axis. This is certainly true of the tombs erected in honour of Emperors Ankan (531–535) and Kimmei (539–571), but there are so many inconsistencies that it is difficult to come to any conclusion regarding exact orientational implications.

4. Before the built shrine, man worshipped nature and thus there evolved an unintentional but nevertherless obvious pattern of orientation with regard to topography. The main symbol of worship was the mountain, but if no conveniently placed mountain existed a waterfall, trees or river took its place. One of the earliest known examples of such a shrine

意図はされないが，にもかかわらず，はっきりとした方位の形式ができ上った．信仰の主対象は山であったが，適当な山がない時は滝や川が代わりとなった．このような神域で，現在知られている最初期の例は奈良の正倉院である⑦．神殿が建てられる前は，拝所は３本の樹木によって構成され，拝む方向は山に向っていた．その山に神が座していたのである．神社建築の配列はこのささやかな起源から明確な発展の跡をたどることができる⑧．

これら四つの例は，日本の歴史の初期に見られる定位の形式や信仰を説明するために選んだ．それらは相互に関係がなく，定式化された方位の法則と無縁である．

方位の法則（方位学）は，6世紀頃中国文化の流入に伴って日本に紹介された．当初は，社寺や都市の配列にのみ影響を与えたが，すぐに建築全般に派及し，日常生活にも浸透した．

しかしながら，あらゆる種類の建築の基準を定めた16世紀の『匠明』までは，総合的な体系としては書き留められることはなかった．特にこの中の『万象識釈』と呼ばれる一巻は構法や木割の他に，方位の基準も定めていた．これらの前の時代では，世代から世代へ口伝されていた．かくも早く一般に拡がった理由としては，一つには日本の気候風土に都合よく適用できた

ことが考えられる．

方位の体系

1 中国における発生

方位学の基本理論の多くは伝説に基づいており，伏義によるとされている．伏義は数学（算術）とも結びつけられる伝説上の中国文化の創始者である．方位学に関しては，都市の構成に適用された数字は陰陽学の哲学と密接に統合されている⑨⑩．

陰と陽の概念は詳しくは後述するが，ここでは初期の都市計画に基本的ないくつかの要点に触れておく必要がある．

陰と陽の要素は万物の中に存在し，相互に作用し合って互いに制し合っていることにより物の存在を可能にしている．しかしながら，これら根本的に相反する要素の直接的あるいは完全な均衡は，発展の制止ひいては単調をもたらすと信じられていた．このため，どちらか一方に必ずわずかな優位が与えられている．

このことが都市計画にとってどういうことを意味したかというと，都市は基本的には対称型であったが，非対称でもあった．周時代より，中国の都市は長方形として計画され，多くは厳格な対称な格子状であったが，建物の配置は厳格に対称ではなく，均衡の感覚によって軸の左

precincts was the Shosō-in in Nara (fig. 7). Before the shrine was built the place of prayer was formed by three trees and the direction of worship was directly aligned on a mountain. It was here that the God resided. A definite progression in the arrangement of shrine architecture can be traced from this humble beginning (fig. 8).

These four examples are listed to illustrate some of the orientation patterns and beliefs discernible at this early period of Japanese history, they are unrelated to each other and independent of any fixed orientation laws.

The laws of orientation entered Japan in the 6th century during the wave of Chinese cultural influence. Initially they affected specifically temple and town layout but soon spread to determine all aspects of architecture and even daily life.

However they were not written down in a comprehensive form until the 16th century in the Shomei scrolls which defined the standards for all types of architecture. One scroll in particular, the Banshōshiki shaku determined orientational standards in addition to those of construction and measurement. Before this the laws were passed on from one

generation to the next. One reason why they gained such widespread acceptance so rapidly was perhaps because they conveniently fitted the climatic characteristics of Japan.

The Patterns of Orientation

1. Their origins in China

Much of the theory in the principles of Orientation is founded on legend, and its origination is attributed to Fu-hsi, the legendary founder of Chinese culture who is especially significant since the science of mathematical calculation is also linked to his name. In the context of orientation the mathematics applied to town organisation are closely integrated with the philosophy of the Yin Yang School (figs. 9, 10).

The concept of Yin and Yang will be dealt with in greater detail in a later section but it is important to introduce a few key points which are fundamental to early city planning.

The elements Yin and Yang exist in everything and are the two factors which interact with and control each other, thus enabling existence. However it was believed that a direct or perfect balance of these two, essentially conflicting

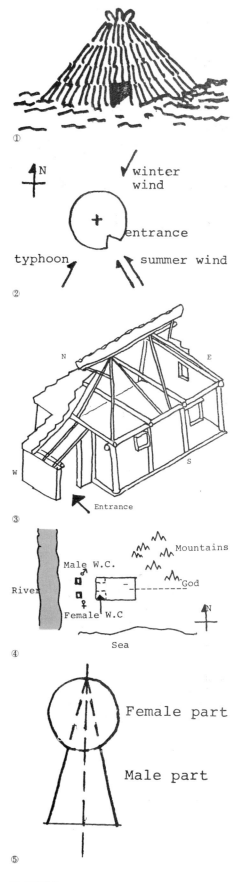

① 縄文住居.
② 縄文住居の平面
③ アイヌの住居.
④ アイヌの住居配置図.
⑤ 古墳.

1. Jōmon house.
2. Plan of Jōmon house.
3. Ainu house.
4. Plan of Ainu house.
5. Kofun.

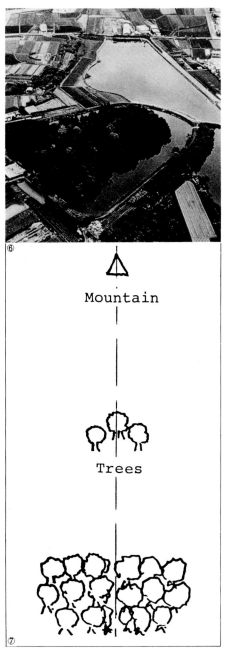

Mountain

Trees

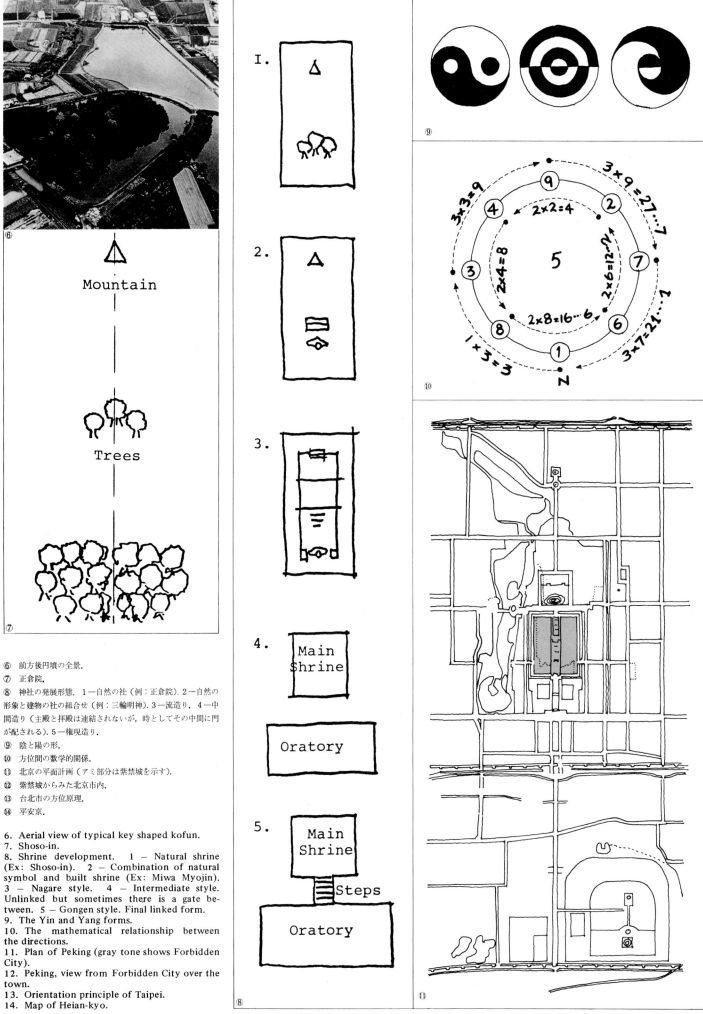

⑥ 前方後円墳の全景.
⑦ 正倉院.
⑧ 神社の発展形態. 1—自然の社（例：正倉院). 2—自然の形象と建物の社の組合せ（例：三輪明神). 3—流造り. 4—中間造り（主殿と拝殿は連結されないが, 時としてその中間に門が配される). 5—権現造り.
⑨ 陰と陽の形.
⑩ 方位間の数学的関係.
⑪ 北京の平面計画（アミ部分は紫禁城を示す).
⑫ 紫禁城からみた北京市内.
⑬ 台北市の方位原理.
⑭ 平安京.

6. Aerial view of typical key shaped kofun.
7. Shoso-in.
8. Shrine development. 1 – Natural shrine (Ex: Shoso-in). 2 – Combination of natural symbol and built shrine (Ex: Miwa Myojin). 3 – Nagare style. 4 – Intermediate style. Unlinked but sometimes there is a gate between. 5 – Gongen style. Final linked form.
9. The Yin and Yang forms.
10. The mathematical relationship between the directions.
11. Plan of Peking (gray tone shows Forbidden City).
12. Peking, view from Forbidden City over the town.
13. Orientation principle of Taipei.
14. Map of Heian-kyo.

1.

2.

3.

4. Main Shrine

Oratory

5. Main Shrine

Steps

Oratory

(13)

(14)

右の絶対的対称が避られていた⑪⑫.

市街地を形成する基本の格子も重要であった.「陰」は奇数で,「陽」は偶数であり,この二つの間に間接的平衡が計られた. このため, 都市の格子の1:1の比率は許されず, 従って街は正方形でなく長方形であり, 格子の長辺と短辺は意識的に平衡を破って, 長安で9:8, 台北⑬で5:4の比率になって東西辺が南北に比べて長い. 日本について述べる時には, このことより詳述する.

さらに, 中国の都市は常に城壁に囲まれており, 日本の例とは対照的である. これは, 陰陽との関係のもう一つの側面を表わしている. 易経によれば, 陰は人体の皮膚に関係しており, 陽は血の循環になぞらえられていた. このため, 都市では城壁は陰, 街路網は陽であった. このように都市と人間の間に順次明確な関係が確立され, 住居においては家の外壁は陰で, 居住・動線空間が陽であった.

この考え方に基づくと, 陰である市の城壁は陽との相互作用のための空間を囲み込んで造り出すとされていた. しかし, 陰陽二元の方向の軸は厳密に関係づけられておらず, この部分こそが直接に方位に係わってくる.

台北を例にとると, 街路網は南北の主街路を中心に構成され, その街路の北端に宮殿があり,

南端には重要な教育を目的とした寺院が配されていた. 中心街路の軸は中国語で天一と呼ばれる北極星に合せられ, 万物がそのまわりを廻る宇宙の中心と考えられていた. 地上でそれにたとえられた天子は, このようにして, 都市の中心軸の北端に位置してこれとの最も近い位置を占めたのである. これは宇宙を地上で表わす構成と考えられている. 陽は天をも示すとされていたので, 街路網も天に合せられた.

陰の要素は地に関していたので, 城壁は周囲の支配的自然形態に合せられることによって, その陰との関係を強化された. 悪い影響(霊)は, 市の北東より迫まってくると考えられ, 市の外に防御のための障害物が必要であった. このため城壁は街路と平行な関係からねじまげられ, 東西の壁の消点が重要な山に合わされ, また北壁が北東の脅威を真正面に受け止めて, 都市を守るように設定されていた.

2 日本の状況

このような中国の思想を日本で最初に実際に適用したのは奈良の前身平城京においてであった. 私は現在の京都となった, より有名な平安京を例にしたいと思う. ここでは日本での状況を紹介し, 中国から日本に輸入され, 都市の配置, 特に方位に影響を与えたいくつかの別の思想的基準を示したいと思う.

elements, resulted in non development and thus monotony. Owing to this one of the two powers was always permitted a slight superiority.

Its relevance to city planning on this level was that although the town plan was fundamentally symmetrical, it was also assymetrical. Nearly all cities in China from the Chou Period were laid out in a rectangular manner, often in a strong symmetrical grid form, the formal grouping of the buildings was marked not by rigid symmetry but by a feeling for balance since an exact duplication on each side of the axis was avoided (figs. 11, 12).

The basic grid which composed the city was also of importance. Yin is representative of 'odd' numbers and Yang of 'even' numbers and thus an indirect balance between the two was formulated. For this reason an exact ratio of 1:1 in city proportion was not permissible and we therefore discover that the town is rectangular rather than square and that the ratios of the grid organisation are set up in a conscious imbalance resulting in a ratio of 9:8 as at Tchang ngan (fig. 13), and 5:4 at Taipei with the East and West sides of the city forming the

longer sides. This we will study in greater detail when the situation in Japan is discussed.

Further to this the Chinese cities were always walled cities, unlike their Japanese counterparts, and with regard to this there is an additional relationship with Yin and Yang. According to the 'I Ching', the element Yin is related to the skin of the human body and Yang with the blood circulation. Therefore in the city, the wall around it represents Yin and the street organisation, Yang. Thus an obvious reduction relationship is established between city and man which passes through the house where the outer boundary of the house again is represented by Yin, and the living and moving space by Yang.

The city wall element, Yin is therefore seen to prepare within its confines a space for its interaction with Yang. The directional axis of the two counterparts however, are not precisely related and it is this part which directly involves orientation.

In the example of Taipei, the street organisation is centred around a North/South main thoroughfare with the Emperors Palace at its northern end and an important edcuational temple to the

794年，首都は戦禍で荒れ果てた平城京から新しく設置建設された平安京に移された⑭．この都市は中国の長安をモデルにして，日本では条坊制と呼ばれた中国の都市構成原理の日本的解釈にのっとり配置されていた．当初の市域は5.4×4.6キロメートルの範囲に拡がり，朱雀大路と呼ばれた主街路が南北に走り，市街地を半分に分断していた．

市の敷地は中国思想「四神相応」（四神に基づいた思考）の原理に基づいて選ばれた．これは天と地の要素を組み合わせて，それらの間の均衡に基づく方位に関する思想であった．四神相応は方位を表わす四神と都市構成とを関連づけていた⑮⑯．

この他に，ある特定の地勢的または人工的要素が都市の各辺に対応して必要であった．
北——高い山や丘　　　　東——流水
南——田または湿地，沼地　　西——大道

日本では，条坊制や天平伽藍⑰のような計画手法は，このような思想を具体的な形として表わしたものとして発達した．これらの技法は単に都市の方位を設定するためだけでなく，都市の中のあらゆる要素の方位をも設定するために用いられた．これらの原理の適用は首尾一貫した形態として現わされ，強固な方位的秩序をもたらした．それらは，平安京のような都市に明確な統一性を与えただけでなく，周囲の地勢とも強力な関係を築いた．

都市の正確な配置は前に述べた例と全く同一ではないにせよよく似ていた．市街地は9条8坊の条坊の格子に造られ，従って縦横の比は9：8であった．条は南北に走り，坊は東西方向であった．しかし，都市には城壁がないので，実際の姿は中国のものとは違っていた．

建物はこの格子に同様な方法ではめ込まれた．天皇の宮殿は中心街の朱雀大路の北端に位置し，壮大な寺院は都市の格子組の他の重要な点にあった．この秩序は一般市民の住居を含む段階まで延長されていた．北東には比叡山山頂に仏教の強大な天台宗の僧院が建てられ，市街地を北の方向の邪悪な力から守っていた．

実際には，平城京と平安京のみがこの「真」または模範的な都市計画の日本での忠実な例である．しかしながら，条坊制とは無縁ではあるが，地勢に市街地を合わせるという主題は江戸においてもみられる

東京の旧名である江戸は，1603年江戸時代の始まりより日本の首都となった．平安京とは対照的に宮殿は市街地の中心にあった⑱．手法は続けて用いられており，中でも北東の方角に対する不穏な迷信は特記に値する．筑波山がこの方向を守っており，この山からは少し離れてい

るが，日光の寺院群も防御の意味で建立されている．市内では，上野の寺院群がこの役に当っている．市街路も市を囲む山々，主として富士山，筑波山，高尾山に合わせて配列されていた．江戸が発展した頃は，これらの山は皆市内から容易に望見でき，いくつかの主街路はそれらに向けられていた．例えば，日本橋本町は南西100キロメートルにある富士山に向っており，現在銀座と日本橋を結ぶ街路は北東の筑波山に向っていた⑲．

このことや，江戸の地図を見るとわかるように，前に調べた基本的計画法則は，日本人が街全体を建設する際多かれ少なかれ使われなくなっていたが，地勢に合わせた方位の考えは，特に借景のような庭園計画手法の場合には強く残っていた．市街地内の一般民家の段階では，方位に関する主たる基本的古法則は守られ続け，根本的には羅針盤上の方位にまつわる迷信や意味づけは本質的には大きな変更を受けなかった⑳→㉔．次にこの側面について述べてみよう．

方位角と家相

方位角は日本でこの分野の研究に使われる言葉であり，それは当然今まで述べてきた中国の思想に根をもっている．方位は方向，向きを意味し，角は隅，角度を意味する．

south. The axis of the street is fixed according to the North Star, named 'the Emperor of the Big Heaven' in Chinese and which represents the steadfast centre of the cosmos about which everything revolves. Its earthly equivalent, the Emperor, was thus situated closest to it — at the northern end of the central axis of the city. This organisation was intended as an earthly realization of the cosmos. Since Yang was indicative of heaven, the street pattern was also aligned to the heavens.

The Yin element was earth based and the city wall therefore was further connected with its Yin association by being aligned to a predominant natural form. Evil influences were believed to attach the city from the north east and thus a barrier beyond the city was needed as protection. The city wall was therefore twisted out of a parallel relationship with its streets so that the vanishing point of the east and west walls were located on the summit of an important mountain, and so that the full face of its north wall would then be facing north east to further protect the city from the evil influences of that direction.

2. The Situation in Japan

This then was the Chinese situation, the first example of this philosophy put into practise in Japan was at the city of Heijō Kyō, the former name for Nara. I intend to look at the more famous example of Heian Kyō, present day Kyōto, in order to introduce the Japanese situation as well as drawing upon some additional philosphical criteria imported from China which influenced the layout and more particularly the orientation of the city. In the year 794, the capital of Japan was moved from war torn Heijō Kyō to the newly founded city of Heian Kyō (fig. 14). This city was modelled on the Chinese town of Tchang ngan and laid out according to the Japanese interpretation of the Chinese city organisation principles which is known as Jōbosei in Japan. The original city occupied an area of 5.4 × 4.6 kms with a major street named 'Suzaku-Ōji' meaning 'red bird', running from north to south and dissecting the town in half.

The site of the city was chosen according to the principles of the Chinese philosophy 'Shishin Sōo' which literally translated means the 'thinking according to four Gods'. This was a philosophy related to orientation which combined

⑮ 四神相応に則った方位図．
⑯ 方位四神とそのシンボル．A—東：青龍．B—南：朱雀．C—西：白虎．D—北：玄武．
⑰ 天平伽藍．完全に対称またはほとんど対称となって表現される．A—中国の例（Shen-nung 寺）．B—日本の例（薬師寺）．
⑱ 江戸の市街図．
⑲ 江戸の街路方位図．
⑳ 現代の家相の適用例（東京日比谷の地下鉄駅）．
㉑ 典型的な民家の北側．
㉒ 典型的な民家の東側と南側．
㉓ 典型的な民家の西側．
㉔ 民家の北西隅部．

15. Orientation according to Shishin sōo.
16. The Gods of direction and their symbol. A — East: Seiryu, Blue Dragon. B — South: Suzaku, Scarlet Sparrow. C — West: Byakko, White Tiger. D — North: Genbu, Black Turtle.
17. Tenpyo Garan or the principles of temple layout usually realised in a wholly or almost symmetrical plan. A — Chinese example (Shen-nung Temple). B — Japanese example (Yakushiji Temple).
18. Map of Edo.
19. Edo street orientation plan.
20. Modern day application of Kasō, Hibiya subway station, Tokyo.
21. North side of a typical Minka house.
22. East and South sides of a typical Minka house.
23. West facing wall of a typical Minka house.
24. Northwest corner of Minka house.

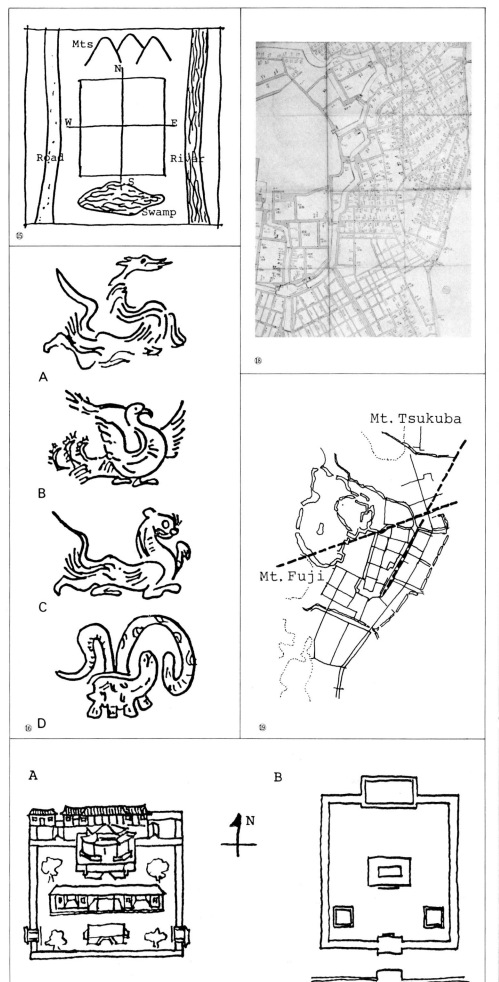

⑮

⑯ A B C D

⑰ A B N

⑱

⑲ Mt. Tsukuba Mt. Fuji

⑳

㉑

㉒

㉓

㉔

エイモス・ラポートは，著書『住居，形，文化』の中で，「日本の方位学の方位体系は地勢に無関係に住居の位置を決定する」と指摘している．これは市街地の配置法と矛盾し，厳密には正しくないが，（住居の周囲への）応対は気候的条件や迷信により強く影響を受け，そのために目を見張る眺望を無視することもある．しかしながら，北向きは迷信だけでなく，気候的に望ましくない方向なので，住居は同時に地勢的にも対応しているように見える．例えば，この方位には丘や木をあてがって寒風を防ぎ，この向きの壁にはほとんど開口部をとらないといったように．このような場合は，どちらが第一義的なデザインの決定要因であるか判断するのは難しい．

部屋の配列については，利用において明確な序列があるが，少なくとも歴史上でより重要なのは迷信からくる部屋の序列である．住居の形態と方位は，日本では「家相」と呼ばれ羅針盤の方位のみならず，五行の要素，十二支，さらに手相や人相が加わり，生と死にまつわる迷信が加味されて決定される．

このように，この概念は非常に複雑であり，一つの条件が他にどのような影響を及ぼすか厳密に判断するのは難しい．また家相がいつ頃発展したかもはっきりしていない．平安期の住居以後では重要な概念であったことは確かなようであり，それ以前にも重要な意味合いを持っていた可能性もあるが，江戸中期まで家相の日本的な解釈は確立されなかった．この頃いくつかの本が家相に関して出版された．これらの中で重要なのは，1760年刊行の神家コレキによる「家相鑑チ録」と後に松浦トケイと益浦銀鶴とによって書かれた江戸末期の書物である．家相も，その前身を中国にあった「宅相」を模範としていた．

現代の家相は，大規模な宅地開発や敷地の不足のため摘用することもむずかしくなっているが，江戸時代の家相に基づいている．それはさらに中国思想より基本法則をとっていた．今あげた理由のため，現在家相は必然的住居設計上の強力な基準とはなっていないが，家相に関して出版される書物や表の数から見る限り，まだかなり多数の信者を有している．

ここでは簡単に家相に係わる種々の様相について述べる必要がある．しかしそれらは皆相互に関連づけられているため，個々に分離することは多くの場合むずかしい．いろいろの様相の中では，特に都市計画に関係が深く重要であったものもあるが，ここでは基本的には住居計画に関する要素について述べる（必要上，多くの説明は図版，表によって行う）．

旧の時刻は方位と陰陽相方に関係しており，2時間毎にさらに十二支の一つに対応する㉖．

さらに，日本語で十干と呼ばれる次のような暦の区分がつけ加えられる．

表①

木	火	土	金	水
甲（きのえ）	丙（ひのえ）	戊（つちのえ）	庚（かのえ）	壬（みずのえ）
乙（きのと）	丁（ひのと）	己（つちのと）	辛（かのと）	癸（みずのと）
東	南	中央	西	北

上表における二つずつの組は五行よりきており，「え」は先のものまたは「兄」を意味し，「と」は後のものまたは「弟」の意味である．

東西南北の主方位は，「四聖」と呼ばれ，図㉖では30°ずつを形成する．十二支はそれぞれ30°ずつを表わすが，丑と寅が合わさって丑寅となるように二つずつ組み合わされ，図上では60°の範囲を与えられる．この四つの組は「四隅」と呼ばれる．このように方位は全部で8つに整理される㉗㉞．

四聖 30×4＝120°
四隅 60×4＝240°

これらの方位にはそれぞれ門があり，四聖の門は，北：休門，東：疾門，南：景門，西：驚門という．また，四隅の門は，北東：鬼門，南東：風門，南西：病門，北西：天門という．

ここで重要な点は，どの方位の表また図解に

---

the elements of heaven and earth and the balance between them. Shishinsōo related to the concept of the orientation of city towards the Gods who represented direction. Each god was symbolized in a group of stars from which he took his name (figs. 15, 16).

In addition to this, certain topographical features or man made elements should occur to each side of the city.
North – High hills/Mountains
South – Rice swamps or large pond
East – Flowing river
West – Main highway

Planning procedures such as Jōbosei and Tenpyō Garan (fig. 17) evolved in Japan to manifest this thinking in the built form. These techniques were used not only to clearly establish the city orientation but also the orientation of all elements of the city. The application of these principles resulted in the strong directional order expressed in a coherent form which gave obvious unity to cities such as Heian Kyō as well as forming a powerful relationship with the surrounding topography.

The precise city layout was similar if not identical to that discussed earlier. The city was founded on a Jōbo grid form of 9 Jō by 8 Bo thus forming a 9:8 ratio. The Jō divisions ran from north to south and the Bo from east to west. However, since the Japanese cities had no surrounding wall their actual appearance differed from the Chinese city.

The buildings were inserted into the grid in a corresponding manner. The Emperors Palace was located at the extreme north end of the central Suzaku-Ōji, the main street, with the impressive temples positioned in other key parts of the lattice network of the city. This order extended to include the ordinary dwellings of the citizens. To the north east, the monastery of the powerful Tendai sect of Buddhism was built on top of Mount Hie to protect the city from evil forces.

In real terms, Heijō Kyō and Heian Kyō are the only two true examples of this type of city/town plan and are referred to as the 'Shin' or model form of town plan in Japan. However, although not associated with Jōbosei, the theme of orientating the city to topography can be further illustrated by Edo.

Edo, the old name for Tokyo, became the capital of Japan at the beginning of the Edo Period in 1603. In contrast to Heian Kyō, the Palace formed the heart of the city (fig. 18). Some techniques were continued, perhaps most notably, that of the adverse superstition concerning the North East direction. Mount Tsukuba protects this direction and although some distance from this mountain the Nikko temples were constructed by Tokugawa Ieyasu for further protection. Within the city, the temple complex at Ueno was built for this purpose. The streets of the city were also arranged according to the mountains which surrounded the city, most notably, Mounts Fuji, Tsukuba and Takao. At the time that Edo evolved these were all easily visible from within the city and certain main streets were aligned to them. For example, Nihonbashi Hommachi Street was aligned on Mt. Fuji 100 kms to the south west, and the present day street which links Ginza and Nihonbashi was deliberately aligned to Mt. Tsukuba in the north east (fig. 19).

It can be observed from this and by looking at the map of Edo, that the fundamental planning laws examined earlier had more or less been dispensed with by the Japanese when applied to the whole city as a built entity, but the idea

Time				Direction		
11p.m–1a.m	子	SU	PAT	(1st Zodiac Sign)	NORTH	
1a.m–3a.m	丑	CHU SHU USHI	COW	(2nd Zodiac Sign)	N.N.E ⌉ 艮 Gon	Ushitora Represnts N.E
3a.m–5a.m	寅	TORA IN	TIGER	(3rd Zodiac Sign)	E.N.E ⌋	
5a.m–7a.m	卯	BO	RABBIT	(4th Zodiac Sign)	EAST	
7a.m–9a.m	辰	SHIN TATSU	DRAGON	(5th Zodiac Sign)	E.S.E ⌉ 巽 Son	Tatsumi
9a.m–11a.m	巳	MI	SERPENT	(6th Zodiac Sign)	S.S.E ⌋	Represents S.E
11a.m–1p.m	午	GO UMA	HORSE	(7th Zodiac Sign)	SOUTH	
1p.m–3p.m	未	HITSUJI	SHEEP	(8th Zodiac Sign)	S.S.W ⌉ 坤 Kon	Hitsujizaru
3p.m–5p.m	申	SHIN SARU	MONKEY	(9th Zodiac Sign)	W.S.W ⌋	Represents S.W
5p.m–7p.m	酉	YU	BIRD	(10th Zodiae Sign)	WEST	
7p.m–9p.m	戌	JUTSU INU	DOG	(11th Zodiac Sign)	W.N.W ⌉ 乾 Ken	Inui
9p.m–11p.m	亥	GAI INOSHISHI	HOG	(12th Zodiac Sign)	N.N.W ⌋	Represents N.W

㉕

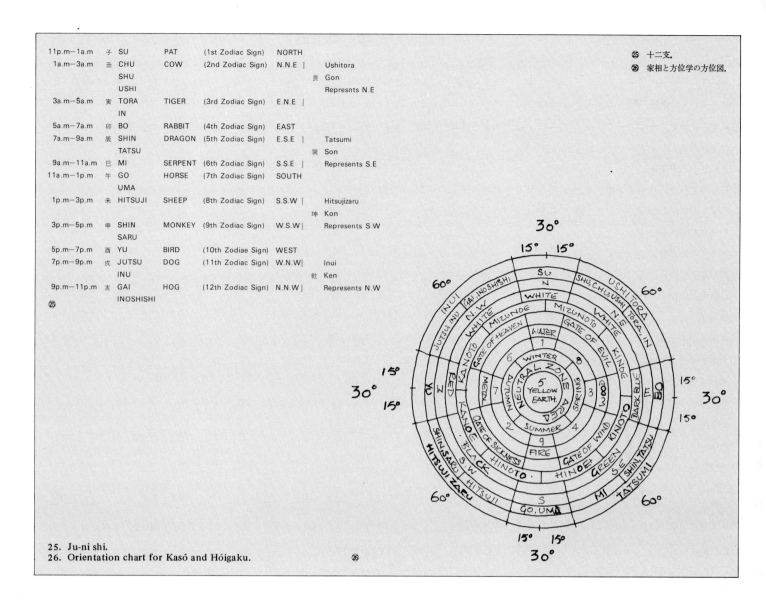

㉕ 十二支.
㉖ 家相と方位学の方位図.

25. Ju-ni shi.
26. Orientation chart for Kasō and Hōigaku.

㉖

of orientation according to topography remained a powerful theme particularly in garden design techniques such as Shakkei. Within the city on the level of individual houses, the main fundaments of the ancient rules of orientation were maintained, and essentially the superstitions and meanings associated with the compass points remained unchanged to a large extent (figs. 20–24). It is this aspect I would like to examine now.

Hoigaku and Kasō

The term Hoigaku is the Japanese word which applies to this study and naturally it too has its roots in the Chinese philosophy already discussed. Hoi – means direction, and gaku – angle or corner.

Amos Rapport points out in his book, 'House, Form and Culture' that 'The Hoigaku system of orientation in Japan determines the location of Japanese houses without regard to topography'. Although this is contradictory to the principles of city layout and is not strictly true, the response is certainly more connected with climatic characteristics and superstition, and an impressive view may well be ignored for this reason. However, since North is an unsatisfactory

direction climatically as well as superstationally, it often appears that the house is responding to topography as well since it may employ a hill or trees to shield it from the cold winds or contain few or no windows in this wall. It is difficult in such a case to decide which is the primary consideration in the design.

With regard to room arrangement there is a clear hierarchy in respect of use, but perhaps more importantly, historically anyway, with regard to superstition. House form and orientation is referred to as 'Kasō' in Japan and is not only determined by the individual compass points but also by the five elements 'Go gyō' and the Zodiac signs, added to this are the science of palm reading, 'Tesō' and face reading, 'Ninsō' and the superstition of birth and death.

The concept is thus immensely complex and the precise influence of one upon the other is difficult to determine, as is the point at which each stage of the history of Kasō developed. It seems certain that it was an important concept from the Heian Period dwellings onwards and possibly before but an entirely Japanese interpretation of Kasō did not

develope until about the middle of the Edo Period when a number of books were published on the subject. The most important of these works are the 'Kasō Kanchi roku' by Koreki Kamiya, written in about 1760 and later books by Tokei Matsuura and Ginkaku Masuura, who was writing at the very end of the Edo Period. Kasō also has its original parallel and forerunner in China where it was referred to as 'Takusō'.

The modern interpretation of Kasō which has become increasingly difficult to apply due to large scale housing developments and the scarcity of sites, is based on the Edo Period Kasō which in turn takes its main principles from the Chinese philosophy. For the reasons mentioned, Kasō is now inevitably not a strong criteria in house design although it still has a large following partly illustrated by the number of books and charts published on the subject.

It is necessary to look briefly at all the various aspects involved in Kasō and since they are all inter related it is often difficult to separate them satisfactorily. Within the various categories there are certain aspects which have relevance to and were important in city planning,

おいても北は下にあるということである．これは，南が主たる方位と考えられたからである（ただし，ここではなじみの深い北を上にした方法をとる）．さらに方位は磁北ではなく真北に従っている．

基本的方位の表を明らかにしたので，次にそれぞれの方位に与えられた意味と結びつける必要がある．ここでまた陰と陽が再び関係してくる．陰陽思想は，陰陽と呼ばれ「陰」と「陽」の二つの漢字で表わされる．

前者，即ち陰の要素は女性，陰性，鬱，深部，性器，秘，闇を表わす．これとは反対に，陽の要素は男性，陽性，天，太陽，高み，行動，昼間を表わす．前にも述べたように，陰と陽は全てのものの中に存在する．

陽は光と昼を表すので，その影響は朝は非常に強く，正午の太陽とともにその極に達する．夕闇とともに，その影響は陰と月の光にとってかわられる．このように夕方以後は人体に悪影響が働きかけはじめる．

この思想に従えば，不運が真夜中に頂点に達すると考えるのが自然と考えられ，それにつれ北が最も運勢の悪い方位を表わすと考えられる．しかしながら，奇妙なことに事実はそうではなく，北東の方向になぜ悪運があるのか説明することは困難であるが，中国の陰陽思想とは無関

係で，中国においては，初期の侵略の脅威がこの方向にあったというだけかもしれない．陰と陽の要素を基礎にして関係の深い他の因子を加味することにより，各方角に影響をもつ力を図に表わすことが可能である㉗．

図㉗の正方形は敷地に対応し，前で述べたその方向に与えられる幸，不幸の運勢はそこに示された軸に沿ってのみ働いている．これらは敷地の外にも拡がっており，そのため敷地を中からではなく，外から影響する．住居の実際の計画に当っては，配置を決める前に部屋とその機能を注意深く決める必要がある．敷地の形状も重要な因子であり，これについては後に述べる．

さらにこれに方角に関するおばあさんの知恵的とでも言うべき迷信が付加されている．実際の住居の計画には特に重要ではないが，住居内での活動に関連が深い傾向がある．そのうちの一つは寝る習慣に関連しており，枕即ち頭を北にしてはならないとしている．それは死者をその向きで安置するからである．また妊婦は子の健康を守るために頭を南にして寝るべきだとしている㉘．

住居の平面計画

平面計画にみられる方位方角の影響に関しては，二つに分けて述べる．はじめは，住居の形と部屋の位置を含む平面における凹凸について述べる．次に個々の部屋の位置とこれが全体の平面計画にどのように影響するかを述べる．

第一部に関しては，ブルーノ・タウトの『日本の家屋と生活』の中に載せられていたものが最良なので，ここではその全部を示すことにする㉙．

個々の部屋や地勢的要素の吉凶を示す最も簡明な方法は，やはり一連の表にするのがよい．

表㉒㉓

表㉒

	北	北東*1	東	南東*2,*4	南	南西*3	西	北西*4
神棚	大吉	凶	大吉	吉	凶	凶	吉	大吉
仏壇	吉	凶	大吉	吉	凶	凶	吉	大吉
井戸	凶	凶	吉	凶	凶	凶	凶	凶
台所	凶	凶	凶	吉	吉	凶	凶	凶
便所	凶	凶	凶	凶	吉	凶	凶	凶
浴室	凶	凶	吉	凶	凶	凶	凶	凶
窓	吉／凶	凶	吉	凶	大吉	凶	吉	凶
玄関	大凶	凶	吉／凶	大吉	吉	吉	凶	凶
倉	凶	凶	吉	大吉	吉	吉	吉	大凶
客間	凶	大凶	凶	吉	吉	大吉	吉	吉
築山	凶	凶	凶	凶	凶	凶	大吉	大吉
池	凶	凶	凶	吉	凶	凶	吉	大吉
門	凶	凶	吉	吉	吉	吉	凶	吉

*1 隅は守られるべきで，壁に開口部があってはならない．特に便所はこの位置に設けてはならない．そこから悪運勢が入り込んでくる．意外であるが，防護に対して明らかに有利であっても，倉もここに建ててはならない．中の品物が悪運勢によって壊される．

*2 玄関には吉．良い運勢が家に入る．

*3 この隅は守られるべきで，開口部があってはならない．雨戸をしまう戸袋はこのためここに置かれる

but essentially here the factors involved refer to the problems of house layout. Necessarily, a considerable amount of explanation will be done through the use of illustration and charts.

The time of day is related to both the compass points and to Yin and Yang, and each pair of hours further corresponds to a Zodiac sign (fig. 25).

Added to this are the 10 Calender signs referred to as Jukkan in Japanese.

Chart 1

WOOD	FIRE	EARTH	METAL	WATER
甲 Kinoe	丙 Hinoe	戊 Tschinoe	庚 Kanoe	壬 Mizunoe
乙 Kinoto	丁 Hinoto	己 Tschinoto	辛 Kanoto	癸 Mizunoto
EAST	SOUTH	CENTRE	WEST	NORTH

The five pairs relate to the five elements. The 'e' ending in each pair denotes the leader of the pair or 'elder brother' and the 'to' ending, the follower or 'young brother'.

The precise directions – North, South, East and West are referred to as 'Shisei' and they form an angle of 30° each within the figure 26. Each zodiac sign represents 30° but because the four pairs become combined as in 'ushi' and 'tora' which becomes 'ushitora', they are designated an angle of 60° on the chart. These four groups are referred to as

'Yosumi' or 'the four corners'. The total number of orientation points can therefore be reduced to eight (C.f. also figs. 27, 34).

$$Shisei\ 30 \times 4 = 120°$$
$$Yosumi\ 60 \times 4 = \frac{240°}{360°}$$

Each of these points has its own gate – the four gates corresponding to the Shisei directions are as follows:

N   Kyūmon : Gate of Rest
E   Shomon : Gate of Injury
S   Keimon : Gate of Scenic Beauty
W   Kyōmon : Gate of Surprise

and the four Yosumi direction points,

N.E   Kimon : Gate of the Devil
S.E   Fumon : Gate of Wind
S.W   Byōmon : Gate of Sickness
N.W   Tenmon : Gate of Heaven

It is important to remember that in any chart or illustration concerning orientation the North point is at the foot of the page or paper, and not the top. This was because South was thought to be the commanding direction, (we will however, use the method familiar to Europeans in this article; North to the top of the page). In addition to this, the orientation calculation is according to real north and not magnetic north.

Having clarified the basic orientation chart it is necessary to connect with it the meanings accorded with each direction and their evolution. It is here that Yin and Yang is again relevant. The Yin Yang philosophy is referred to as 'inyo' in Japan and is represented by the two characters 陰 and 陽 . The former, the 'in' or 'yin' element is representative of female, negativity, melancholy, the depths, the sexual organs, secrecy and darkness. The opposite of this is the 'yo' or 'yang' element which is identified with the male, positivity, heaven, the sun, the heights, movement and daytime. As has been stated before Yin and Yang exist in all things.

Since Yang is representative of light and daytime, its influence is very strong in the morning, peaking with the sun at midday. As dusk falls its influence is replaced by Yin and the rays of the moon. Thus from dusk onwards bad influences begin to act on the human body.

Based on this philosophy, it would seem natural that the period of ill luck would climax at around midnight and therefore North would represent the direction of most ill fortune. Curiously this is not the case and quite why mis-

ことが多い.

＊4　倉と寝室には吉. この方角の良運勢を保護する.

その他の方角に関しては次の表の通りである.

表③

	北東北	東北東	東南東	南南東	南南西	西南西	西北西	北北西
神棚	凶	凶	吉	凶	凶	凶	大吉	大吉
仏壇	凶	凶	吉	吉	凶	凶	吉	吉
井戸	凶	凶	吉／凶	吉	凶	凶	吉	吉
台所	凶	凶	吉	吉	凶	凶	吉	吉
便所	凶	凶	吉	吉	凶	凶	吉	吉
浴室	凶	吉	吉	吉	凶	吉	吉	吉
窓	凶	吉	吉	吉	吉	吉	吉	吉
玄関	凶	凶	吉	大吉	吉／凶	凶	凶	凶
倉	凶	凶	大吉	大吉	吉	凶	大吉	大吉
客間	凶	凶	凶	凶	吉／凶	吉／凶	凶	凶
築山	吉／凶		凶	吉	凶	凶	大吉	大吉
池	凶	凶	吉	吉	凶	凶	大吉	大吉
門	凶	凶	吉	吉	凶	凶	吉	吉

前述した「十干」表①もここでは関係をもっているので, 次の表にその影響を列挙する. 基本的には, 北東南西の主方位の影響と同様である表④.

表④

	壬	癸	甲	乙	丙	丁	庚	辛
神棚	大吉	大吉	凶	凶	凶	凶	吉	吉
仏壇	吉	吉	凶	凶	凶	凶	吉	吉
井戸	吉	吉	凶	吉	凶	凶	吉	吉
台所	吉／凶	吉／凶	凶	吉			吉	吉
便所			凶	吉	吉	吉	吉	吉
浴室	吉		吉	吉	吉	吉	吉	吉
窓	吉		吉	吉	吉	吉	吉	吉
玄関	凶	吉	吉	吉	大吉	大吉	吉	吉
倉			吉／凶	吉	凶	吉	吉	吉
客間			凶	吉	凶	凶	吉	吉
築山	凶	凶	凶	凶	凶	吉／凶	大吉	吉
池	凶	凶	凶	凶	凶	凶	大吉	吉
門	凶	凶	凶	吉	吉	吉	吉	吉

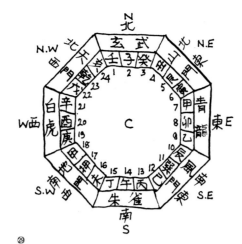

㉙

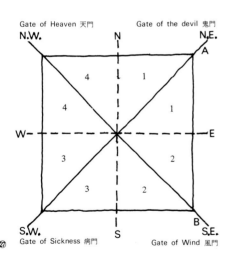

Gate of Heaven 天門　N.W.　　Gate of the devil 鬼門 N.E.
W　　E
S.W.　　Gate of Wind 風門 S.E.
㉗ Gate of Sickness 病門

㉘ Death

Birth

㉗　陰陽の領域図. A—凶線（凶運の方角線）. B—吉線（幸運の方角線）. 1—この領域は万物の始りと終りを共に表わすので, 特に複雑である. 2—ここは陽が最も強いので, 田の中で幸運が来る. 3—陰が陽に取って代わりはじめるので, 吉凶相なかばである. 4—この領域は陰が最も強くなっているにもかかわらず, 吉凶はない.

㉘　枕の方角.

㉙　建物における方位角の吉凶.

1—倉や納屋は吉. この方角の土地がへっこんでいる場合は大吉. 便所は吉凶なし.

2—この方角の門は憂うつを導き入れる. ほこりが家内騒動の原因となる.

3—この方角の井戸は他人に心配をかけ, 虚栄をもたらすが, 真の幸福ではない, 門は吉凶なし.

4—この方角における住居の拡張は家を滅ぼす. 井戸, 便所も破滅させる.

5—この方角の神棚は不運をもたらす　築山は吉, 門は凶.

6—この方角の倉は一世代に限って家を繁栄させる. 暖炉は幼児の病をもたらす. 神棚は吉.

7—この方角で住居に欠込があると願事の成就を妨げる. 住居の突出は上司の引き立てがある. 井戸は健康をもたらす.

8—この方角にある倉は再婚をもたらす. 門があると病が絶えない.

9—この方角に浴室または暖炉を設けると吉運をもたらす. 泉と水路は長寿. 神棚は他人の尊敬と名誉をもたらす.

10—この方角の門は明るさと居心地の良さの印であり, 倉は繁栄をもたらす. 住居の突出は平和をもたらす.

11—神棚は繁栄を, 土地は破滅をもたらす.

12—井戸, 倉, 便所は大吉. 庭は健康と幸福をもたらす.

13—この方角に突出した門は幸運と幸福の印である. 神棚は神々の加護をもたらす.

14—この方角に広い空地があると平和の印である. 井戸は眼の病をもたらす.

15—この方角のかまどは病気をもたらす. 倉の類は大吉.

16—この方角の過度の突出は女性の力が支配することを意味する. 離れまたは倉は主人の早死, 早い引退, 家の破滅をもたらす.

17—この方角の池は水難や主人の酒乱をまねく. 便所は病が絶えない. 庭や木は吉凶なし.

18—この方角の井戸は健康を害す. 門は争い事や不運を増す. 倉は土から幸運を得るのを妨げる.

19—倉の類は繁栄をもたらす. この方角で東を向くかまどは火事をまねく. 仏壇は幸運の印である.

20—この方角にある住居の突出は女性の力が支配的となる. 門は見栄と贅沢をもたらす. 井戸は兄弟姉妹の平和をよぶ.

21—この方角の大道は浪費をまねく. 住居は欠込まれていれば心優しさと繁栄をもたらし, かまどは遠方よりの富をもたらす.

22—この方角の納屋や倉はより大きな繁栄を, 小さな神棚はより大なる神々の加護を, 住居の突出は官庁での出世をもたらす.

23—この方角の隠居所は長寿, 門は富と幸福を, 水路は家内の平和をもたらす.

24—この方角のかまどは富を, 井戸は良水と幸運をもたらし, 便所の類は大吉.

27. Yin and Yang. The sphere of influence. A — Kyosen: Direction line of bad luck. B — Kissen: Direction line of good luck. 1 — This area is particularly complex since it represents the end and the beginning of all things. 2 — This is the luckiest segment of the diagram since Yang is at its strongest. 3 — Both a lucky and unlucky area since Yin begins to take over from Yang. 4 — This area is neither lucky nor unlucky even though Yin is at its strongest in this sector.

28. The direction of the pillow.

29. Significance of the Cardinal Points in Building.

1 — Good for building a storehouse, a barn etc.; receding ground at this point promises good luck; a lavatory does not harm.

2 — A gate here lets in melancholy; dirt is the cause of family troubles.

3 — A well here brings worries over others and vain glory but no true happiness; a gate does not harm.

4 — Extension of the homestead at this point will bring destruction; a well or lavatory promises ruin.

5 — A Shinto shrine built here brings misfortune; a miniature hill in the garden, good luck; a gate, misfortune.

6 — A storehouse built here promises the prosperity of the family for one generation; a fireplace will cause infantile diseases; a Shinto shrine brings good luck.

7 — If the house recedes at this point, it is a hindrance to the fulfilment of hopes; a projection thereof brings the favour of superiors; a well here, health.

8 — A storehouse of the like in this direction is the agent of a second marriage, and a gate, of perpetual illness.

9 — A bath-room or a fireplace built here is the assurance of best luck; a water course of a spring, that of longevity; a Shinto shrine, that of respect of others and honour.

10 — A gate here is a sign of cheerfulness and comfort; a storehouse, the source of prosperity; a projection of the house at this point, the assurance of peace.

11. A Shinto shrine brings prosperity; dirt, ruin.

12. A well, a storehouse or a lavatory brings the best of luck; a garden, good health and happiness.

13 — A projecting gate here is the sign of good luck and happiness; a Shinto shrine promises unsparing divine protection.

14 — Wide, open space in this direction is the sign of peace; a well that of eye diseases.

15 — A cooking stove facing this way is the source of illness; a storehouse or similar, that of the best of luck.

16 — An excessive projection at this point means the predominance of feminine power; a pavilion or a storehouse, the master's early death; a recession, ruin of the household.

17 — A pond here causes deaths from drowning or the intemperance of the master of the house; a lavatory, perpetual diseases; a garden or a wood does not harm.

18 — A well here causes ill health; a gate increases troubles and misfortunes; a storehouse prevents one from getting good from the soil.

19 — A storehouse or similar is the source of prosperity; a cooking stove here facing east is apt to cause a fire; a Buddhist niche is the sign of good luck.

20 — A projection of the home here leads to the predominance of feminine power; a gate, to vanity and extravagance; a well, to peace among brothers and sisters.

21 — highway here invokes unnecessary expenditure; if the house recedes, there will be tenderness of heart and prosperity; a cooking stove brings wealth from after.

22 — A barn of a storehouse here leads to greater prosperity; a small Shinto shrine, to greater divine protection; a projection of the house, to a successful career in government service.

23 — A retreat built here for the elders gives longevity; a gate, wealth and happiness; a water course or similar, peace in the family.

24 — A cooking stove brings wealth; a well gives good water and luck; a lavatory or similar brings the best of luck. (Translated by Shiro Hirai, Tokyo)

中央の土の要素「つちのえ」と「つちのと」は相反する要素をその交錯する点で中和する．そのため，家の中央は平穏と安全を意味するが，特定の影響が特に強い時には時たま荒れることがある．

住居の中心の位置

家相設定の古い例では③⓪③⓵③⓶，全ての方位が含まれている．しかし，近年の例では四聖と四隅の8つの方向のみの場合の方が多い．いずれにせよ，敷地の幾何学的分析は住居の中央を表わす点から分割され，その点から各々の方角に運勢の範囲が決定される．この中心点は住居の形から算出されるが，また一方では五行の要素「土」をも表わしており，敷地の中性的領域でもある③⓷③⓸．

はじめに，敷地の地勢を考慮して建物にとって最良の位置を決定する．つづいて可能な種々の異なった住居の型に対し，それぞれに家相を調べる．決定された住居平面の複雑さや形状に従って，住居の中央はいくつかの違った基準で決定することができる．

1　最も簡単な方法は，農家の田の字型平面*1に明らかなように大黒柱*2によって中央を決定する方法である．

2　主人の居室の場所により決定する方法．

3　住居の均衡的中心によって決定する方法．

4　平面の形の幾何的中心によって決定する方法③⓹→③⓻．

実際の敷地の形状も重要である．当初は形状のみによって好ましい敷地が決定され，続いて主人の支干と多くの場合男の支干が考慮加味され，敷地の地勢も加味された．図③⓼は敷地の形状の良形，不良形を単純化して示している．また，図③⓽は地勢と主人との関係を示す．

周期的再生（相生相剋）

方位角の基本的理念の中で，支配的な考え方の一つに「周期的再生」というのがある．これは，陰陽と天地万物の四季の周期に現われている．五行の考え方の中にも同様な思想があり，各要素は正と負の関係で互いに関係している．正の方向は，相生と呼ばれ次のような周期となる．

1　火を起こすには木が必要である．

2　木は燃えると灰になり，これは土を表わす．

3　土の中を掘ると金属が出てくる．そして金属の表面には水が結露し，

4　水を得て木が生成する．このようにして周期が一巡する．

負の方向では，次のような型が見られる．負の方向は日本では，相剋と呼ばれる．

1　水は火を消す．

2　火は金属を溶かす．

3　木は土なしでは育たない．

4　土は水の流れを支配する．

次の表がこの理念を示している④⓪．これらの要素はまた，四季との直接関係で変化の第一側面をも表わす．これを通して前述したように方角とも関連している．

⓪　方位角に基づく江戸時代の民家の平面図．1—宮．2—倉．3—浴室．4—書院．5—主要居室．6—客室．7—倉．8—井戸．9—築山．10—居室．11—玄関ホール．12—台所．13—庭．

⓵　江戸時代の建物の平面．北はこの図の下の方である．1—客室．2—廊下．3—庭．4—主家．5—縁．6—庭．7—倉．8—店．9—玄関．10—坪庭．11—空地．12—倉．C—家の中心．

⓶　北西隅に倉をとり込んだ住居．

⓷　五行と方位．

⓸　四聖と四隅別方位角の範囲．

30. Layout of Edo Period house in accordance with orientation principles. 1 – Shrine. 2 – Warehouse/store. 3 – Bathhouse. 4 – Shoin. 5 – Main living space. 6 – Guest room. 7 – Store. 8 – Well. 9 – Artificial hill. 10 – Subsidiary living room. 11 – Entrance hall. 12 – Kitchen. 13 – Garden.
31. Plan of Edo era building. North is thus to the bottom of the plan. 1 – Guest room. 2 – Linking corridor. 3 – Garden. 4 – Main house. 5 – Veranda. 6 – Garden. 7 – Warehouse. 8 – Shop. 9 – Entrance. 10 – Courtyard. 1 – Open space. 12 – Warehouse. C – House center.
32. House with an inbuilt 'Kura' or warehouse in its northwest corner.
33. The elements according to direction.
34. Dividing up the Orientation chart according to Shisei and Yosumi directions.

fortune is found in the direction of the North East is difficult to say, but it may be that it has no connection with the Yin Yang philosophy of China, but simply be the result of the fact that the threat of invasion in China came initially from this direction. We can build up a chart using the Yin and Yang elements as a basis in conjunction with other relevant influences to illustrate the potent forces associated with the directions (fig. 27).

The square section in the diagram corresponds to a plot of land with the good and bad fortunes associated with the directions discussed earlier extending only along the exact axis with which they are indicated. These latter influences extend beyond the site and therefore influence the site from outside and not from within. In the actual planning of the house, the position of the room and its function must be carefully considered before the location is decided. Site shape is also an important affector and will be dealt with at a later point.

Added to this there are a number of superstitions attached to direction which are the equivalent of what we refer to as 'old wives tales'. They are not particularly important considerations in actual house layout but tend to be more connected with activities within the house. One particular example concerns sleeping habits, — one should never sleep with the pillow, thus the head to the North since this is the position in which the dead are laid also a pregnant woman should sleep with her head to the south thus assuring the health of the child (fig. 28).

House Layout

As regards layout in respect of orientational influences this will be discussed in two parts. The first refers to the house shape and the position of any recess or projection in the plan, including room location. The second part refers only to the position as regards individual rooms and how this affected the overall layout of the house.

For the first part there is no better reference than that published in Bruno Taut's, 'Houses and People of Japan' and it is therefore reproduced in its entirety (fig. 29).

The simplest way to illustrate the favourable and unfavourable aspects of the individual rooms and landscape features, is again by a series of charts with relevant notes:

Chart 2

	N	NE*1	E	SE*2	S	SW*3	W	NW*4
Household Shrine	V.G	B	V.G	G	B	B	G	V.G
Buddhist Altar	G	B	V.G	G	B	B	G	V.G
Well	B	B	B	G	B	B	B	B
Kitchen	B	B	B	G	B	B	G	B
Toilet	B	B	B	B	B	B	B	B
Bathroom	B	B	B	G	B	B	B	B
Window	O.K	B	B	G	V.G	B	G	B
Entrance	V.B	B	O.K	G	B	B	B	B
Storehouse	?	B	G	V.G	G	B	G	V.G
Guest Room	B	V.B	B	B	V.G	B	G	G
Artificial Hill	B	B	B	B	B	B	V.G	V.G
Pond	B	B	B	B	B	B	G	V.G
Gate	B	B	B	G	G	G	B	G

Key: V.G – very good. G – good. O.K – good nor bad. V.B – very bad. B – bad.

*1 The corner should be protected and there should be no openings in the wall. The toilet in particular should not be positioned here since evil influences can enter the house through it! Surprisingly, the storehouse should not be put here despite its obvious protection advantage because the goods will be destroyed by evil forces.
*2 Good for entrance, good influences can freely enter the house.
*3 The corner should be protected and there should be no opening. The 'tobukuro' or wooden closet in which the rain doors or 'amado' are stored is often positioned here for this reason.
*4 Good for storehouse and sleeping; the good influences from this direction give protection.

For the secondary directions:

Chart 3

	NNE	ENE	ESE	SSE	SSW	WSW	WNW	NNW
Household Shrine	B	B	G	B	B	B	V.G	V.G
Buddhist Altar	B	B	G	G	B	B	B	G
Well	B	B	O.K	G	B	B	G	G
Kitchen	B	B	G	G	B	B	G	G
Toilet	B	B	G	G	B	B	G	G
Bathroom	B	G	G	G	B	B	G	G
Window	B	G	G	G	G	G	G	G
Entrance	B	B	G	V.G	O.K	B	B	B
Store	B	B	V.G	G	B	B	V.G	G
Guest Room	B	B	B	B	O.K	O.K	G	G
Artificial Hill	O.K	?	B	B	B	B	G	G
Pond	B	B	B	B	B	B	V.G	V.G
Gate	B	B	G	G	B	B	G	G

Key: V.G – Very good. G – Good. B – Bad. O.K – Good nor bad.

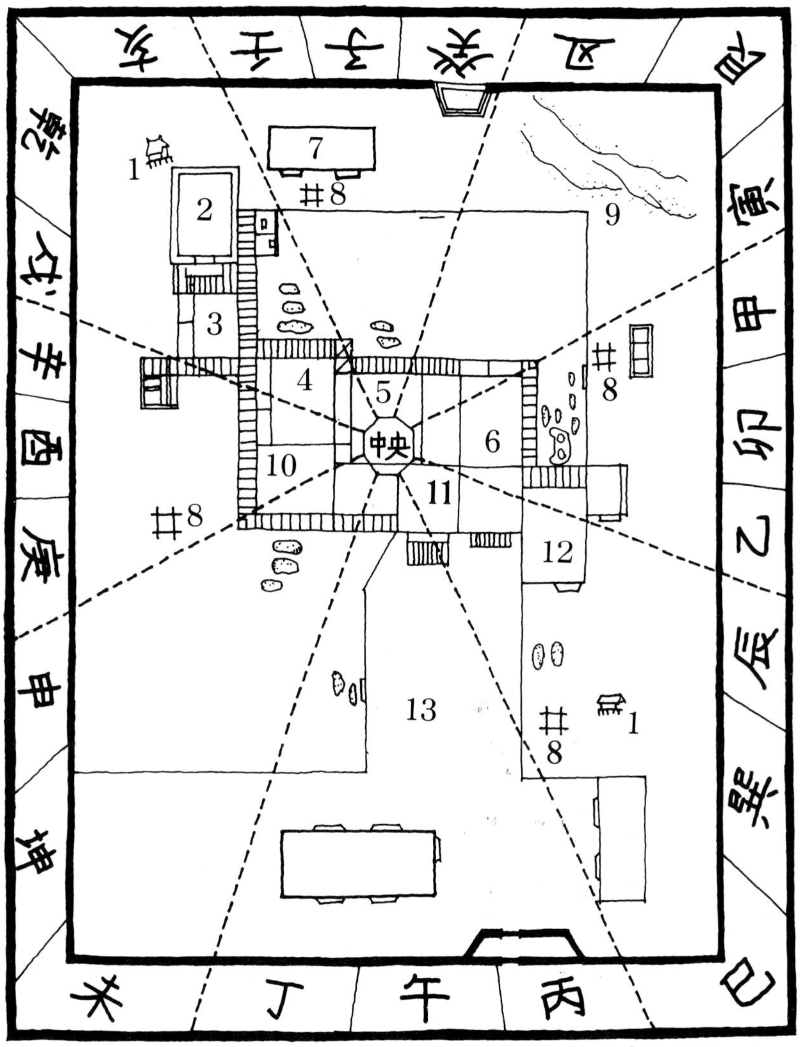
1
2
3
4
5
6
7
8
9
10
11
12
13
中央

㉚

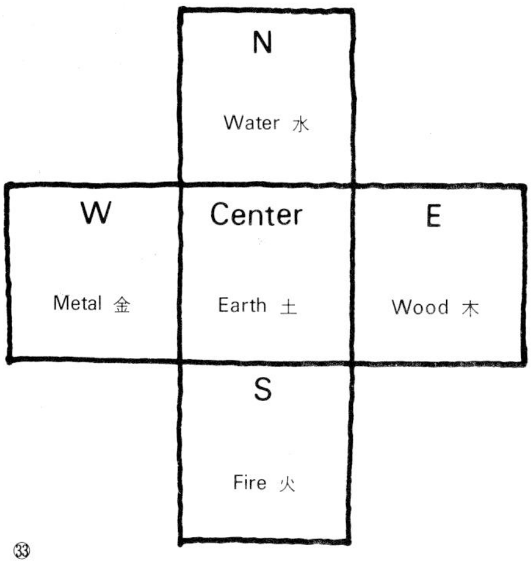
N
Water 水
W
Metal 金
Center
Earth 土
E
Wood 木
S
Fire 火

㉝

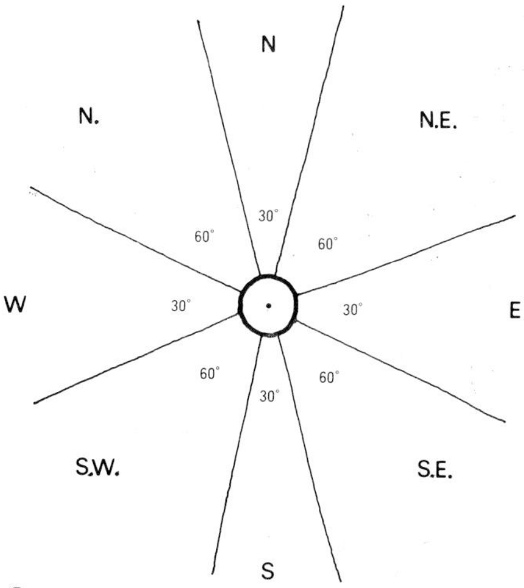
N
N.
N.E.
W
E
S.W.
S.E.
S
30°
60°

㉞

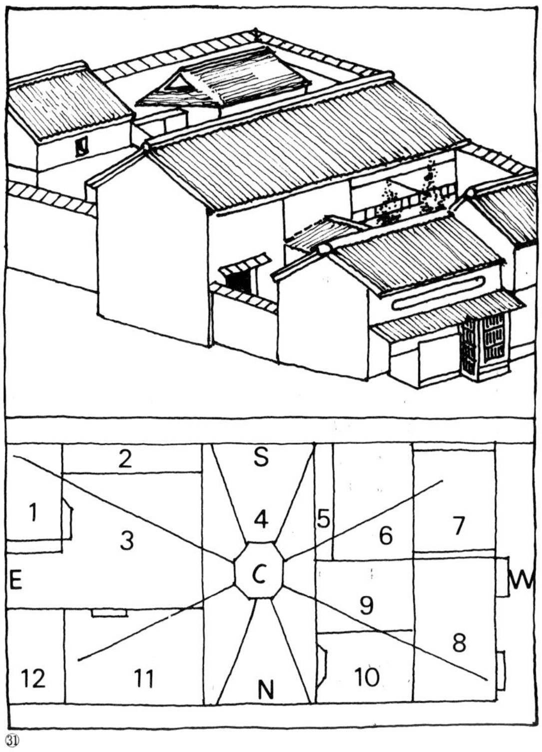
S
E
W
N
C
1
2
3
4
5
6
7
8
9
10
11
12

㉛

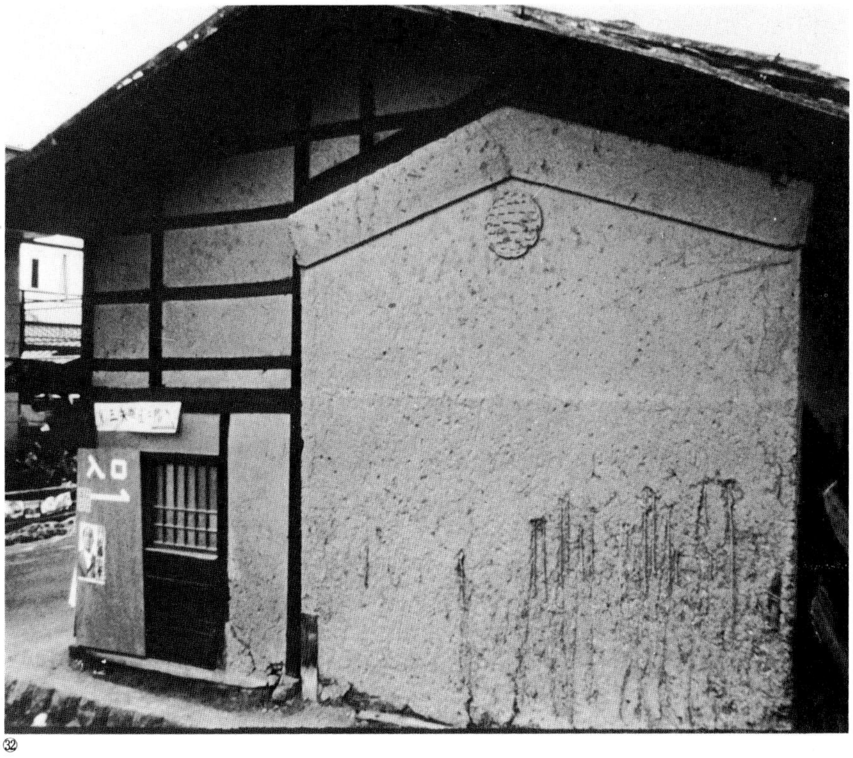

㉜

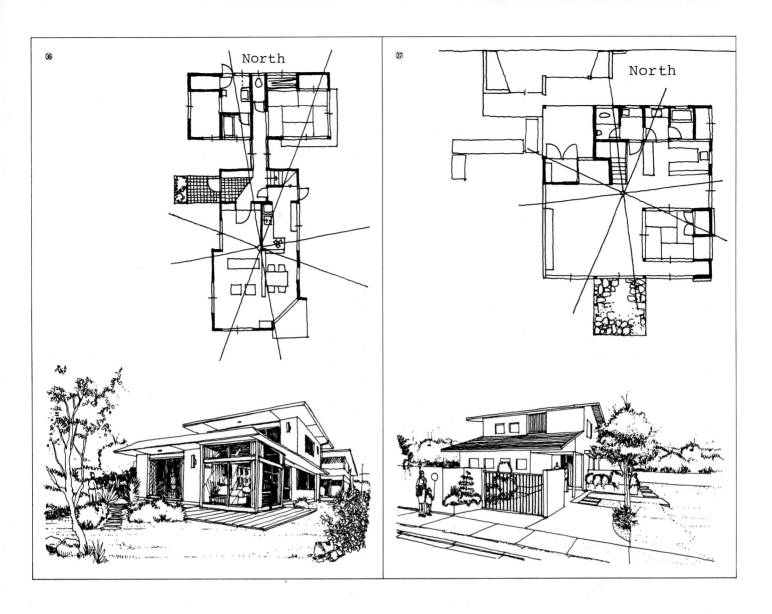

The 'jikkan' referred to earlier (Chart 1), also have their part to play here and therefore are worth listing, essentially they come under the sphere of influence of N.E, S and W (Chart 4).

Chart 4

	Mizunoe	Mizunoto	Kinoe	Kinoto	Hinoe	Hinoto	Kanoe	Kanoto
Household Shrine	V.G	V.G	B	B	B	B	G	G
Buddhist Altar	G	G	B	B	B	B	G	G
Well	G	G	G	G	B	B	G	G
Kitchen	O.K	O.K	G	G	?	?	G	G
Toilet	?	?	G	G	G	G	G	G
Bathroom	G	G	G	G	G	G	G	G
Window	G	B	G	G	G	G	G	G
Entrance	B	G	G	G	V.G	V.G	G	G
Store	G	?	O.K	G	G	G	G	G
Guest Room	B	B	G	G	B	B	G	G
Artificial Hill	B	B	B	B	O.K	V.G	G	G
Pond	B	B	B	B	B	B	G	G
Gate	B	B	G	G	G	B	G	G

Key: V.G – Very good.   B – Bad.   G – Good.   O.K – Good nor bad.

The earth element Tsuchinoe and Tsuchinoto at the centre neutralises the conflicting influences at their point of intersection and therefore the centre of the house represents calm and security but with the occasional flare up when one influence may be particularly strong.

Position of the House Centre

In older examples of the plotting of Kasō (as in figs. 30–32), all the compass point angles are included. In more recent

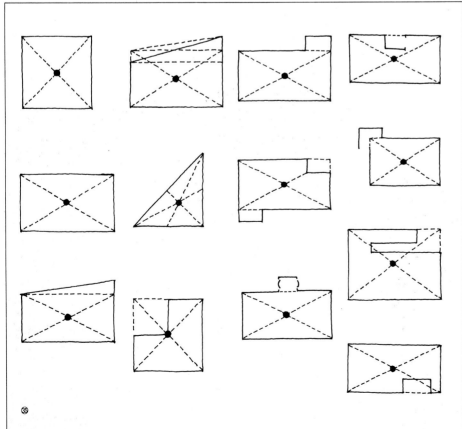

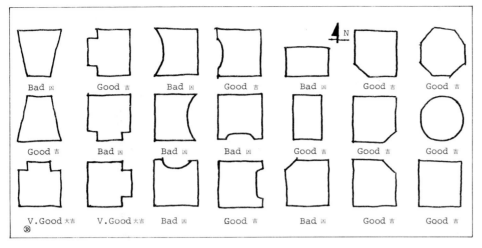

Bad 凶 | Good 吉 | Bad 凶 | Good 吉 | Bad 凶 | Good 吉 | Good 吉
Good 吉 | Bad 凶 | Bad 凶 | Bad 凶 | Good 吉 | Good 吉 | Good 吉
V. Good 大吉 | V. Good 大吉 | Bad 凶 | Good 吉 | Bad 凶 | Good 吉 | Good 吉

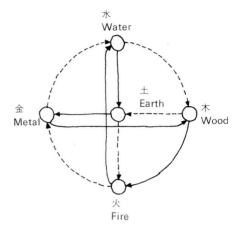

水 Water
土 Earth
金 Metal
木 Wood
火 Fire

...... Sojo directions 相生方向
——— Sokoku directions 相克方向

		Wood	Fire	Earth	Metal	Water	None
Birth Element	Site Shape	1	2	3	4	5	6
木 Wood		貧困 Povery Destituton	繁栄 Prosperity	破滅 Destruction	幸福 Happiness	平和 Peace Calm	凶運 Bad Luck
火 Fire		裕福 Enrichment	貧困 Poverty Destitution	病気 Disease	死 Death	幸福 Happiness	凶運 Bad Luck
土 Earth		病気 Illness	裕福 Enrichment	繁栄 Prosperity	病気 Disease	貧困 Poverty Destitution	凶運 Bad Luck
金 Metal		災難 Disaster		貧困 Poverty Destitution	繁栄 Prosperity	幸福 Good Luck	凶運 Bad Luck
水 Water		大吉 Very Good	病気 Disease	裕福 Enrichment	貧困 Poverty Destitution	病気 Sickness	凶運 Bad Luck

SITE SHAPE : 1—High in West & low in East. 2—High in North & low in South. 3—High in East & low in West. 4—High in South & low in North. 5—Low centre & high surround. 6—High in centre & low surround.
敷地形状: 1—西に高く、東に低い. 2—北に高く、西に低い. 3—東に高く、西に低い. 4—南に高く、北に低い. 5—中央に低く、周囲が高い. 6—中央が高く、周囲が低い.

㉟ 住居の中央の求め方. 不整形は拡張または簡略化し整形として求める.
㊱㊲ 現代住居の例.
㊳ 敷地形状の吉凶 (江戸時代の図版より). Good＝吉, Bad＝凶, V. Good＝大吉.
㊴ 敷地形状と五行との関係.
㊵ 五行の循環変転図.

35. Calculating the position of the house center. Irregular shapes are extended or simplified to make regular shapes and then calculated.
36, 37. Modern house example.
38. The good and bad fortune of various site shapes. From an Edo Period chart.
39. Fortune according to site shape and birth element.
40. The cyclic association of the five elements.

examples however it is more likely that we will find only the 8 orientation points of the Shisei and Yosumi groups. Which ever is the case, the geometrical breakdown of the site will be done from a point representing the house centre and from this point generate all the spheres of influence relevant to their particular direction. This centre point is calculated according to house shape, but it is also representative of the element 'earth', and is the neutral zone of the site (figs. 33, 34).

In the first place the topography of the site is considered to establish the best position for the actual building. Following this, the aspects of Kasō are studied in regard to various different possible house types. According to the complexity of the decided plan and its shape, the house centre can be established by a number of differing criteria:

1. The simplest method which was often apparent in the Ta no ji form of farmhouse*1, was by locating the centre according to the Daikoku bashira*2.
2. According to the position of the master of the houses' room.
3. According to the position of the balance centre in the house.

4. According to plan shape and its geometric centre (figs. 35—37).

The actual site shape is also important. Originally a favourable site on which to build was decided by the shape only and then more specifically in relation to the birth element of the owner, often considering the elder son as well, and also the exact topography of the site was relevant. Fig. 38 is a simplified analysis of the favourable and unfavourable site shapes, and fig. 39 illustrates the relationship between site topography, and the owner.

Cyclic Renewal

One of the most dominant ideas in the principles of orientation is that of 'cyclic renewal'. This is evident within Yin and Yang and in the seasonal renewal of all things. The five elements 'Go gyō' also contain such a philosophy since they are related with both a positive and negative directional force. The positive force is known as 'So jō', and it works something like the following:

1. For fire we need wood.
2. Wood — when it burns makes ash which represents earth.
3. When we dig in the earth we find metal, and on the surface of the metal

water is formed as condensation.
4. Wood in turn grows from water, and thus the cyclic pattern is completed.

In the negative direction, the following pattern is discernible; the negative direction is called 'Sōkoku' in Japanese.

1. Water puts out fire.
2. Metal melts in fire.
3. Wood cannot grow without earth.
4. And earth controls the flow of water.

The following chart illustrates this principle (fig. 40).

The elements also represent certain aspects of change in direct connection with the seasons and thus are related to direction as discussed earlier.

ki (Wood) — This represents penetration touching and feeling. It coincides with the East direction because plants start growing and insects moving in the Spring and is therefore indicative of movement. This is a Yang element.

hi (Fire) — This represents change and the shape of the Chinese letter indicates flame. It is necessarily associated with South because of its 'heat'. Incubation and conception are connected with this element. This is also a Yang element.

tsuchi (Earth) — Representative of 'exuding', it is the element from which

49

木——これは貫ぬくこと，触覚を表わす．これは春に草木が伸びはじめ，虫も活動を始める動きを示すとされ，そのため東の方角と一致する．これは陽の要素である．

火——これは変化を表わし，漢字の字形は炎を表わしている．これはその「熱」，「暖かさ」のため南の方角と関連づけられる．これも陽の要素である．

土——これは生み出すものを表わしている．それはこの要素から万物の生成が生じ，死んだ人，滅んだ物はこれに帰る．このため，これは陰と陽の合わさったもので，他の要素の中心に置かれる．

金——これは秋を表わす．成長のないことを象徴し，西の方角と収穫とに関連する．これは陰の要素である．

水——水平線と「究極」を表わす．これはまたほとんどのものが冬眠する冬の静けさと平穏さとに関係づけられる．このため，季節では冬にあたり，もう一つの陰の要素である．

　四聖の主方角（東西南北）と四隅の主方角（東北，南東，南西，北西）は数に基づく周期により算定される．四聖の方角は奇数が当てられ，陰の方角であり，四隅の方角は偶数が当てられ，従って陽の方角である．

北＝1

1×3＝3　これは東．

3×3＝9　これは南．

3×9＝27　これは十の位の2を落して7と考え，西を表わす．

3×7＝21　これはまた十の位の2を落して1と考え，1はもとに戻り北となる．

南西は2で表わす．

2×2＝4　これは南東．

2×4＝8　これは北東．

2×8＝16　これは十の位の1を落して6と考え，北西を表わす．

2×6＝12　これは2と考えまた南西に戻る．

これは次の周期の表⑤に表わすこともできる．

表⑤

		成男	適用
1	一白	中年男	友情
2	二黒	母	
3	三碧	青年	発展
4	四緑	客人	成功
5	図表に書かれていず		
6	六白	主人	現実
7	七赤	少女	隠遁
8	八白	少年	変化
9	九紫	成女・中年男	不規・不離＊

＊これは不貞とは無関係で，混同してはならない．

これらの方角の数字は，唐代の中国で書かれた『洛書』で定義された方角に関する基本的法則を構成する．これらの数は，現代の方位角の算定とはほとんど関係がないようであるが，当初の図表の基礎をなしたものであり，頭の中に入れおく必要がある．

（訳：日野水　信）

註
＊1　田の字型の住居平面の発展は，漢字の田の形となる四間で構成される住居のことである．

1空間　2空間　3空間　4空間（田の字平面）

＊2　大黒柱は民家構法の特殊形態における主要中心柱のことである．

---

all growth comes and all destroyed or dead matter returns. It is therefore a combination of Yin and Yang and is positioned in the centre of the other elements.

kin (Metal) – This represents autumn since it is symbolic of no growth and is associated with West and harvest time. This is a Yin element.

mizu (Water) – Representative of the horizon and 'the end'. It is further associated with peace and tranquility of winter when most things are hibernating. It therefore symbolizes North and is the other Yin element.

The major direction signs of Shisei – North, East, South and West and Yosumi – North East, South East, South West and North West are also calculated according to a cyclic but numerical pattern. The Shisei directions are the Yin directions in that they are represented by odd numbers and the Yosumi are the Yang directions since they are calculated by using even numbers.

North = 1

    $1 \times 3 = 3$ which is East
    $3 \times 3 = 9$ which is South
    $3 \times 9 = 27$ which becomes 7 because the 2 is omitted and 7 represents

West
    $3 \times 7 = 21$ which becomes 1 because the 2 is again omitted and thus we arrive back at North
South is represented by 2
    $2 \times 2 = 4$ which is South East
    $2 \times 4 = 8$ which is North East
    $2 \times 8 = 16$ which becomes 6 because the 1 is omitted in this case and represents North West
    $2 \times 6 = 12$ which becomes 2 and therefore arrive back at South West

This can also be represented in the following cyclic diagram (Chart 5).

Chart 5

	Form	Application
1. IPPAKU	Middle aged Man	Friendship
2. JIKOKU	Mother	?
3. SANPEKI	Young Man	Development
4. SHIROKU	Guest	Success
5. (not represented in the chart)		
6. ROPPAKU	Master, Host	Reality
7. SHICHISEKI	Little Girl	Seclusion
8. HAPPAKU	Small Boy	Change
9. KYUSHI	Middle Aged Woman	Detachment/Attachment*

* This is not to be confused with infidelity with which it has no connection.

These orientational numbers form a basic principle of the rules of orientation as defined in a book called 'Rakusho', written in China during the To Dynasty. They appear to have little relevance on the present day orientation calculations, but were the basis for the original charts and therefore important to bear in mind.

Notes:
*1. The Ta no Ji development of house plan is the term used to describe the four space house which forms the shape of the letter 田 'ta' meaning field in Japanese.

1. space   2. space   3. space   4. space Ta no Ji plan.

*2. The Daikokubashira is the main central column in one particular form of Minka construction.

*

References:
Nihon no Toshi Kukan, Itoh Teiji, Shokokusha 1968.
Houses & People of Japan, Bruno Taut.
"House of the Ainu", Masahiro Chatani, *Detail*, July 1979.
Science & Civilisation in China, Vol. 4 Part 3., Joseph Needham.
Edo – Tokyo: Toshi no Naka no Machiya, Hosei Daigaku: Tokyo no machi kenkyukai.
Kasō, Chisō, Hōi, Bosō no kenkyu, Ryusuke Shiga, Shubunkan.
"Gendai no Kasō", Kiyosi Seike, *Sumai no Sekkei*, Jan.1978.
"Mabsysteme im chinesischen Stadtebau", Alfred Schinz, *Architectura*, Vol. 6, 1976.

FRONTAL PERCEPTION IN ARCHITECTURAL SPACE

by Jorge M. Ferreras

建築空間における正面の知覚

ホルヘ・M・フェレーラス

日本の伝統的な建築に見出すことのできる正面性について私の考えを紹介するに当たって，私がそのことに初めて気づいたいくつかの個人的な経験について述べたいと思います．人間が一生の内でも最も熱心に筋肉運動的な冒険を求める年代である幼少と青年期を，私はアルゼンチンのパンパスで過ごしました．そこでは我々をとり囲む風景は天と地の無限の平面をへだてるかのような，ひたすら遠く手の届かない広がりのある地平線だけであると言えるでしょう．ここでは数百キロの範囲に一つの山も丘も林も川もあるいは湖もありません．唯一つあるのは，人の進路に対して永久に垂直であり，永久に水平であるあの真直な地のはての線です．町を歩き回ってみても到るところにあるこの地平線から逃げるわけにはいきません．というのも，あ

らゆる街路の景観の最終には地平線が現われるからです①→⑥．小さな町では１階の高さを越える建物がわずかしかないため，私の筋肉運動的な経験をしたいという欲求を満すには，全くうらやましい身分の友達が住む２階建ての家に行くか，そこからふり返ると広場が見え，普通の視点よりは少しばかり高いことが楽しみな教会の入口へ続く階段を登るしかなかったのです．家での地形的な変化といえば，入口の二段の階段と，居間とパティオをつなぐ一段の階段だけでした．こうした階段は息をのむような峡谷であり，プラントボックスは人をこばむジャングルであり，パティオの囲りの溝は大きな河であるという風に誇張して考えながら家の囲りを歩きまわったことを思い出します．建築的な世界に入るために必要なスケールの操作を学んでい

たわけです．こうした非常に彫刻的なものに対する好奇心，つまりはスケールを楽しみたいという欲求は自然環境の平坦さへの反動だったと言えるかもしれません．17才の時，山や川や湖そして建築的な変化の非常に富んだ「もっと豊かな」環境に移り住んだのですが，知的な好奇心のために，パンパスに住んでいたかくも長い間夢みていた物質的な豊かさに無関心になってゆきました．何年も後になって，日本の風景と建築とが長い間忘れていた子供のころの環境をみなおさせたのでした．

日本の形⑦や色彩の感覚的な表現によって子供のころの欲求が満され，伝統的な建築に備っているある種の比喩的な性質にふれ，ついに初めて私はパンパスを評価し，再認識するに到りました．パンパスは私に，長い間眠ってはいた

By way of introduction to my thoughts on the Frontality which can be perceived in Japanese traditional architecture I would like to describe some of the personal experiences which made me first sensitive to it. I spent my childhood and adolescence, that period of life when man most avidly seeks kinaesthetic adventures, in the Argentinian pampas where the surrounding scenery can be described as being simply a distant, unreachable, stretched horizon separating the seemingly infinite planes of heaven and earth. There there are no mountains, hills, forests, rivers or lakes within several hundred kilometers. The only presence was that straight line of horizon, eternally perpendicular to one's route, eternally horizontal. Even when moving around the town one is not freed from this ubiquitous horizon since it appears at the end of every street perspective (figs. 1–6). The small town had only a few buildings over one storey high therefore my lust for kinaesthetic experiences could be comforted only by either going to the two-storey house in which a much-envied friend of mine lived, or by climbing the stairs leading to the atrium of the church, a place from where I would

look back towards the square, delighted by the slightly higher than normal view-point. Topographical variation at home was restricted to the two steps at the entrance and the one step between the living area and the patio. I can remember wandering around the house magnifying these steps into breathtaking cliffs, the plant boxes into impenetrable jungles and the small gutter surrounding the patio into a large river . . . I was learning to manipulate scale, to approach the architectural world. It can probably be said that this curiosity for the highly sculptural, this necessity of playing with scale was a reaction to the flatness of the natural environment. Although at seventeen I moved to a comparatively "richer" environment of mountains, rivers, lakes and great architectural variety, rising intellectual curiosities made me become indifferent towards the physical richness which I had dreamed of for so long while living in the Pampas. Many years later, my experience of the Japanese landscape and architecture was to cause me to reidentify with my long-forgotten childhood environment.

I finally came to appreciate and reidentify myself with the Pampas when, after satiating my childhood lust in the sensuous appeal of shapes (fig. 7), colours and textures of Japan, I began to communicate with a certain metaphorical quality inherent in the traditional architecture. The Pampas had imprinted on my mind a sensitivity towards flatness which although dormant for a long time, was revived when I first noticed the beauty of a tatami-mat floor as a surface abstracted from the room. Quietly sitting in a traditional Japanese room I felt a paradoxical Pampas-like vastness despite the small size of the room. I was perceiving a "metaphysical space" (fig. 8).

There must be some common factor in my perception of both the Pampas and the metaphysical aspects of the Japanese interior. This common factor could be the dissociative character of that process which allow us to perceive abstracted surfaces in their geometrical beauty. As one example, the geometrical patterns of the tatami-mats suggested to me the patterns made by the boundaries between large Pampas fields as seen from the air (figs. 6, 8–10). Driving through the Pampas I used to imagine such abstract patterns in order to avoid boredom. The monotony and solitude of the Pampas

ものの，平坦さに対する感性を刻みつけていた
のでした．そしてこの感性は部屋から抽出され
た面としてのタタミ敷の床の美しさに私が初め
て気づいた時によみ返ってきたのでした．伝統
的な日本間に静かに座っているうちに，部屋の
規模が小さいにもかかわらず，私は逆説的にパ
ンパスのような広大さを感じていました．「形
而上的な空間」⑧ を感知していたわけです．

パンパスと日本の室内の形而上的な傾向の相
方の知覚の中には，何らかの共通な要素があっ
たにちがいありません．この共通な要素とは，
幾何学的な美しさの中に抽象的な面を感知させ
る分離的な過程の性格であると言えるかも知れ
ません．一つの例として，畳の幾何学的なパタ
ーンは私に空から見た時の壮大なパンパス原野
の間にある境界でできたパターン⑥，⑧→⑩を暗
示させました．パンパスをドライブする時，私
はよく退屈しのぎにそうした抽象的なパターン
を想像したものでした．パンパスの風景の単調
さと孤独とが，私をその形而上的な美しさに感
じやすくしていて，何年も後になって，多分，
パンパスの広大さに対するホームシックのせい
か，日本の伝統的な部屋の限られた空間の中に
同じような性格を発見したのでした．限られた
この文章の中で，私は日本的な空間とは全く違
った経験を通じての基本的には日本空間の認識

①

② ③

landscape made me susceptible to its
metaphysical beauty and many years
later, perhaps inspired by homesickness
for the Pampas vastness, I discovered a
similar quality in the limited space of
a Japanese traditional room. Within the
space of this article I intend to introduce
some points of a much larger analysis
which is basically the result of my identification with the Japanese space through
my experience of its antipodean opposite.

④ ⑤

①→⑥　アルゼンチンのパンパス風景．
⑦　鹿児島県坊津町の風景．
⑧　高大寺，京都．
⑨⑩　東京近郊の住居．

1, 6. Argentinian pampas (photos by Agustín
Ferreras).
2–5. Argentinian pampas (photos by Daniel
Garavelli).
7. Bonotsu, Kagoshima Prefecture.
8. Kodai-ji, Kyoto.
9, 10. Residence in Tokyo suburbs.

⑥

⑦

⑧

⑨

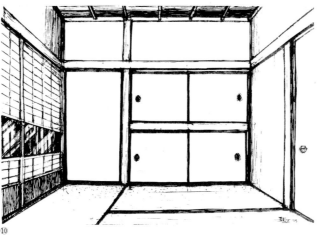

⑩

の結果である，より大きな分析のうちのいくつかを紹介しようと思ったわけです．

正面性

一部には表面のテクスチャーや色彩の不統一さ，そして一部には退屈さに触発され，ベッドにしばられた人は自分の面している天井とか壁とかに想像の絵を画いて自らを慰めるものです．空間を構成するこうしたあらゆる要素から一つの要素だけを分離することを通じて，人はこのように普通と違う建築的な空間を知覚することを楽しめるわけです．その上に，彼の考えを集中する表面はやがて独立しはじめ，彼の想像のためのスクリーンの役をはたし，それが物質的でないという意味で形而上的な性格をもった「抽象的な」空間の中での主たる構成要素になってゆくのです．スクリーンのような表面はこのようにして部屋の他の部分から分離されます．人に表面を独立したものとして認知させるこの「分離」の過程は，誰かがある部屋で物質的な空間をボリュームとして感じるような「連合的」な過程とは相対するものです．従って抽象的な空間とは，それによって物理的な空間が組み立てられる他の要素の中から抽出された特別な要素の上に，精神を集中させることによって生成され，またそのように認知されるものなので

Frontality

Partially inspired by surface texture and colour irregularities and partially out of boredom, a person confined to bed learns to entertain himself drawing imaginary pictures on the ceiling or on the wall facing him. Through the dissociation of a single element from all of those composing the space a person can thus enjoy a way of perceiving architectural space which is different from the usual. The surface upon which he concentrates his thoughts becomes autonomous and, acting as a screen for his fantasies, this surface becomes the main composing element in an "abstract" space having a metaphysical nature – in the sense that it is non-physical. The screen-like surface is thus dissociated from the rest of the room. The "dissociative" process which allows a person to perceive a surface as autonomous is opposed to the "associative" process which makes the same person in the same room perceive the physical space as a volume. The abstract space therefore, is generated and so perceived through mental concentration upon a particular element abstracted from the others with which it combines to make the physical

す．組立てられている表面の上に続けて集中することで空間を読みとることは，日本の伝統的建築を認知する方法としては美学的に最も役立つことであり，それ以上に目的とする表面への集中はその表面が視線に対して垂直の時，いわばその表面が正面として見られる時により容易になるということに気づきました．日本の伝統的な空間を構成する表面の全ては床や天井に到るまで，正面として見られる時に，極めて訴える力を持つという特殊性をさずけられています．従って私がこの主たる知覚的な特徴に「正面性」という名前を選んだのもその理由からです．幾何学的なパターンと隣接した要素との分節における視覚的な空間デザインの暗示が，この正面性を気づかせたのでした①→㉒．

正面性に気づくためには，西洋人は自分が異なった種類の知覚を必要とする異なった空間の中に居ることに気づく必要があります．何もない部屋の壁や天井や床の幾何学的なパターンがどんなに美しくとも，西洋人の第一印象は不満足に類するものか，またはせいぜい良くも悪くもないといった程度です．彼は部屋と家具の表面が彫刻的に相互作用し合うものとして空間を認知するのに慣れているのです．こういうわけですから，日本の部屋に入ることによって彼が認知する初めてのことは空虚さでしょう．それ

も哲学的な意味ではなく，単に家具が無いことからもたらされる感覚にすぎないのですが，西洋式に歩き廻って空間を知覚するということをすれば表面に対して正面から集中するという（できれば日本式に静かに座りながら）すばらしい全く新たな知覚的経験をすることができるでしょう．ちょうど寝たきりの想像力豊かな人が天井に空想を投映して楽しめるように，部屋の面はそれ以外の二次元的な芸術からでは知ることのできない多くの抽象的な構図を楽しませてくれます．我々西洋人は最も偉大なモンドリアンを，それも彼が理想としていたモンドリアンを楽しむことができるでしょう．そして，もし彼が知覚的な冒険にすごす時をもっていたなら，壁面や天井面をずっと見つづけながら，さらにモンドリアン的な楽しみを他の表面にも捜し求めることでしょう．さらに，もし彼が好奇心一杯で（あるいは冒険心一杯で）あれば，想像の中で彼は重力の束縛を忘れ畳の配列から生じる絵画的な構図を鑑賞するまでになるでしょう．家具がほとんど無いということは床面を露出するだけでなく，家具を置くための場所としての床の概念を弱めてもいます．家具を置かなければその場所からも表面を十分に楽しむことができるわけです．このように壁や天井と同じレベルとして床を知覚することがより簡単にな

ってきます．一度経験してしまえば，我々冒険心に富む西洋人は，自分が集中できる「正面性」の数に等しいだけの多くの「抽象的空間」を部屋の限られた空間の中で楽しめるということに気づくでしょう．

日本建築における正面性は全ての開口部から引き戸であることによって強調されます．このため少し開いていると，台形として知覚される開き戸と違い，開いていても開きかけであっても閉じていても，同じ幾何学的効果が得られるわけです．

起し絵図対透視図（正面性対ヴォリューム性）

空間を表面の抽象的な正面性として知覚する傾向と，表面によって限定されたヴォリュームとして知覚する傾向との違いは，起し絵図と線による透視図との違いに象徴されます．起し絵図は立方体の幾何学的な発展形と考えることができます．それらの表面が平面としての性格以上のものを暗示しないため，起し絵図は正面性の領域に属します㉓．一方，線による透視図は二次元を用いながら三次元を暗示しているため，立体性の領域に属するものです．江戸時代を通じて（1603〜1868）用いられた建築的表現方法である起し絵図は，見る者の心の中で絵画的な抽象となる日本の伝統的空間の特筆すべき傾向

space. I found that reading a space by successive concentrations upon the composing surfaces was the most aesthetically rewarding way of perceiving Japanese traditional architecture and moreover, that concentrating upon a given surface was easier when that surface was perpendicular to the visual axis, that is to say, when it is frontally viewed. All of the surfaces composing a Japanese traditional space, even the floor and ceiling, share the peculiarity of being very appealing when seen frontally and it is for this reason that I chose "Frontality" to name this main perceptional attribute. Hints in the space design visible in the geometrical patterns and in the articulation of adjacent elements lead to the perception of this Frontality (figs. 11−22).

In order to perceive Frontality a Westerner must be conscious that he is in a different kind of space requiring a different kind of perception. No matter how beautiful the geometrical patterns on the walls, ceiling and floor of an empty room are, the Westerner's first impression is one of discomfort, or at best, indifference. He is used to perceiving a space as being the sculptural interplay of the room and furniture surfaces. For this reason the first thing he will perceive upon entering a Japanese room will be emptiness, not in its philosophical sense but merely as the feeling produced by the absence of furniture. If the tendency to perceive the space in the Western way of walking around it can be resisted long enough to concentrate frontally on the surfaces (preferably while quietly sitting in Japanese style) a delightful and completely new perceptual experience will result. Just as the ceiling can amuse the bedridden imaginative person projecting his fantasies, the surfaces of the room can amuse with many abstract compositions previously unknown outside of two dimensional art. Our Westerner will enjoy the biggest Mondrian he ever dreamed of and if he has the time to spend in this perceptual adventure, he will look for more Mondrianesque delights in the other surfaces, concentrating successively on the walls and the ceiling. Then if he is curious enough (or adventurous enough) he will forget the force of gravity and imaginatively rise to appreciate the pictorial composition resulting from the lay out of the tatami-mats. The scarcity of furniture not only exposes the floor but weakens the concept of the floor as a place to put furniture from which the other surfaces can be comfortably enjoyed. Thus the perception of the floor on the same level as the walls and ceiling becomes easier. Once the experience is over our adventurous Westerner will find that within the limited space of the room he was able to enjoy many "abstract spaces", equal in number to the "frontalities" he was able to concentrate on.

Frontality in Japanese architecture is strengthened by the fact that all openings are sliding, so the same geometric appeal remains whether they be open, ajar or closed, unlike hinged doors which are perceived as trapeziums when ajar.

Okoshiezu vs. Perspective (Frontality vs. Volumetry)

The difference in tendencies to perceive the space as the abstracted frontality of the surfaces or as the volume defined by them can be represented by comparing the okoshiezu with the linear perspective. The okoshiezu can be likened to the geometrical development of a cube. It belongs to the realm of frontality as its surfaces suggest nothing more than their

⑬

⑪→⑱　私がスケッチするためにこれらの場所を選んだのは，私が特殊な空間の経験をしているのだと感じたためです．今私は大きな明らかに意味をもった表面が私に訴えかけるのを感じましたし，そのためこの訴えかけは私のスケッチの中で無意識に強調されたのでした．（⑪：作田邸．⑫：太田邸．⑬：清水寺．⑭⑮：園城寺．⑯：伊勢神宮．⑰：熊本城．⑱：笹川邸）．⑲→㉒　（⑲⑳）：東京にある門．ここでは門の独立性が塀の平らな面の素材の選択によって強調されています．（㉑：西芳寺．㉒：出雲大社）．ここでは幾何学性もしくは断片の統一性を破る過渡的な要素のない「序列の乱れた」レベルの変化が見られます．

11—18. I chose these places to sketch because I felt I was experiencing a particularly special space. I realize now, that the large, clearly defined surfaces appealed to me and that I subsequently unconsciously emphasized this in my sketches. (11 — Sakuda house, Nihon Minka-en, Kawasaki. 12 — Ota house, Nihon Minka-en, Kawasaki. 13 — Kyomizu-dera, Kyoto. 14 — Onjo-ji, Shiga. 15 — Onjo-ji, Shiga. 16 — Ise shrine, Ise. 17 — Kumamoto castle, Kumamoto. 18 — Sasagawa residence, Niigata).
19—22. (19—20) Here, the autonomy of the gates are emphasized by the choice of materials and the fragmentation of the plane of the fence. (19—20 — Gates in Tokyo). (21—22) Here, there is a "dislocated" level change without any transition elements braking the geometry or unifying the fragmentation. (21 — Saiho-ji, Kyoto. 22 — Izumo Taisha, Izumo).

planer natures (fig. 23). The linear perspective however belongs to the realm of volumetry since it attempts to suggest three dimensions by using two. Okoshiezu, a method of architectural representation used during the Edo Period (1603—1868) clearly illustrates the peculiar tendency for Japanese traditional spaces to become pictorial abstractions in the mind of the viewer. The linear perspective answers the necessity of representing in two dimensions the volumetry of corners as seen from a given viewpoint. After the Renaissance rediscovery of linear perspective during the transition to Baroque, European architecture moved toward a sensous enjoyment of plasticity. In Japan, a country characterized by its speed and efficiency in adopting foreign things, it is surprising that perspective should take so long to diffuse through the arts. If no unwelcome, it was unnecessary. It is also significant to note the eagerness with which Western artists and architects experiment with the Japanese aesthetic of frontality and autonomy of surface in pictures, furniture and architecture. This aesthetic of frontality, stubbornly maintained through the centuries, should be

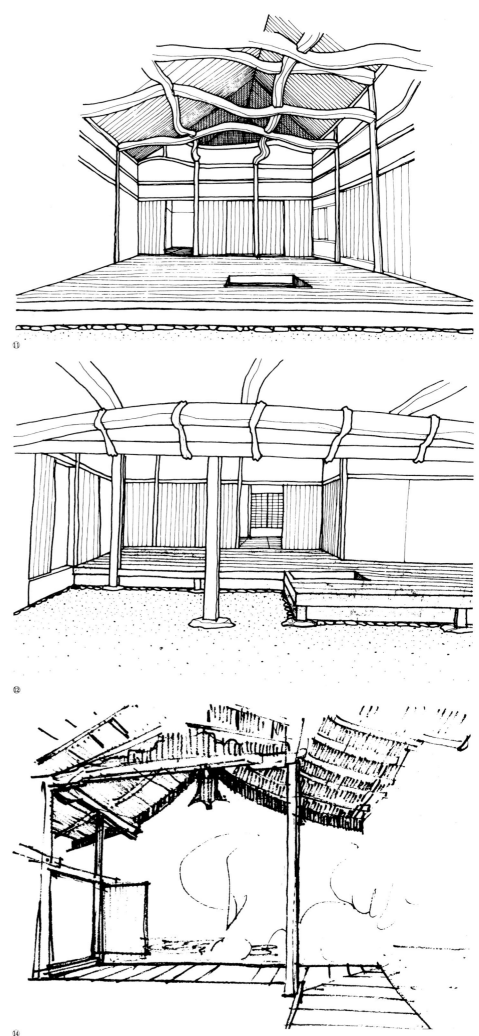

⑪

⑫

⑭

⑮

⑯

⑰

⑱

⑲

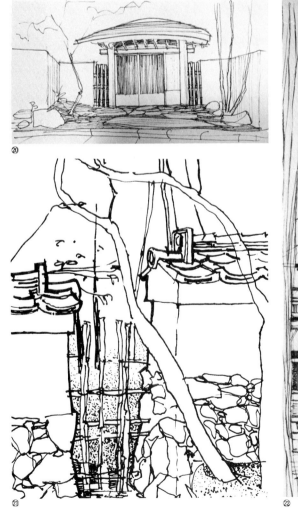

⑳

㉑

㉒

をはっきりと例証しています．線による透視図は二次元の中で，与えられた視点から見た角部の立体性を表現する必要性に対する解答です．ルネッサンス期に線透視を再発見した後，バロックへの過渡期の間にヨーロッパの建築家は可塑性の感覚的な嗜好へと移り変っていったのでした．外国の物事を採用することの速さと効果において特筆的な国である日本においては，透視図が芸術の分野に流布するのにかくも長い時間を要したことはおどろくべきことです．歓迎されなかったわけではないにしても，必要とはされなかったわけです．同時に西洋の芸術家や建築家が絵画や建築で日本的な正面性や表面の独立性の美学を試したその熱意には顕著なものがありました．世紀にまたがって強固に続いたこの美学的な正面性は，日本が西洋にもたらした主たる貢献の一つに数えられるべきでしょう．

京都，大徳寺の茶屋「高林庵」の起し絵図のスケッチのいくつかは，これまでに述べた日本の伝統的な空間の特色を図示しています．この部屋を選んだのはそれが何といっても代表的だからという理由からではなく，その単純さのために，スケッチを通じて空間を理解するのがより簡単なためです㉔．起し絵図をみれば，各々の面が異なった幾何学的パターンを持っていることがすぐ解ります．この部屋では中央に半畳

の畳が敷かれていますが，こうした軸をもったパターンは，機能の大きさあるいは形の点で異なる畳の敷き方をしたほかの部屋には表われてきません．垂直な位置に「壁」を起してみると，四つの面に見出される共通な要素は，まぐさのような木製の水平部材である「長押」です㉕．知覚における非常に初歩的な訓練の基礎として，たった一つの室内透視図を使うことで我々は日本的な室内空間の極めて特長のある性格を評価することができます㉖．たとえその空間が逆さにスケッチされていようと正しくスケッチされていようと，そのバランスは保たれており，同じことをした場合に他の空間では起きるであろう奇妙な感じは起きません．このバランスは，その面を正面から見た時にだけ明らかになる水平線の視覚的な強さによるところが大です．見る軸が90度ずれれば，逆さにしてもバランスのとれていた安定した空間の特質は失われます㉗．この特質が失われるのは，水平線の上にある対角線の優位性に基づくものでしょう．

時として日本の部屋の調和と落ち着きとは，二つの相対するイメージの同時知覚によってもまた失われてしまいます．このことの一つの明確な例は，京都の北部にある三千院の宝泉院の書院から見た庭の景観です．西の壁を正面から見ると，スクリーンのような竹やぶが建物の内

側の構築物に額どられて見えます㉘㉙．庭のこの部分での竹のやさしさと新鮮さと繊細さとは，見る者の心に女性的な優美さの印象を残します．しかし，南の壁を正面から見ると庭の全く異なった部分が見えます㉚．五百年を経た松の木が，今度は粗く力強い男性的な特質を見る者に暗示します．次に南西の角を見るために再び方向を変えると，左手の松の木の力強さと右手の竹やぶの繊細さとの相対する印象を同時にもつことになります㉛．南と西の壁は単に異なる額どられた風景であるばかりではなく，「そのもの自体」が異なっています．なぜならば，それらが異なるモデュールに従って分離されているからです．角の所を見る時，隣合った壁がつながったものであると考えることはむずかしいことです．なぜなら，それらは同じ水平線に従って分離されていないからです．加えて，同時に二つの異なる性格を表わしている庭の二重性は一層の緊張を生み出します．そこでこの特殊な角について次の二つの並置を見出すことができます．一つは二つのグリッドから成っているということであり，もう一つは二つの庭が女性的なものと男性的なものの要素の対比であるということです．別の言い方をすれば，物理的な並置と感情的な並置とがお互いを補強していると言えます．このように各々の面を正面から見れば明確

considered one of the main contributions of Japan to the West.

Some sketches of the okoshiezu of the tea ceremony room "Koorin-an" at the Kyoto temple Daitoku-ji are included to illustrate the above mentioned characteristics of Japanese traditional space. This room was chosen not because it is by any means representative but because its simplicity makes the space easier to understand through sketches (fig. 24). Looking at the okoshiezu it is quickly noticeable that each surface has a different geometric pattern. Although in this room half a tatami-mat is placed at the centre, axial patterns such as this do not appear in other rooms having a different tatami-mat lay out because of function, size or shape. Raising the "walls" to their upright positions we find that the only common element to be found on the four surfaces is the "nageshi", a lintel-like horizontal wooden member (fig. 25). By using a single interior perspective as the base for a very elementary exercise in perception we can appreciate a very unique characteristic of Japanese interiors (fig. 26). Even if the space is sketched upside-down or at right angles its balance remains and the space does not become as

strange as any other space would if subject to the same exercise. This balance is greatly due to the visual strength of the horizontal line which becomes evident only when the surfaces are viewed frontally. When the visual axis deviates from 90° the characteristic of the space to appear balanced and calm even when upside-down, is lost (fig. 27). This loss could be attributed to the predominance of diagonals over horizontals.

Sometimes the harmony and calmness of a Japanese room can also be dissolved by the simultaneous perception of two conflicting images. A very clear example of this is the view of the garden from the Sho-in of the Hosen-in, in the Sanzen-in a temple to the north of the city of Kyoto. Looking frontally to the west wall a screen like forest of bamboo appears framed by the interior structure of the building (figs. 28, 29). The tenderness, freshness and delicacy of the bamboo in this part of the garden leave an impression of feminine grace on the mind of the viewer. However, looking frontally to the south wall a completely different part of the garden is viewed (fig. 30). A five hundred year old pine tree now suggests to the viewer the

masculine qualities of roughness and strength. Thus changing the direction again to view the south-west corner we have the simultaneous yet conflicting impressions of the strength of the pine tree to the left with the delicacy of the bamboo to the right (fig. 31). The south and west walls are not only framing different scenes, but are different *in themselves* since their divisions follow different modules. Looking towards the corner it is difficult to read the adjacent walls as being continuous, because their divisions are not following the same horizontals. In addition the duality of the garden presenting two different qualities at the same time creates more tension. So in this particular corner we find two juxtapositions; one being the two grids and the other being the two garden elements contrasting feminity with masculinity. In other words a physical juxtaposition and an emotional juxtaposition mutually reinforce each other. Thus when either surface is viewed frontally a clear, strong image results, but when apprehended together an obvious tension arises.

Using the photographs in a rotation exercise we find that each photograph

で強い印象を得ることができます．しかし，両方を認知しようとすると明らかな緊張感が生じます．

「組合せ」の試みをした写真を使うと，各々の写真が非常に異なった絵になっていることが解ります．視線が角に向けられると，水平線が無いため不安定な感じが生じます．正面性のある写真㉜によってつくられた静的でバランスのとれたモンドリアン的な構図に代って，ダイナミックな風車のような効果が得られるということになります㉝．正面性においてのみ，正方形や矩形は日本文化の中でかくも評価される静謐のメッセージを，水平を通して伝えることができるのです．

パンパスや海の広大な広がりの中では，360度を見渡すことができ，しかも地平線が見えます．日本の室内では見る場合も想像する場合も，正面性を保つ限り人は向い合った面に限定されます．しかしパンパスの静謐を味わう可能性は，正面に見える面から現われてくる地平線を通じて知覚される「抽象的な空間」に見い出されます．

正面からの透視

線透視の二次元に含まれるヴォリュームと平面の方向性および相互作用は，見る者に異なる感

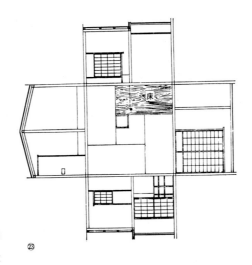

㉓

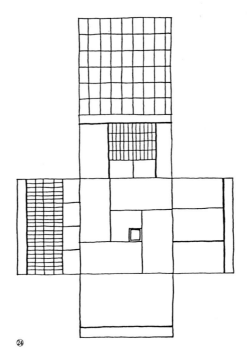

㉔

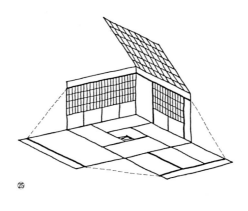

㉕

㉓ 起し絵図（『茶の建築』より）．
㉔ 高林庵の起し絵図（『茶室起し絵図集』より）．
㉕ 起し絵図．

23. "Cha no Kenchiku", *Nihon no Byoyo* 21, Tokyo, plate 63.
24. From the Koorin-an, "Chashitsu Okoshiezu Shu", Bokusui Shobo, Tokyo, 1966.
25. Okoshiezu.

produces very different "combined" picture. When the eye is directed towards a corner, the absence of horizontal lines produces a feeling of instability. Instead of the quietly balanced Mondrian-like composition produced by the frontal picture (fig. 32) we now have a dynamic windmill-like effect (fig. 33).

Only in its frontality is the square or rectangle able to convey through the horizontal its message of calmness so much appreciated in Japanese culture. Within the vast expanses of the Pampas or the sea one can turn a full 360° and yet still see a horizontal. In a Japanese interior, one is restricted to the surfaces either seen or imagined in their frontality, but the possibility of enjoying the quietness of the Pampas is there to be found in the "abstract space" perceived through the horizontals emerging from the frontally seen surfaces.

Frontal Perspective vs. Angular Perspective

The directionality and interplay of volumes and planes contained within the two-dimensions of a linear perspective can evoke different emotions in the viewer. The number of vanishing points is predetermined and this not only per-

情を呼び起こすことができます．焦点の数は前もって決めることができますし，このことによって想像上の観察者の位置を推しはかることができるだけでなく，一つの面やあるいは角から見たマッスあるいはヴォリュームによって示される正面性であろうと，あるいは鳥かん透視による環境との関連性であろうと，空間のより説得力のある面を示すこともできるわけです．正面からの透視図は，一般に構図の中心にある一つの焦点をもっています．見る者が抱く二つの極端な感覚の一つは，無限を示すダイナミックな斜線の暗示する届かぬゴールへ走ってゆきたくなる衝動的な欲求であると言えるでしょう．もう一つの感覚は，スクリーンにあたる無地の広がり㉘を横ぎる地平線としての線の安定感と静謐への欲求であると言えるでしょう．最初のような感覚が我々の物理的な不安感から生じるのに対し，二番目のような感覚は我々の精神的な不安感から生じます．両方ともダイナミズムをもつものです．最初の例では，このダイナミズムはハイウェイ上の車にとっての地平線と変らない遠方のゴールに向けられています．しかし二番目の例では，一軒家の窓に額どりされた地平線と変らない室内的なイメージに類するものに向けられています．時空の中において物としての知覚的な説得力よりも空間としての感覚

mit us to infer the position of the imaginary viewer but shows us the more appealing aspects of the space whether they be the frontality shown by a surface, the massing or volumetry shown by a corner, or the relation to the environment shown by an aerial perspective. Frontal perspectives have a single vanishing point which is usually at the centre of the composition. One of the two extreme emotions evoked in the viewer could be interpreted as the impulsive need to run towards an unreachable goal, suggested by the dynamic diagonals pointing to the infinite. The other could be interpreted as the need for the stability and calmness of a horizon-like line crossing an empty screen-like expanse (fig. 28). The first kind of emotion is born from our physical unrest while the second is born from our metaphysical unrest. Both are endowed with dynamism. In the first case this dynamism is directed towards a goal in the distance not unlike the horizon is for a car on a highway but the dynamism of the second is directed towards some kind of interior image not unlike the horizon as framed by the window of a solitary cottage. Both are interpretational extremes occurring

的な暗示性が強い場合，これら二つの感覚は極めて説明し易くなります．角からの透視図は二つかそれ以上の消点をもってできています．角からの透視図は，はるかに扱い易い二次元の形式で三次元の暗示を与えることによって，見る者に物理的な世界を越えた力の感覚を生じさせます．それは世界の中心としての人間の表明です．

　視覚的な方向が徐々にはっきりしてくると，写真をとる人の手の中で四次元的な存在感は無くなり，建築的な世界はゆっくりと消えてゆきます．一つの感覚は千の絵に値するわけですが，kinaesthetic 知識の感覚と精神的な認識の高尚とも言える性格とは，我々の感覚的な領域を侵している消費者指向のイメージの群れと闘うのにはやはり適していません．しかし，この販売用のイメージの流入の一つの明確な効果は，我我が数多い文化の知覚的な相違を判断できることと，同時に二次元で世界を知覚する能力を増やしてくれることです．二つの文化を代表する二人の写真家が建築的な空間を異なった方法で写しとることに私は気づきました．このことはあたりまえのように聞えるかも知れませんが，それは我々が写真家の知覚的な傾向を，彼の写真に表現される視線の軸の角度に気をつけることで判断できるということを意味します．最も

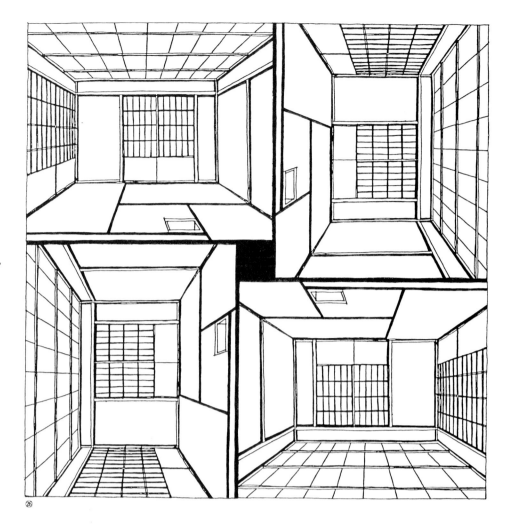

when the emotional sugestiveness of the space is stronger than its perceptional appeal as an object in time and space. Angular perspectives are those with two or more vanishing points. They evoke in the viewer the feeling of power over the physical world by their suggestion of three-dimensionality in a much more manageable two dimensional form. It is the expression of man as the centre of the world.

　As man becomes increasingly visually oriented, the architectural world is slowly vanishing, losing its four dimensional existence in the hands of photographers. Although one emotion is worth a thousand pictures the sensuousness of kinaesthetic knowledge and near-spirituality of metaphysical appreciation are still ill-matched to fight the hordes of consumer-oriented images invading our perceptual territory. However, one positive effect of this influx of ready-to-sell images is that we are able to judge the perceptual differences of various cultures and, at the same time improve our ability to perceive the world in two dimensions. I have found that two photographers, representative of two cultures, will portray architectural spaces in different

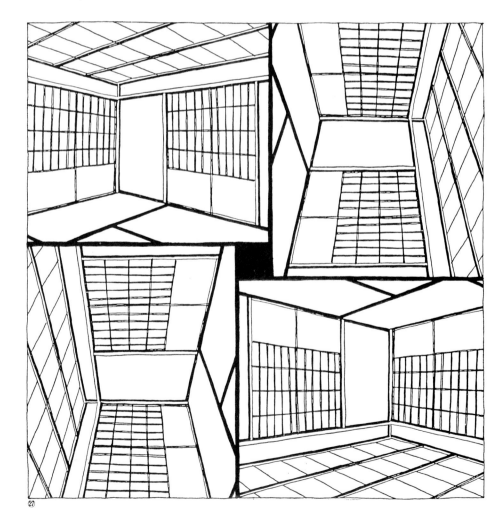

㉖㉗　茶室の展開図.

㉘→㉛　宝泉院の書院, 三千院, 京都

26, 27. Interior perspective.
28. Sho-in of the Hosen-in, Sanzen-in, Kyoto (photo by Horacio Oliva).
29—31. Sho-in of the Hosen-in (photos by Jorge Ferreras).

良い面またはコーナーを表わす写真を撮る時の
視点の選択に気をつければ，彼が正面性を気に
しているか，角度をもった透視を気にしている
かを決めることができます．このように視線の
軸を正面にとろうと角度をもたせようと，写真
を撮るという行為の中で，我々は「正面性」と
「立体性」に対する感性を示していることにな
ります．

　正面性と日本の伝統的空間に関する私の考え
の全てが，私の認識の欠点を主観的に表明した
にすぎないかも知れないという気づかいから，
私は統計をとってみました．そして日本人の写
真家の撮ったほとんどの写真が正面からのもの
で，一方西洋人の撮ったほとんどの写真が角度
をもったものだということを知っても，さほど
驚きませんでした．もし我々は単に「見たいも
のを見る」あるいは我々の文化的な様式が我々
に見せるものを見るのだと考えれば，この統計
は仮に文化的に決定されたものではないにして
も，文化的に強調された空間認識の方法がある
のだという証明として受取らねばならないでし
ょう．このことは，雑誌で写真を発表する写真
家が各自の文化の空間認識の方法を表現してい
るのだという仮定も由なきことではないという
ことを暗示しています．

　建築的空間を写真によって判断することの危

㉜

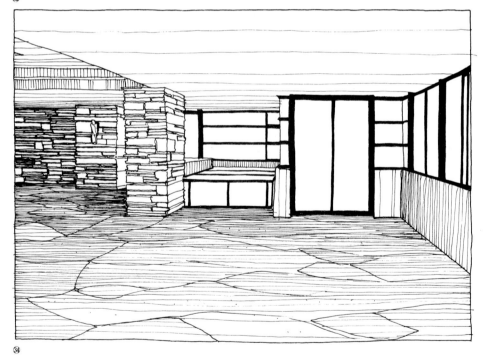

㉞

ways. Although this may sound obvious it means that we can judge the perceptive tendency of a photographer by noting the angle of the visual axis as expressed in his photographs. We can determine whether he is inclined towards Frontal or Angular Perspective by noting his selection of viewpoint when photographing to best show the surfaces or corners. Thus in the act of photography we reveal our sensitivity to "Frontality" or "Volumetry" whenever we make the choice between frontal or angular visual axes.

Concerned that all my thoughts on frontality and the perception of Japanese traditional spaces might be nothing more than the subjective manifestation of my own perceptional vices, I gathered statistics and was not surprised to find that most photographs taken by Japanese photographers were frontal ones, while most of those taken by Westerners were angular. If we think that we only see "what we want to see" or what our cultural patterns will let us see, the statistics must be accepted as proof that there are culturally reinforced if not culturally determined ways of perceiving space. Implicit in this is the nor unreasonable

assumption that photographers who publish pictures in magazines are representative of their respective cultures' way of perceiving spaces.

The risk involved in judging an architectural space through photographs derives from the fact that we are receiving a second hand experience. By selecting to focus on either a frontal wall or on a corner the photographer is restrict-

③③

③④⑤ 落水荘の内部スケッチ.

34. Adapted from photography by Yukio Futagawa, G.A., F.L. Wright's "Fallingwater", ADA EDITA, Tokyo, 1970, p. 22.
35. Adapted from photography by P. Mayen, F.L. Wright's "Fallingwater", ETAS, Milan, 1962, p. 68–69.

All the sketches by the author.

険性は，我々が借りものの体験をしているのだという事実に由来しています．正面の壁であろうと角であろうと焦点を決めるということで，写真家は自らの空間の解釈の提示の限界を，見る者に抱かせる感覚的な反応といった程度に限定していることになります．形体が簡単になるほど，正面性をもった幾何学的な形として形体を認識するのが楽になります．正面から撮られた写真では，写真家の視覚的な軸線に直角の面は，透視図的なゆがみをもつことなしに純粋に幾何学的に表われます．こうした状態ではその面を空間的な文脈から分離することが簡単になります．そこでこの面は，隣合う面の明瞭な透視的変形によって強調された幾何学的単純性をもった独自なものと認識されるわけです㉙㉚．私が出会った日本の室内の写真の多くは，すでに述べましたように，日本の写真家は正面から撮り，西洋の写真家は同じ空間を角を使って㉛，言い換えれば，角度のある透視によって写真に撮る傾向があります．これは西洋人がより立体に敏感で自然に角から写真を撮るのだ，あるいは単に日本空間の正面性の特質が気づかれないか無視されているのだという意味にとれるのでしょうか．時として，日本人の写真家が西洋的空間の正面性を認識するという逆も真実です．
一つは日本人が，もう一つはヨーロッパ人が撮

ing to the extent of proposing his own interpretation of space the kind of emotional reaction he will evoke in the viewer. The simpler a shape is, the easiest it will be to perceive as a frontal geometric figure. In a frontally taken photograph the surface perpendicular to the visual axis of the photographer will appear in its pure geometry, without any perspective distortion. In these

situations it becomes easier to dissociate the surface from the spatial context and so perceive it autonomously with its geometric simplicity enhanced by the sharp perspective deformation of the adjacent planes (figs. 29, 30). I have said that most of the Japanese interior pictures I have encountered were frontally taken by Japanese photographers and that Western photographers exhibit the tendency to photograph the same spaces using corners (fig. 31) that is to say as Angular Perspectives. Could this be taken to mean that the Westerner, being more sensitive to volumetry naturally takes photographs of corners, or merely that the frontal appeal of a Japanese space is unnoticed or ignored? Sometimes the reverse is true as the Japanese photographer will perceive a Western space in its frontality. Comparing two photographic studies of Frank Lloyd Wright's 'Fallingwater House', one by a Japanese and the other by an European, I found that the Japanese photographer took most pictures frontally while the European focussed on corners. Therefore the Japanese published book is composed mostly of views structured by frontal perspective while the European book is

ったフランク・ロイド・ライトの「落水荘」の写真のスタディを比べると，日本人の写真家はほとんどの写真を正面から撮っており，ヨーロッパ人の方が角に焦点を合わせていることが解ります．従って，日本人の出版した本はほとんど正面からの透視による構図で構成され，ヨーロッパの本はほとんどが角からの透視による構図でできているわけです．両方の写真家の認識した通りの同じ空間のスケッチを比較してみると，異なった空間の印象であることが解ります．「日本人の視点」㉞は正面性を通して，質感の多様性と幾何学的なパターンを強調する平行で独立した面同志の複雑な相互作用を強調します．部屋の中央にある柱は，周囲の壁に対する要としてよりは別の面として認識されます．簡単に言えばこの写真は日本の伝統的空間を暗示しているということです．角度をもった透視図によって「ヨーロッパ人の視点」㉟は，空間の要として認識される柱の囲りにあって取り囲んでいる垂直の壁の概念を強調します．独立した矩形で構成された面よりも立体的な空間を特に強調する西洋人は，コーナーウィンドウの枠の連続性を強調します．この住宅は，日本建築と日本芸術の収集の両方に経験をもつ建築家Ｆ・Ｌ・ライトの恐らくは傑作であるために，微妙な日本の影響が日本人の写真家に日本的な方法で空

間の正面性を読み取らせたのだと言えるでしょう．

本論の冒頭は，どんなデザイナーにとっても最も価値のある，認識の背景を呼びさますように読者を刺激したいと考えて風景の認識に中心を置きました．アルゼンチンのパンパスであろうと日本の伝統的空間の中であろうと，認識される「抽象的な空間」の効力を示したいと思ったわけです．「正面性」の概念をその形而上的な力と共に，この「抽象的な空間」への認識的なアプローチとして示したのです．最後に，直接的な文脈から抽象して物事を認識する日本人の特殊な能力は必ずしも美しい空間を生むとは言えません．次の事は銘記されるべきでしょう．注意深く制御された抽象主義は非常に満足できる結果を生むことができますが，不用意な抽象主義（多くの日本人建築家にとっては危険な傾向である）はひどい分裂と離反を生みます．多すぎる建物全ての隣合った立面はお互いが反発しながら，このことを立証しています．

（訳：伊藤真一）

composed mostly of views structured by angular perspective. Comparing through sketches the same space as perceived by both photographers the result is different spatial impressions. The "Japanese viewpoint" (fig. 34) emphasizes through frontality, the complex interplay of parallel, autonomous surfaces emphasizing the variety of textures and geometric patterns. The column in the centre of the room is perceived more as another surface than as a pivot for the surrounding walls. In short, this picture suggests a Japanese traditional space. Through the use of the angular perspective the "European viewpoint" (fig. 35) emphasizes the idea of vertical surfaces surrounding and enclosing the column which is sensed to be the pivot of the space. The continuity of the corner window frames is accentuated by the Westerner so emphasizing a volumetric space instead of the surfaces composed of autonomous rectangles. Since the house is perhaps the masterpiece of F.L. Wright, an architect who both experienced Japanese architecture and collected Japanese art, it could be said that the subtle presence of Japanese influence inspired the Japanese photographer to read the space

frontally, in a Japanese manner.

The beginning of this article centered around the perception of landscape in the hope that the reader would be stimulated into recalling his own perceptional background, a most valuable tool for any designer. This is intended to show the validity of the "abstract space" whether it be perceived in the Argentinian Pampas or inside a Japanese traditional space. The idea of "Frontality" with its metaphysical overtones is proposed as a perceptional approach to this "abstract space". To conclude, the particular ability of the Japanese to perceive things as abstracted from their immediate context does not always result in beautiful spaces. It must be remembered that while consciously controlled abstractionism can produce very satisfying results, unconscious abstractionism (a dangerous tendency for many Japanese architects) can result in severe fragmentation and disjunction — as the mutually ridiculing, adjacent lateral elevations of all too many buildings serve to testify.

REGIONAL STYLES OF FARMHOUSE IN NORTHEAST JAPAN

by Masao Noguchi

風土と民家形式──東日本の農家

野口昌夫

民家という言葉は，日常的には庶民の住まいや家庭を指すが，建築学的には，土着の伝統的な建築様式をもつ庶民階級の住居を意味する．民家は，現存する他の分野の古建築に比べ，最も数が多く，その様式は，住む人の職業の様態，地域的な条件，建築された年代などによって様々に変化する．

現在，日本に残されている民家は，大部分が17世紀以降に建てられたもので，西欧の都市や農村に16世紀以前の木造民家がかなり残っているのに比べると，全体的に新しい．その理由としては，湿度の高い日本の気候が，木材の腐朽を進めることのほかに，建築構造と生活様式の両面において，長期の利用に適合する庶民住宅が成立したのが，比較的遅かったことによるものとされている．現存する日本の民家のなかで，最も古い時期に属する16世紀から17世紀前半までの民家の大部分は，早くから文化が開けた近畿地方の諸府県に分布しているのに対し，東北地方，九州地方では，17世紀前半まで遡る古民家は発見されていない．明治維新以降，日本の民家は，西洋から輸入された建築材料や構造技

術を次第に採り入れていくが，生活様式の近代化に対応して，間取りそのものも変化していく．このような過程のなかで，どの時代までのものを民家とするか，が問題になるが，一般的には，新しい材料や技術が導入されてはいても，間取形式に大きな影響を及ぼしていない大正前期までが，民家の時代的下限とされている．

日本の民家の最も基本となる部分は，江戸時代に被支配階級であった農民・漁民・商人・職人などの住居である．加えて，江戸時代に支配階級であった武士の住居のうち，中・下級の武士の住居で，規模において農家や町家と大きな違いが無いものも民家に含められる．日本の民家は，住む人の職業によって，大きく三つに分けられる．それは，農家，町家，武家屋敷で，主として，家屋の配置と間取りの特色に，それぞれの差異があらわれる．

農家：主屋の周囲に広い空地がとられ，屋内に農作業のための広い土間をもつ．

町家：道路に面し，隣家と軒を接して建ち，営業のための空間「みせ」をもつ．

武家：主屋の周囲に広い空地がとられ，玄関や床の間を備えた客座敷をもつ．

これら三つ以外の職業，例えば，漁業，林業，職人，僧侶，旅籠などの場合も，上のいずれかの様式を基本としている．

民家の地方色

日本は，平野の面積が狭小で山地が多いため，専業農家の比率は比較的少なく，養蚕，畜産，林業，漁業などの副業を営む兼業農家が大半を占めている．このような農業の様態は，多様な気候風土と共に，民家の形式に様々な変化をもたらし，多彩な地方色をもった日本の伝統民家が形成されていった．近世に入る前も，このような地方色は存在したはずだが，地域による差異はそれほど大きくなかったとされている．現在みることのできる民家の地方的特色が成立したのは，この250年以来のことであり，これは，農村形態が確立した江戸時代中期以降にあたる．このような地方的特色が成立した要因としては，以下のようなものが考えられる．

ⅰ）地域的な条件

The word *minka* indicates simply a house of the common man or family, but in architectural parlance it represents the common class of dwelling in indigenous and traditional styles. There are many more farmhouses than other types of extant architecture of similar age, and they vary by the occupations of their inhabitants, regional conditions, and the age in which they were built.

The farmhouses remaining in Japan today are largely from after the seventeenth century, fairly new compared to the relatively large number of pre-sixteenth century wooden structures remaining in Western Europe. Aside from the fact that Japan's climate is very moist and hastens the decay of wood materials, it was relatively plate that common houses were developed that were suited to long-term use in terms of both structure and the way of life of their inhabitants. Of the *minka* still standing today in Japan, most of the oldest, from the sixteenth and early seventeenth centuries, are found in the Kinki area, centering on Kyoto in central Honshu, where cultural development came early; in contrast, no farmhouses dating back to the early seventeenth century have been discovered in the north-eastern or southernmost parts of Japan. Since the Meiji Restoration in the late 1860's the Japanese house has gradually incorporated Western techniques and imported building materials, and as the way of life has modernized, the room arrangements themselves have changed. Against this background, it is hard to tell when development of the *minka* ceased. The early Taisho era,

however, roughly up to 1910's, is usually taken as the limit of the age of the *minka*, when new materials and new techniques had not yet had much of an impact on the plan.

The basic Japanese *minka* served as home for the prescribed classes of the Edo period, farmers, fishermen, merchants, and craftsmen. In addition, the dwellings of the middle and lower classes of *samurai* are included under the rubric of *minka* as they did not differ greatly from farm or townhouses in scale. Japan's *minka* fall broadly into three classifications, by the inhabitants' occupation. These are the farmhouse, the townhouse, and *samurai* residence; there differ mainly by characteristics of orientation and plan.

Farmhouse: Surrounded by wide open

1. 旧伊藤家 Ito-ke
2. 旧清宮家 Kiyomiya-ke
3. 旧作田家 Sakuta-ke
4. 旧太田家 Ohta-ke
5. 旧山田家 Yamada-ke
6. 旧工藤家 Kudo-ke
7. 旧藤原家 Fujiwara-ke
8. 千葉家 Chiba-ke
9. 旧広瀬家 Hiroae-ke
10. 旧渋谷家 Shibuya-ke
11. 旧遠藤家 Endo-ke
12. 旧野原家 Nohara-ke
13. 旧江向家 Emukai-ke
14. 白川郷の Gassho in
　　合掌造 Shirakawa

① 本稿で取りあげた
民家例の位置.
Location of examples
cited in the text.

Condition / Regional styles	Climate/Topography			Secondary occupation		Main examples cited in this article
	warm/ plains area	cold/ mountainous	heavy snow-fall	horse breeding	seri-culture	
Bunto-gata	○					Itō-ke, Kiyomiya-ke
Chūmon-zukuri	○					Sakuta-ke, Ohta-ke
Magariya		○	◎			Yamada-ke
Kōshū-minka		○	○	◎		Kudō-ke, Fujiwara-ke
Takahappō-zukuri		○			○	Hirose-ke
Gasshō-zukuri		○	○		○	Shibuya-ke, Endō-ke
		○	○		○	Emukai-ke, Nohara-ke

2. Climatic conditions and farming considerations and the form of the *minka*. Among the *minka* styles of eastern Japan mentioned in the article, those connected with climatic and farming considerations are particularly strong.

primary spaces	floor finish	alternative names of spaces* ③
DOMA: earth-floored area	pounded earth	NIWA, DAIDOKO, DOJI
HIROMA: main living quarter	wood plank, bamboo	OKAMI, JŌI, CHANOMA, HIROMA, ZASHIKI, DAIDOKO, YOKOZA, IDOKO, NAKANOMA, OUE
NEMA: sleeping space	wood plank	NANDO, HEYA, NEDOKO, NEMA
KYAKUMA: guest room	tatami	DEI, DEE, ZASHIKI, OMOTE, OKU

*Although the basic type of space remains constant, the specific function and name of the space differs in various regions and in different historical periods.
※間取りを構成する各空間(土間, 広間, 寝間, 客間)の呼称は, 地域や時代によって特徴をもち, 呼称が違うことは, その空間の内容にも差があることを示す.

自然条件──気候：気温, 雨量, 積雪量, 風の
　　　　　　　向き, 風の強さなど.
　　　　──地形：平野─山地, 急峻な傾斜
　　　　　　　地, 沿岸地域など.
　　　　──土地の建築材料：屋根葺材など.
社会条件──伝達形式：技術や様式の伝播形式,
　　　　　　　交通機関など.
　　　　──建設方法：手労働, 村人の労力の
　　　　　　　相互交換など.
　　　　──伝統技術：その土地の職人がもつ
　　　　　　　伝統的手法など.
　　　　──支配機構：藩の政策, 身分制度な
　　　　　　　ど.
ii) 住む人の職業の様態
農業, 漁業, 林業, 商業, 職人, 旅籠, 武士,

僧侶, など.
兼業農家, 特に副業として養蚕業, 焼畑農業,
馬の多頭飼育などを営む農家.
家主の社会的階層（名主, 網元など）.
iii）時代的な要因
養蚕業の隆盛, 馬産の奨励, 農業形態の変化な
ど.

　このような要因が複雑に関係し合って, 地域
特有の民家形式, 即ち地方色が生まれ, それは,
外観, 間取り, 構造, 室内意匠, 細部の装飾に
様々にあらわれる. しかしながら, このような
民家形式の中で, 限られた地域に分布し, しか
も地域的な条件との密接な因果関係が推測され
るものはあるが, 一般には, なぜその地域だけ
に, この形式が成立したかを合理的に説明する

ことは難しいとされている. このことは, 民家
に対する環境の影響がいかに複雑にからみ合っ
たものであるかを示している.

　地方的特色の指標として, ある地域における
外観, 間取り, 構造, 手法などを総合的に捉え
たものが,「何々造り」と呼ばれる類型である.
主なものを北から挙げると, 曲屋（岩手）, 中門
造り（秋田, 山形, 新潟）, 高八方（山形）, 赤城
型（群馬）, 土蔵造り（埼玉）, 甲州民家（山梨）,
甲造り（静岡, 山梨）, 本棟造り（長野）, 合掌造
り（岐阜, 富山）, 撞木造り（静岡, 愛知）, 高塀
造りあるいは大和棟（奈良）, 反り棟造り（島根）,
四方蓋造り（香川）, 竿家造り（宮崎）, くど造り
（佐賀）などが知られている.（括弧内は, 分
布する主な県名）.

grounds, the interior has a large *doma*, or earth-floored area, for farming chores.
Townhouse: Facing the road and built right up to the eaves of neighboring houses, the interior includes shop space to accomodate the family business.
Samurai residence: Surrounded by spacious grounds, it has a formal entry and reception rooms.

　Housing occupations other than these three, for instance fishermen, foresters, craftsmen, priests, innkeepers, etc., can all be considered to be basically one of these types.

Regional Characteristics
More of Japan's land area is mountainous than flat, and the number of farmers who do nothing besides farm is relatively small; the majority supplement their farm income with secondary work such as growing silk worms, husbandry, gathering timber or fishing. These various occupations, along with varied climatic conditions, made for changes in the form of the farmhouse and were responsible for the different types of the traditional Japanese house. The same differences ought to have been seen even before the approach of the Edo-period, but regional differences were not in fact so great. The regional characteristics we see among *minka* still standing today appeared only within the last 250 years, or with the establishment of a definite form of farming village in the middle of the Edo-period. Below are listed some factors in the production of these regional characteristics.

i) Natural conditions

—Climate: humidity, amount of rain and snowfall, direction and strength of winds, etc.
—Land formations: plains or mountains, steeply sloped land or swampy coastal areas.
—Regional building materials: materials for thatching roofs, etc.
Social conditions
—Transmission forms: the way of communication of local techniques and styles, traffic facilities, etc.
—Construction methods: hand labor and mutual exchange of labor among villagers.
—Traditional techniques: the traditional skills of local craftsmen.
—Controlling institutions: feudal administration, social class system.

ii) Forms by inhabitants' occupation

条件 民家形式	気候風土			農業の様態(副業)		ここで取り上げた 民家の例
	温暖な 平地	寒冷な 山地	多雪地	馬の飼育	養蚕	
	○					旧伊藤家, 旧清宮家
分棟型	○					旧作田家, 旧太田家
中門造り		○	◎			旧山田家
曲屋		○	○	◎		旧工藤家, 藤原家
甲州民家		○			◎	旧広瀬家
高八方造り		○	○		◎	旧渋谷家, 旧遠藤家
合掌造り		○	○		◎	旧江向家, 野原家

② 気候風土および農業様態と民家形式. 本稿では, 東日本の「何々造り」と呼ばれる民家形式のうち, 気候風土および農業様態との関連が特に強いものを扱っている.

④ 三室広間型の間取り. 手前から, 土間, 竹すのこ床にむしろを敷いた広間, 奥は畳敷きの客間 (旧伊藤家).
⑤ 三室広間型の間取り (旧伊藤家復元平面図).
⑥ 三室広間型, 入母屋造りの民家 (旧伊藤家).
⑦ 四間取り (田の字型). 三室広間 (図⑤) の広間が, 後になって前後に仕切られ, 全体が四室構成の四間取りに変化した例. この場合, 分けられた広間の表側の部屋は客間的な性格をもち, 裏側の部屋は家族の食事等に利用された (旧伊藤家移築前平面図).
⑧ 茅葺き, 入母屋造りの民家 (旧伊藤家正面).
⑨ 茅葺き, 寄棟造りの民家 (旧清宮家).
⑩ 寄棟造りの民家 (手前が旧清宮家, 奥は旧北村家).

ただし, この「何々造り」と呼ばれる, 地域的な形式の差異による類型は, 日本の民家の総体を分類したものではなく, 特色の著しい形式を列挙したものである. 従って, 数量的には最も多い一般的な民家, 即ち, 単純な寄棟造りや入母屋造りの屋根で, 矩形平面をしたものは, そこには含まれていない⑧→⑩.

ここでは, 上述の地方的特色を成立させた要因のなかでも, 特に重要だと思われる, 気候風土および農業の様態が民家形式に与えた影響を考える. 紹介する民家は, 東日本 (中部, 関東, 東北地方) の「何々造り」と呼ばれる民家のうち, 特にこれら二つの要因と関連が深いものである①②.

④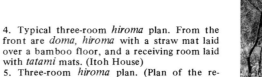

⑤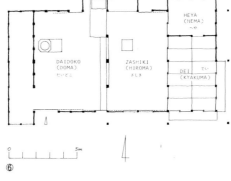

⑥

⑦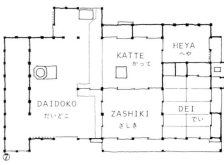

⑧

⑨

⑩

— Farming, fishing, forestry, merchant, craftsman, innkeeper, *samurai*, priest, etc.
— Secondary occupation: especially the raising of silk worms, or of horses in numbers, and plash-and-burn farming.
— Social class of the owner: village head, head fisherman, etc.

iii) Factors by era
— The prosperity of the silk worm industry, encouragement of horse breeding, changes in occupational methods, etc.

Such factors as these combined to produce shades of regional differences in the form of the *minka* and were expressed in the facade, plan, structure, interior design, and ornamentation of details. While we can conjecture that these

4. Typical three-room *hiroma* plan. From the front are *doma*, *hiroma* with a straw mat laid over a bamboo floor, and a receiving room laid with *tatami* mats. (Itoh House)
5. Three-room *hiroma* plan. (Plan of the restored Itoh House)
6. Three-room *hiroma* plan in a *minka* with hipped gable roof. (Itoh House)
7. Four-room plan: a square divided into four quadrants. Example of a three-room *hiroma* plan (similar to figure 5) which has become a four-room plan by dividing one room. The interior room created by the division had a more formal feeling, while the posterior room was used for family meals, etc. (Plan of the Itoh House before renovation)
8. *Minka* with hipped gable roof of thatch. (Facade, Itoh House)
9. *Minka* with hipped roof of thatch. (Kiyomiya House)
10. Hipped-roof *minka*. (Kiyomiya House in foreground, Kitamura House in background)

気候風土と民家形式

日本は南北に長く，複雑な地勢をもつため，その気候条件は様々で，民家の形式に及ぼす影響は大きい．代表的な気象的要因と，それが及ぼす主要分野を挙げると，次のようになる．

気温：主屋の規模，屋内の馬屋の有無，いろりの大きさ，居間の広さ，床の構造，外部に面する間仕切の構造等．

雨量，積雪量：屋根の匂配，屋根瓦の形式，出入口の構造，外部に面する戸口の形式，外壁の構造等．

風の向き：出入口の方向，配置．

風の強さ：屋根構造，棟飾りの形式，敷地の選定，敷地周囲の石垣や防風林．（『日本建築史基礎資料集成』より）．

また，気候に対処するための建物外部の設備装置としては，雨囲い，水屋造り，雪囲い，防風林など，その地域の特殊な気象条件に対応して工夫がなされていた．

しかしながら，気候が，建物の形式そのものに直接大きな影響を与えたとは言い難い．大まかには，北部・寒冷地の一棟多室の形式と，南部・温暖地の小棟分立の形式の相違がしばしば

挙げられる．一年の半分近くを，夜昼，屋内で暮し，作業をしなければならない寒冷地では，戸外生活を自由に過せる温暖な地方とは，広い意味での建物形式に違いは出てくる．ところが，「何々造り」といわれるような，ある地域独特の民家形式のうち，気候風土の影響を著しく受けて発達してきたものは少ない．多雪地帯という特殊な気候条件から生まれた「中門造り」は，その興味深い一例である．

ここでは，まず関東平野の温暖な地方の民家を通して，その間取りと内部機能の概略を説明し，併せて太平洋沿岸を中心に分布する分棟型の民家を紹介する．次にそれとは対照的な気候条件のもとにある日本海寄りの多雪地帯に発達した「中門造り」の民家にふれる．

民家の間取り

民家の間取りで最も基本的な形式は，三室広間型と呼ばれるもので，広間，客間，寝間の３室から構成される③→⑥．部屋の配置は，矩形平面の中央部分に広間，片側に土間，もう一方の側に客間と寝間が前後に置かれる．この三室広間型は，東北地方から九州地方にいたる各地に見

られ，また高冷地から温暖地まで分布しているので，当時の日本の農家の生活様式に適合したものであったと考えられる．住生活の基本機能である食事，接客，就寝に一部屋ずつ割り当てられ，しかも広間が最も大きく，間取りの中心を占めていることが，この間取りの特色である．各部屋の主な機能は次の通りである．

広間：家族の食事，団欒および日常の客の接待．

客間：冠婚葬祭の行事の際の集会．

寝間：家長夫婦の寝室．

もう一つの間取り形式は四間取り（田の字型）と呼ばれるもので，上述の三室広間型の広間を前後に分けて，全体を四室構成にしたものである⑦．この場合，分けられた広間の表側の部屋は，客間的な性質を持ち，裏側の部屋が，家族の食事等に利用される．日本の古い農家の間取りは，上の三室広間型か四間取り，もしくは，それにさらに寝室や客間を付け加えたものが大多数を占める．

農家の間取形式は，時代が下るにつれて規模が大きくなり，部屋数が増し，またその組み合せ方が複雑化する．日常生活空間の間取りの変化では，三室広間型の多くが四間取りに変化す

---

various *minka* styles distributed within a limited area are closely connected to local conditions, it is generally very difficult to give a conclusive answer as to why a certain style is found only within a certain district. This is further evidence of how deeply enmeshed the *minka* was with its environment.

Certain styles are recognized as representing regional differences affecting the facade, plan, structure, and construction methods together. Following is a list of some of these styles by name, with the prefectures where the type is primarily found in parentheses: starting from the north, the *magariya* style (Iwate), *chumon* style (Akita, Yamagata, Niigata), *takahappo* style (Yamagata), *Akagi* style (Gunma), *dozo* style (Saitama), the Koshu *minka* (Yamanashi), *kabuto* style (Shizuoka, Yamanashi), *hon-mune* style (Nagano), *gassho* style (Gifu, Toyama), *shumoku* style (Shizuoka, Aichi), the *takahe*, or *Yamato-mune*, style (Nara,) *sori-mune* style (Shimane), the *shihobuta* style (Kagawa), the *saoya* style (Miyazaki), and the *kudo* style (Saga).

These names, while identifying regional styles, do not really classify the body of Japanese *minka* types, but simply name the obvious characteristic of a style. The quantitatively most numerous *minka* style, then, with its simple hipped roof or hipped gable roof and rectangular

plan, is not covered by any of these specific type names. (figs. 8–10)

We will here examine two of the factors mentioned above which determine regional characteristics, climatic conditions and farming methods. The *minka* we will introduce are among the popularly-named styles in eastern and northeastern Japan and have a deep relation with these two factors. (figs. 1, 2)

Climatic Conditions and Minka Form
As Japan stretches narrowly from north to south with a complicated topography, climatic conditions have had a large effect on the form of the *minka*. Representative climatic factors each have their important field of influence.

Temperature: Size of the main roof, the presence or absence of horse stalls under the roof, the size of the hearth, the size of the rooms, the floor structure and structure of exterior walls.

Rain and snowfall: Roof slope, type of roof tiles, structure of the entryway, form of exterior openings and structure of exterior walls.

Wind direction: Direction and location of the entryway.

Wind strength: Roof structure, roof ridge ornamentation, selection of site, windbreaks of stone or plantings around the site.

In addition, many appurtenances and equipment outside the dwelling were

devised to deal with the particular weather problems of a region, for instance rain doors, well sheds, snow fences, wind breaks of trees, etc.

Still, it is hard to say that climate has had a large direct influence on the form of the building itself. In general, the difference between the many large rooms under a single roof of the cold range in the north and the separated, many-roofed buildings of the southern; warmer areas is often mentioned as an example of the direct influence of climate. In a broad sense, differences in building form are apparent between the cold regions where for nearly half the year life must be spent indoors day and night in doing both daily chores and work, and the warmer areas, where life can freely be lived outside. But there are few distinctly regional *minka* forms or classified styles which owe their development to the remarkable influence of climate. The *chumon* style of the heavy snowfall belt is a very interesting example of the development in response to climatic conditions.

We will first look at *minka* from the warm Kanto plain, near Tokyo, and explain the plan and functions of the interior spaces, and will introduce the separate-roof style distributed primarily along the Pacific coast. We will then take a look at the *chumon* style minka found in contrasting climatic conditions in the

①

⑫

⑬

⑭

⑯

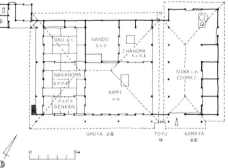

⑮

⑰

11. Facade of *betsumune minka*. On the left is the main roof (living areas), on the right, the kitchen (earth-floored), with a gutter built between the two of them.

12. Roofs of *betsumune minka*. Main roof on right, kitchen on left. The T-shape formed by the meeting of the two roof ridges earns this the name of *Shumoku* style in the Tokai (east Inland Sea) region of Honshu. (Sakuta House)

13. Interior of a *betsumune*-style *minka*. The separate structures are apparent only from the outside; the interior is arranged on a wholly unified plan. (Ota House)

14. Rain trough of a *betsumune minka*. (Sakuta House)

15. Plan of *betsumune minka*. The plan is connected, with the two roofs (indicated by dotted lines) over the living area and kitchen, crossing. (Sakuta House)

16. Section through a *betsumune minka*. A gutter pipe is located between the eaves of the living space and kitchen roofs, carrying rain water to the front of the house. (Sakuta House)

17. The gutter between the two roofs. (Sakuta House)

⑪ 分棟型民家の正面. 左が主屋(居室部), 右が釜屋(土間部)で, 両棟が接する谷に樋が設けられる(旧作田家).

⑫ 分棟型民家の背面. 主屋(右)と釜屋(左)の棟がT字型をつくるため, 東海地方では「撞木造」と呼ばれる(旧作田家).

⑬ 分棟型民家の内部. 外観は別棟になっているが, 内部空間は一体化した間取りとなっている(旧太田家).

⑭ 分棟型民家の樋部分(旧作田家).

⑮ 分棟型民家の平面図. 間取りは連続しているが, 居室部(主屋)と土間部(釜屋)に別々の屋根(点線部分)が棟を直交させて, かかっている(旧作田家).

⑯ 分棟型民家の断面図. 主屋と釜屋の軒が接する部分に樋が設けられ, 雨水を前方に流す(旧作田家).

⑰ 両屋の軒の接線に雨樋が設けられる(旧作田家).

る傾向がある．伊藤家の場合も，そうである．即ち，大きな空間を柔軟に使い分ける多目的室が，機能別の専用室に分化していく過程である．また，養蚕などは居住目的以外の要素が家屋内にもちこまれた場合も，四間取りへ変化することが多い．

しかし，気候の寒冷な東北日本では，広間の中央（家屋の中央）に大きないろりを設け家屋全体を暖める必要があるため，三室広間型から四間取りへの進展は比較的少ない．むしろ，厩を土間前方に統合した「曲屋」形式や，積雪時の通路を併せて設ける「中門造り」のような特殊な間取形式に発展を遂げる．

住生活の基本的要素としては，前に述べた食事，就寝，接客の各々に対応した部屋があればよいわけだが，それ以外に産業上の要素，気候風土，あるいは格式（客間部分の充実）等の要素が組み込まれて，間取りは複雑に発展し，地方的特色もそこに生まれてきたのである．

分棟型の民家

「分棟型」あるいは「別棟型」と呼ばれる民家形式は，主屋と釜屋，即ち居室部と土間部（炊事その他の作業場）の二つの家屋が軒を接して並び建てられたものである⑪→⑰．この形式は，南方の島々や太平洋岸のいくつかの地域に分布しているが，関東地方では伊豆諸島，安房地方，茨城県の一部に見られる．主屋（居室部）と釜屋（土間部）が別棟になっているにもかかわらず，内部空間は分割できない一体化した間取りとなっている．外観は，平入の主屋の片側に，妻入の釜屋が接して建ち，両棟の屋根が接する谷に，雨水を前方に流すための大きな樋が設けられている．上から見ると，この樋を狭んで主屋と釜屋の棟がT字型になっているところから，東海地方では「撞木造り」（撞木とは鐘を叩くために用いるT字型の棒）といわれている．このように別棟とする利点としては，一つの大きな屋根をつくるより，棟が低くできるために台風の被害を軽減できることなどがあるが，むしろ，そのような実利面よりは，同じ形式を継承してゆくこと，即ち伝統のなせるわざであると考えられる．実際のところ，屋根葺きの手間，両屋根の隣接部の雨仕舞などを考えると合理的な形式とは言い難いからである．このような不都合に対処するため，本来は分棟型だった建物が後に直屋に改造された例は多い．千葉県，九十九里町にあった分棟型民家，作田家も，川崎の日本民家園に移築復元される前は，一つの連続した屋根で覆われていた．現在，この九十九里地方では，分棟型民家は，全く見ることができないが，この復元によって，房総地方にも古い時代に分棟型が存在していた事実が明らかになった．

多雪地の民家

「中門造り」は，屋根の棟がL字型で，入口がその正面突出部の妻面にある草葺農家で，長野県東北部から東北地方の日本海寄り地域即ち多雪地帯に分布している．多雪地では，雪囲い（屋内の保温のために，茅やわらで外壁を覆う）や雁木道（道路に面して主屋から庇をおろして歩廊を設け，積雪時の通行に使う）など，雪に対処するための様々な工夫が見られる．このような防雪対策の中でも，雁木道にみられるような屋外と屋内の間の緩衝地帯の必要性から生まれた民家形式が，「中門造り」である⑱→㉕．

深雪時で，台所への入口が，積雪や屋根のおろし雪で塞がってしまう場合は，この中門口か

---

snow belt along the Japan Sea.

Interior Plans

The basic minka plan is the so-called three-room *hiroma* plan composed of a living, or family room, receiving room and bed room. In small plans, the living area is located in the middle, with an earth-floored area to one side, and a receiving room and bed room side by side on the other. This three-room plan is seen everywhere from Tohoku to Kyushu, in cold and warm areas alike, and was eminently well adapted to the Japanese lifestyle of the time. The three basic functions of daily life, eating, receiving guests and sleeping, are afforded one room apiece, yet the living room is characteristically the largest, and occupies the center of the plan. The functions of each room are as follows. (figs. 3-6)

Living room, Hiroma: for family meals and relaxation and the reception of familiar guests.

Receiving room, Kyakuma: for assemblies of guests at times of weddings or funerals or festivals.

Sleeping room, Nema: master bedroom.

Another type of plan has four rooms arranged symmetrically within a square, like the living room of the above plan divided, with a total of four rooms. The front room of the living area has a more formal air while the interior room is used for family meals and gatherings.

The plans of Japan's old farmhouses are similar to those above, and the majority have a version of the three-room *hiroma* plan with a sleeping room and receiving room added. (fig. 7)

The plan of the farmhouse grew in scale with time, increasing the number of rooms and further complicating their relationships. There is a tendency for the three-room *hiroma* plan to become the four-room plan. The Itoh House is an example. In short, the large multi-purpose rooms become differentiated in use and their functions specialized; there are many examples of a secondary occupation, such as silk worm raising, coming indoors and changing the arrangement to a four-room plan.

In the cold northeastern part of Japan, however, where there is a need to warm the whole house by the heat from the hearth located in the center of the living areas, specifically the living room, there are relatively few examples of the three-room plan shifting to the four-room plan. There is instead the development of characteristic plans such as the *magariya*, with earth-floored horse stalls added at the front and the *chumon* style with its buffer entrance room attached.

It is sufficient to have a room for each of the three basic functions of life mentioned above — eating, sleeping, and receiving guests — but other factors also enter into consideration, such as possible cottage industries, climate, family status and adequacy of the spaces for receiving guests, complicating the plan; it is from such considerations that regional characteristics are born.

Separate Roof Style

In the separate-roof style *(betsumunegata)*, the living spaces and earth-floored, strictly work spaces (for cooking and other work) are built adjacent to but separate from each other. (figs. 11–17) This type is found in the southern islands and in many places along the Pacific coast, in the Kanto (Tokyo) area, in the Izu islands, in the Awa region and part of Ibaraki Prefecture. Although the main living spaces, called an *omoya* and the earth-floored work spaces, called a *kamaya* are under separate roofs, the interior arrangement is a whole and cannot be divided. On the exterior, the living space, entered from the long side, is built adjacent to the earth-floored area which is entered from the gable end. Rain water is made to run along the valley formed by the two roofs and empty into a trough beneath the eaves at the front. In the Tokai area between Tokyo and Kyoto this is called the *shumoku* style (the *shumoku* is a T-shaped mallet used to strike temple bells), due to the T-shaped formation of the roofs where they join. The advantage

ら出入する．また，かなり雪が深い場合，中門
2階の窓から出入する例もあるといわれている．
吹雪の吹き荒れる時節は，中門口から入ってす
ぐの通り土間で衣服に着いた雪を取り払い，台
所に入る．もし，この中門部分が無かったら，
台所や土間は，入口から直接吹き込む雪や，屋
根から落ちる雪が，屋内の暖気で溶けてぬかる
みになってしまうだろう．

　このような緩衝地帯としての意味を持つ中門
部分は，長いほど有効で，しかも道路から近い
ほど都合が良い．従って家屋の配置を南向きに
することよりも，道路との位置関係によって中
門の突き出す方向が決まってくる．このように，
中門造りは，積雪と密接な関連を持ちつつ広く
普及した形式であるが，正面に妻を見せる出入
口をもつ中門は，上に述べた実用面のほか，家
の格式の表現としての意味も併せて持っていた
のである㉒．

　山田家は，長野県北端部の秋山郷に見られる
中門造りの例である．主屋の間取りは典型的な
三室広間型で，中門部分には，左手に厩と便所，
右手に通り土間がある．外観は，寄棟造りの主
屋から入母屋造りの中門が突き出している．外

of two structurally separate roofs is that
they can be built lower than a single
large roof and so lessen damage inflicted
by typhoons. However, it may be less
for practical advantage and mainly due
to the weight of tradition when the
trouble of thatching such a roof and the
business of carrying off the rainwater
that falls between them is considered.
To cope with this inconvenience, many
former separate-roof types have been
remodeled into *sugoya,* simple continuous roof.

When the Sakuda House of Kujukurihama in Chiba Prefecture was moved to
Open-air Museum of Traditional Houses
in Kawasaki and restored, it was discovered that although it had been under
a single continuous roof structure, it
was originally a separate-roofed structure.
Separate-roof *minka* are no longer to be
found in the Kujukurihama area but,
based on the restoration of the Sakuda
House, it is clear that the separate-roof
minka once existed on that peninsula
as well.

Minka in Areas of Heavy Snowfall
The thatched roof of the *chumon* type
assumes an L-shape with the entrance
under the eaves of the gable end and is
distributed through the belt of heavy
snowfall on the Japan Sea side of northeastern Japan, from the northeastern part
of Nagano Prefecture northward. In this

⑳

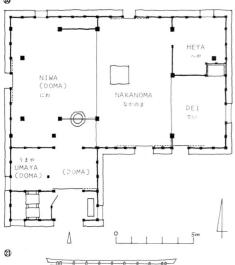

㉑

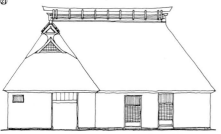

㉒

㉕

HEYA
へや

NIWA
(DOMA)
にわ

NAKANOMA
なかのま

DEI
てい

UMAYA
(DOMA)
うまや

(DOMA)

0　　　　　5m

㉓

㉔

⑱　正面に妻を見せる入口部分（中門）は実用面のほか，家の格式の表現としての意味も持つ（⑱→㉒㉔㉕は旧山田家）.

⑲　積雪時の採光のために，窓部分にはすべて，障子張りの棟間がつくられている.

⑳　中門造りの民家．左手の突出部が中門部分．深雪時に室内を保温するため，開口部は少なく，外壁は茅が段状に葺かれている.

㉑　中門造りの民家の間取り．主屋部分は三室広間型．突出した中門部分があるため，入口から雪が直接吹きこまない．また

出入の際に，中門部の通り土間で衣服に着いた雪を取り払って土間に入るため，主屋に雪をもちこむことが無い（旧山田家）.

㉒　中門造りの民家は，突出部の妻側に正面入口をもつ（旧山田家）.

㉓　雁木道．道路に面して主屋から庇をおろして歩廊を設け，積雪時の通行に利用される（新潟県高田市）.

㉔　主屋から直角に突出する中門部分（左手）.

㉕　左手が広間，右手が土間，間仕切りの奥が中門部分で，主屋と屋外の間の緩衝地帯の役割を果たす.

18. Entry at the gable end of a *chumon* style *minka;* it served formal as well as functional purposes. (Photographs 18 through 22 and 24 and 25 are of the Yamada House)

19. To obtain as much light as possible when snow drifted high, all windows had transoms of sliding paper doors.

20. *Chumon minka.* The projection on the left is the *chumon,* or buffer room. To conserve the heat of the interior in cold snowy weather, the opening is small and the exterior wall is thatched clapboard-style.

21. Plan of a *chumon minka.* The living area has the three-room *hiroma* plan; the projecting *chumon,* buffer room, protects from snow blowing inside at the entry and, by creating

a space where snow may be brushed from the clothes before entering the living area, snow is not tracked inside. (Yamada House)

22. The *chumon minka* has its formal entry in the projection of the gable end of the roof. (Yamada House)

23. *Gangi-michi.* Secondary eaves along the living area facing the road create a passageway for use in the snowy season. (Takada, Niigata)

24. A *chumon* projecting perpendicularly from the main-roof living area (on left).

25. Living spaces on the left, the earth-floored area to the right and the *chumon* to the back of the room arrangement, acting as a buffer zone between inside and out.

壁は茅の段葺きによって覆われている．この茅壁は，深雪時の室内の保温や湿気に対して有効であり，隙間風も防いだ．開口部が少なく，その面積も小さいのは，防雪対策であり，積雪時の採光のために，窓部分にはすべて欄間が設けられている．

農業の様態と民家形式

これまでみてきたように，気候風土は，温暖地と寒冷地とで，大まかな形式の差を生み出したが，「何々造り」のような建物自体の形式を多様につくりあげるほど著しい影響を及ぼしていない．一方，これから述べる農業の様態（ここでは特に屋内で営む副業の様態を指す）は，現在，日本に見られる多彩な地方色をもつ民家形式を生みだした最も大きな要因である．

　主として屋外で行われる農業，林業，漁業は家屋の形式に大きな影響を与えないが，屋内で副業を営む場合は，そうはいかない．副業としては，養蚕業，馬の飼育，煙草葉の加工，製茶，製紙，製織，木工，薬細工，農鍛冶などさまざまであるが，とりわけ養蚕業と馬の飼育は，他の副業に比べて，広い場所と人手を必要とする

ため，家屋に大きな変革がなされ，各地に特色ある民家形式が生まれた．山地や中部以東北の寒冷地は，専業農家として十分に生活が成り立つ温暖な近畿以西の地域とは逆に，ほとんどが米の単作地帯であり，さまざまな副業を営む兼業農家の比率が高い．従って，副業がもたらした特色ある民家形式は，主に中部，関東，東北の山地および寒冷地に形成されてきた．

　ここでは，各地方の様々な民家形式を生み出す要因となった副業として，最も大きい影響力をもった，馬の飼育と養蚕業を取りあげ，それによって発達した各地の民家形式をいくつか紹介する．

馬の飼育

日本では，馬は古くから耕作，運搬，厩肥の製造などに利用されており，農家にとって大きな役割を持っていた．東北日本の中でも，旧南部藩に属していた地方は，藩の政策として古くから馬産が奨励されたため，売馬による収入は，その地方の農家にとって大きな経済資源であった．それゆえ，農民と馬との結びつきは強く，馬は家族の一員として愛護され，厩の建築にも

力が注がれていた.

　厩の規模と構造は，収容頭数，日照，通風，保温等の条件から決まってくるが，その配置形式には，大別して二つある．即ち，主屋と別の棟に建てる場合と，主屋と同じ棟に建てる場合である．日本の寒冷な山地では，後者の場合（内厩式と呼ばれる）が多い．それは，一つ屋根でつながっていれば，寒い時節でも馬の世話のために外に出る必要はなく，厩内の保温に対しても有利であるためとされている．内厩式の農家には，直屋の場合（主屋の矩形の輪郭の一部に厩をもつ），と曲屋の場合（厩が主屋から直角に突出してL字型の輪郭をもつ）とがある㉖→㉞.

　既に述べた「中門造り」の形式と「曲屋」の形式はよく似ているが，別系統のものとされている．主屋はどちらも，三室広間型系の間取りであるが，その相違は，突出部の間取にある．すなわち，「曲屋」の場合，大きな厩が突出部前寄りの梁門全体を占めるが，「中門造り」では，片側を土間の通路にして，その脇の手前に便所，奥に小さな厩が配される．従って「中門造り」では，木戸口を中門の妻に設けるが，「曲屋」では，「ほらまえ」と呼ばれる突出部の入隅位置

area may be seen many devices to deal with the snow, such as snow fences erected under the eaves on all sides of the house to help insulate it and to protect exterior walls from the ravages of the snow, and snow-shelter-eaves added on the side of the house facing the road to preserve a passable corridor when snow drifts over first-floor heights. The *chumon* type is born of the need for a buffer zone between interior and exterior under the eaves. (figs. 18–25)

In heavy snowfalls, when the kitchen entrance is blocked by snow drifts or snow shovelled off the roof, access is gained through the *chumon,* or central, opening. Or, when snow is extremely high, access is through a second story window of *chumon.* At times when snow is blowing badly, one enters the *chumon* entrance and brushes off the snow clinging to clothes in the earth-floored "mudroom", and then enters the kitchen area. If there were no buffer space, snow from outside would be more likely to blow directly in to the earth-floored areas, melt in the heat of the interior and disturb the floor surface, making it wet and muddy.

The *chumon,* then, acts as a buffer zone, as effective as it is deep and as convenient as it is close to the road. So rather than simply orient the house toward the south, its location is determined by the relationship of the ex-tension for the *chumon* entry to the road. The *chumon* type is closely bound to life with drifting snow and is widely distributed; its gabled entrance, though, besides accomplishing its primary purpose was also used to present the best face to guests. (fig. 22)

The Yamada House is an example of the *chumon* type in the village of Aki-yamago at the north end of Nagano Prefecture. The plan of the main house is a typical three-room *hiroma* plan; on the left of the buffer space are horse stalls and a toilet and on the right is an earth-floored passageway. On the exterior, *chumon* part with half-hipped roof extends from main building with hipped roof. The exterior walls are thatched with layers of *kaya* grass, which acts as effective insulation in the cold months and helps prevent drafts. There are few openings and their limited area is also an anti-snow measure; however, in order to take advantage of the light in the snowly months, all windows are provided with transoms.

Side Occupations and House Types

As we have seen so far, the influences of climate alone on the formation of types has not been remarkable aside from the differences seen between warm and cold areas. However, the different farming conditions – here referring especially to secondary occupations or cottage industries – we will now consider constitute the largest factor in the formation of types with a strong regional flavor seen in Japan today. Strictly speaking, farming, forestry, and fishing, etc., have little influence on the form of the house, but cottage industries, secondary occupations practiced within the house, do. There are many such cottage industries, silk worm raising, processing tobacco leaves and tea leaves, paper making, weaving, carving, straw work and smithing. Silk worm and horse raising, especially, compared to the others, require space and labor and make the greatest demands on the house, giving rise to regional characteristics in the form of the *minka,* Unlike the area around Kyoto and westward where an adequate living can be made from the land alone, in the cold mountainous areas from there east and northeastward the percentage of households which plant only rice and which must turn to side industries, is relatively high. Accordingly, the areas in which *minka* acquired characteristics of these cottage industries are primarily the mountainous and cold areas of Chubu, Kanto, and Tohoku, or the eastern half of Honshu.

Below are considered *minka* types which developed from horse and silk-worm raising, the two cottage industries with the largest regional influence on the *minka.*

につけられるのである㉛㉞.

　曲屋形式は，東北地方では旧南部藩領内，特に盛岡付近に多く分布している．厩は，正面から見て右手にある場合と左手にある場合があるが，どちらも日あたりが良いように，ほぼ南東方向をL字型に抱くような向きに配置される．曲屋形式の間取りでは，ジョイと呼ばれる広間と厩とが，大きい土間（ニワ）を隔てて直角に配置される．厩は土間の方に開かれて，馬栓棒で仕切られ，馬はそこから顔を出す．土間には，飼料釜，秣切場があり，ふつうはその奥にダイドコロが設けられる．厩の屋根には破風があり，カマドや炉でたく煙は，そこから排煙されるため，馬の背を暖めるといわれるし，屋根裏の乾草の乾燥にも役立つ．

　曲屋のような，特殊な外観と平面を持つ形式が生まれた要因としては，次のようなことが挙げられている．

　1）寒冷地で，馬の多頭飼育を屋内で行う場合，直屋形式では桁行方向の長さが大きくなり過ぎ，敷地との釣り合いが悪い．

　2）南東向きにL字型で囲むことによって，寒い北西の季節風を避けた日だまりが，前庭にで

Horse Raising

Horses have long been used in Japan for tilling and the production of fertilizer and have performed many roles on the farm. Even in northeastern Japan, in areas that once belonged to the old southern fiefs which encouraged the raising of horses as a matter of policy, the income derived from the sale of horses was very important to the farmers of the area. For such reasons, horse and farmer were closely bound, the horse being cared for almost as a member of the family, and great attention was paid to the construction of stables.

　The scale and construction of the stable was decided by the number of animals kept and the available light, ventilation, and insulating factors; there are two main categories of location: housed outside the main structure of the house, and within it. In Japan's cold mountainous areas, most are within. Of these, one type is attached to the interior of the house, making it unnecessary to go outside to care for the horses in winter and keeping the stable area some warmer. In such cases, the stable is sometimes an extension, attached to the main roof at one end, while in other cases it sticks out perpendicularly from one end of the main roof, in an L-shape. (figs. 26–34)

　As we have already noted, the *chumon* and *magariya* forms are similar but

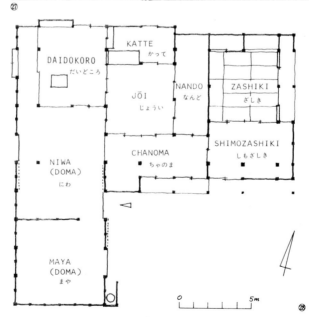

㉖　曲屋の概観．厩が主屋から直角に突出（左手）して，全体としてL字形の輪郭をもつ（旧工藤家）．

㉗　曲屋の内部．手前から広間（板張），土間，その奥が厩（旧工藤家）．

㉘　曲屋の間取り．厩は突出部前寄りの梁間全体を占め，入口は入隅位置にある．南東方向をL字で囲った前庭ができ，陽だまりをつくっている（旧工藤家）．

㉙㉚　曲屋の背面．寒冷な北西の季節風を背に受け，南東方向をL字形に抱いて前庭に陽だまりをつくる（千葉家）．写真：

栄美智子．

㉛　突出部の入隅位置にあるほらまえ，と呼ばれる出入口（旧藤原家）．

㉜　左手が主屋部分，右手が厩のある突出部分．カマドや炉でたく煙は厩の屋根の破風から排煙されるため，馬の背を暖めるといわれる（旧藤原家）．

㉝　遠野の曲屋（菊池家）．写真：栄美智子．

㉞　突出部の入隅位置にある戸口（千葉家）．写真：栄美智子．

26. *Magariya* exterior. The stable projects perpendicularly from the main structure at the left, making an L-shape. (Kudo House)

27. *Magariya* interior. From front to back are the *hiroma* (board-floored), *doma* (earth-floored), and stable. (Kudo House)

28. Plan of *magariya*. The stable occupies the whole span between beams at the front projection and the entrance is in the inside of the corner. The garden plot enclosed by the ell of the building faces southeast and gets abundant sun. (Kudo House)

29, 30. Rear facade of *magariya minka*. The house turns its back to the cold northwesterly winds and accepts the sunlight from the south-east in the front garden made in the ell of the front of the house. Tono.

31. The entrance, called *horamae,* located in the inside corner of the house and the projecting part. (Fujiwara House)

32. On the left is the main structure, on the right the projection of the stable. Smoke from the rice oven and hearth is vented out through the roof over the stable, giving the horses some warmth. (Fujiwara House)

33. *Magariya* in Tono. The exterior wall is a reconstruction.

34. Door in the inside corner of the projection. Tono.

③⑤

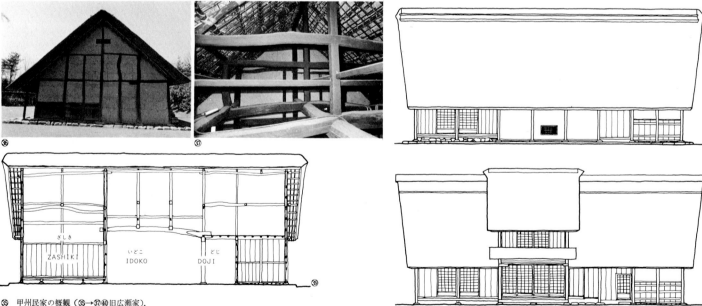

㊱

㊲

㊳

㊳

⑤ 甲州民家の概観（⑤→⑦④旧広瀬家）.

㊱ 妻側の壁面には，棟木まで延びる棟持柱が立つ.

㊲ 蚕室を確保するために，のちになってこの部分が改造され，屋根が突き上げられた.

㊳ 甲州民家，旧広瀬家. 上は復元立面図. 下は移築前立面図. 建築当初は切妻造りの民家であったが，のちに養蚕の目的に適うように屋根が押し上げられ，通風，採光のための窓を表側にもつ中2階の蚕室がつくられた.

㊴ 旧広瀬家復元断面図. いどこ上部の三つのスパンの小屋組を改造して突き上げ屋根がつくられた.

㊵ 茅葺き，切妻造りの甲州民家.

35. Exterior of a Koshu *minka*.
Photographs 35, 36, 37 and 40 are of the Hirose House.
36. The full length of the post supporting the roof ridge pole is seen in the wall of the gable end.
37. This part was rebuilt at one time to accomodate the raising of silkworms, lifting the roof.
38. Koshu *minka*, Hirose House. Above is an elevation of the restoration; below, an eleva-

tion of the building before moving. When first built it was of simple gable construction but the roof was later raised to accomodate raising silk worms and a second floor added for the worms with a window provided in front for light and ventilation.
39. Section of the restoration of the Hirose House. Three spans of the roof structure over the living areas was rebuilt and a hipped projection added.
40. Gabled and thatched Koshu *minka*.

養蚕民家の形式 Regional styles of sericultural farm houses	屋根の形状 Roof configurations	主に分布する県 Prefectures of major concentration
Kōshū-minka 甲州民家		Yamanashi-ken 山梨県
Akagi-gata 赤城型		Gunma-ken 群馬県
Kabuto-zukuri 甲造り		Shizuoka-ken 静岡県
Takahappō-zukuri 高八方造り		Yamagata-ken 山形県
Gasshō-zukuri 合掌造り		Gifu-ken Toyama-ken 岐阜県，富山県

屋根裏に蚕室を設け，通風，採光をとるという改造の目的は同じなのだが，土地の伝統技術や改造前の屋根形式が異なるため，その工夫や変革の仕方は様々で，各地に興味深い養蚕農家の形式が生まれた．
Although sharing the purpose of creating room for the raising of silk worms and providing that space with light and proper ventilation, the traditional techniques of the region and the form of the roof prior to remodeling differed by area and various interesting forms of minka for silkworm-raising farmers were devised.

きる．

3）主屋の各室から，厩の動静を見通せる．

4）主屋の梁間寸法に拘束されずに，必要な大きさの厩が建てられる．また，構造的にも直屋より安定する．

このように，曲屋形式は馬の多頭飼育との関連が強く，これに積雪，季節風などの気候的要因が加わって発達したものである．

養蚕

養蚕は，古くから日本に伝えられたが，盛んに行われるようになったのは，明治初期から第2次大戦前にかけての時期で，特に中部の山岳地（山梨，長野，岐阜），関東山地（群馬，埼玉），東北南部，を中心に行われた．養蚕の飼育法は，清涼育（天然飼育法の一種），温暖育，条桑育の順に発達したが，このうち民家形式にもっとも大きな変革をもたらしたのは温暖育であり，明治10年（1877年）に初めて行われたといわれる．その後，大正末期から条桑育が一般に流行したが，屋内よりも屋外に条桑を建てる場合が多いため，民家形式には大きな影響を与えなかった．従って，現在みられる，特色ある養蚕農家の形

式は，温暖育が盛んに行われた時期，即ち明治中期から大正にかけて成立したものである．

温暖育といわれる飼育法の特色は，蚕の各年令に応じて，飼育室を分化し，生育状態に適応した飼育環境をつくることにある．稚蚕では，密閉した室内で飼育するため，天井を板張とし，熱の拡散を防いだ．五齢（壮蚕）になると，通風および室内の乾燥が要求され，また飼育のための広い場所が必要であった．従って，飼育場所を確保するために，屋根裏を2層，3層に改造し，その通風，採光のために，屋根の形式を大きく変革していかねばならなかった．屋根裏に蚕室を設け，通風採光をとるという目的は同じであるにもかかわらず，それぞれの土地の伝統や，改造前の屋根形式が異なるため，その工夫，変革の仕方が様々に変化し，各地に興味深い民家形式が形成されていった．著しい特色をもつ養蚕農家の形式としては，甲州民家（山梨），赤城型（群馬），甲造り（静岡，山梨），高八方（山形），合掌造り（岐阜，富山）が挙げられる．

甲州民家

甲府盆地とその周辺の丘陵地帯に分布する草葺

different in origin. In either case, the room arrangement is some form of the three-room *hiroma* type, with variations in the plan of the stable extension. In the *magariya* style, the stable fills the full span at the front of the extension but in the *chumon* style one side is an earth-floored passage with a toilet on the other side at one end and a small stable located deeper in. Accordingly, in the *chumon* style a large door is built in the center of the wall under the gable while in the *magariya* the door appears in the inside corner of the extension with the main house. (figs. 31, 34)

The *magariya* style is found in the northeastern parts, within the old southern fiefs and especially in the vicinity of Morioka city in Iwate Prefecture. The stable appears on both the right and left of the facade, in either case being situated to receive good lighting, usually in an L-shape open to the southeast. In the plan of the *magariya*, a living room called a *jo-i* and the stable bound a large earth-floored area at right angles. The stable is open to the earth-floored area with a tethering bar on that side over which the horses may poke their heads outside. A feeding trough and mill stone are found in the earth-floored area, at the far end of which is usually the kitchen. The stable roof has vents from which the smoke of the rice oven and hearth are exhausted; this system gives

some warmth to the horses and dries hay in the attic.

The following are offered as factors in the development of a style with a characteristic facade and plan, such as the *magariya*.

1) When keeping a number of horses inside in cold areas, the beams required for the *sugoya* style become too large, all out of proportion to the site.

2) With an L-configuration oriented to the southeast, cold northwesterly seasonal winds are blocked and the front garden is open to sunlight.

3) Activity in the stable can be seen from all rooms of the house.

4) The stable can be built only as large as necessary since it need not conform to the span of the main house, and it is structurally more stable than the *sugoya*.

The *magariya* style is thus closely related to the keeping of a number of horses and developed from that as well as climatic factors, such as snowfall and seasonal winds.

Silk Worm Raising

Silk worm raising has long been practiced in Japan but was most enthusiastically pursued from the beginning of the Meiji period to before the Second World War (1870's to 1930's) and especially in the mountainous reaches of central Japan (Yamanashi, Nagano, and Gifu Prefectures), the mountainous Kanto area

切妻造りの民家は甲州民家と呼ばれ，次のよう
な特色を持つ民家形式である③⑤→④⓪.
1）屋根は草葺の切妻造りである③⑧上.
2）妻の壁面に棟木まで延びる棟持柱（むなもちばしら）が立つ.
3）屋根の中央部を一段高く切り上げて，その
表側に窓が設けられる③⑧下.

　もともとこの地方の民家は，1），2）の特徴を
もつ形式であったが，養蚕業が行われるように
なって，改造され，3）のような独特な外観を持
った養蚕農家の形式が生まれたもので，突き屋
根，櫓造りなどと呼ばれる．屋根が突き上げら
れた部分は，中2階に相当し，さらにその上部
の屋根裏にもう一層の床を設けて，全体で三層
にする場合が多い．養蚕時は建物全体が蚕室に
かわるのだが，蚕室の面積をできるだけ広くす
るために，上のような屋根裏の改造がなされ，
採光と換気のために，煙出（けぶだし）と呼ばれる窓が表側
に設けられたのである．旧広瀬家は，甲州民家
のなかでは古い時期に属するもので，建築当初
は，草葺の切妻造の民家だったが，19世紀の初
め頃に，養蚕の目的に適うように中2階を設け，
屋根が突き上げられた③⑧③⑨.

㊶

(Gunma and Saitama Prefectures) and in the southern part of Tohoku, the northeast. There are three methods of raising silk worms — the "clean and cool" method, the warm-temperature method and the on-the-leaf method — and of these, the one which had the greatest effect in restyling the *minka* was the warm-temperature method, which is said to have first been practiced in 1877. From the early 1900's, the on-the-leaf method was predominant, but as it called for sheds to be built outside for the worms rather than have them under the home roof, its effect on *minka* styles was negligible. So the houses we see today which were heavily influenced by silk worm raising are those built between the late 1870's and early 1900's.

The warm-temperature method of raising silk worms characteristically separates the worms by year and attempts to provide the best environment for that age. To keep the youngest in warmth, the room was enclosed and a ceiling suspended to prevent the temperature from dropping. At maturity (about five years) ventilation and dryness are desired, and more room needed. To obtain these spaces, two or even three levels were built under the roof; securing the necessary ventilation and light entailed great changes in the roof itself. And, despite the shared goals of providing space, ventilation and light for silk worms, with different regional traditions and

㊷

41, 42, 43. *Takahappo minka* in Tamugimata. Endo House in the foreground.
44. Section of a *takahappo minka*. The roof was originally hipped (shown by dotted lines), but as silkworm production prospered, a cupola was built to provide light and air for their benefit. A window called a *takahappo* was built high under the gable, and a window called a *happo* was built in the roof. Three levels were built for the raising of the worms,

a second floor, loft and attic loft.
45. Elevation of the gable end of a *takahappo*. The gable is brought up high, with a window at the second floor and loft levels. (Shibuya House)
46. *Takahappo* in Tamugimata.
47. Windows in the gable end are called *takahappo* and windows in the roof are called *happo*.

㊸

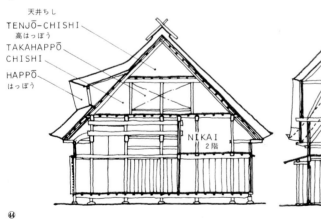

天井ちし
TENJŌ-CHISHI

高はっぽう
TAKAHAPPŌ
CHISHI

HAPPŌ
はっぽう

NIKAI
2階

㊹

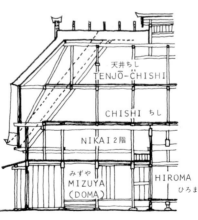

天井ちし
TENJŌ-CHISHI

CHISHI ちし

NIKAI 2階

みずや
MIZUYA
(DOMA)

HIROMA
ひろま

㊻

0   5m

㊺

㊼

㊶→㊸　田麦俣の高八方造りの民家（手前は遠藤家）．写真：
堀川幹夫．
㊹　高八方造りの断面図．もともとは寄棟造り（点線部分）で
あったが，養蚕の隆盛に伴い屋根裏の蚕室の通風，採光のため
に甲造りに改められた．妻側の破風に「高はっぽう」と呼ばれ
る高く切り上げた窓をつくり，屋根面には「はっぽう」という
屋根窓を設けた．屋根裏の蚕室は，3層（2階，ちし，天井ち
し）になっている．
㊺　高八方造りの妻側立面図．破風が高く切り上げられ，2階
とちし（3階）の窓がつくられている（旧渋谷家）．
㊻　田麦俣の高八方造り．写真：堀川幹夫．
㊼　妻面の窓は高「はっぽう」，屋根面の窓は「はっぽう」と
呼ばれる．写真：堀川幹夫．

高八方

山形県の朝日山地には高八方と呼ばれる独特の養蚕農家の形式がみられる㊶→㊼この地方の屋根は，もともとは寄棟造が基本形であったが，養蚕の隆盛に伴い，屋根裏の蚕室の通風と採光のために甲造りに改め，屋根窓のはっぽうを拡大するなどの改造がなされた．養蚕に用いられる屋根裏は，二階，ちし（3階），天井ちし（4階）と多層にわたる．屋根面にははっぽうという屋根窓を設け，妻側の破風には「高はっぽう」と呼ばれる高く切り上げた窓がつくられた㊹．この地方の民家は，平家建てでも建物の建ちが高く，天井の高い上屋造りであったため，その天井高を低くして多層建てに改変することは，それほど難しくなかった．平家建て寄棟造りが，多層の高八方形式に改造された例が，渋谷家である㊺．この形式の民家集落として有名な山形県田麦俣は，明治末の大火により部落の大半を焼失したが，それ以後に建てられた家屋は，その頃盛んになった温暖育に適するように，総2階建てとすることが多かった．

㊽ 合掌造りの民家集落（白川郷）．写真：中沢敏彰．
㊾ 五箇山地方の妻入の合掌造り．階上（2階と3階）は蚕室で，大きな三角形の妻面に，換気，採光のための障子窓が，層ごとに並ぶ（旧江向家）．
㊿ 桁の上に巨大な合掌（又首）を三角形に組み，その小屋裏を数層にわけて，板を渡し，蚕室の面積を広げた（旧江向家）．
51 旧江向家の広間．奥の梯子を登って蚕室に至る．
52 合掌造り民家の断面図．1階は居住部，階上（屋根裏）は，2〜4層の蚕室である．
53 合掌造りの民家．写真：中沢敏彰．→

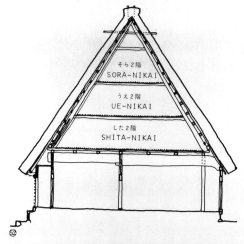

roof-forms already in existence, the solutions and changes themselves varied, making for very interesting *minka* forms in different locales. Remarkable changes in houses engaged in silk worm production are found in the Koshu *minka* (Yamanashi), *Akagi* style (Gunma), *kabuto* style (Shizuoka, Yamanashi), *takahappo* style (Yamagata), and the *gassho* style (Gifu, Toyama).

Koshu Minka

The simple, thatched *minka* seen in the Kofu basin and surrounding hills is called the Koshu *minka* and is characterized by the following. (figs. 35—40)

1) The roof is gabled and thatched. (fig. 38 above)

2) The gabled end shows a post supporting the roof ridge.

3) The center portion of the roof is raised and the front of that portion fitted window. (fig. 38 below)

This style had always incorporated features (1) and (2) but with the advent of the silk worm industry, the style was modified and the third features also became characteristic of the facade as a silk worm *minka* style was formulated, sometimes also called the "jutting roof", or turret, style. In most cases, the raised part of the roof indicates a second level and another above it, for a total of three floors. Silk worm raising changed the whole building to its purpose, and to achieve the greatest possible floor area,

48. Shirakawa-go, a village of *gassho* style *minka*.
49. *Gassho minka* of the Gokayama area with the entry in the gable end. The upper (second and third) floors were for raising silkworms and windows protected by sliding paper doors were provided for each floor in the large wall of the gable end of the house. (Emukai House)
50. A huge roof structure was built over the beams, beneath which a number of levels were created by laying boards over the beams to increase the space alotted to the raising of silkworms. (Emukai House)
51. *Hiroma*, living area, of Emukai House. The ladder in the background leads to the worming rooms.
52. Section through a *gassho minka*. The first floor was for living areas, upper floors (from two to four under the roof) were for raising silkworms.
53. *Gassho* style *minka*.→

合掌造り

合掌造りは㊽→㊼, 日本の多彩な民家形式の中でも, ひときわ印象的な美しさを持っている. その巨大な三角形の切妻に3～5尺の明り障子が並ぶ特異な外観は, 富山湾にそそぐ庄川の上流地域, 即ち岐阜県荘川, 白川地方から, 富山県五箇山地方を中心に分布する. その地域の中には, 荘川では入母屋造りの平入, 白川では切妻造りの平入, 五箇山では切妻造りの妻入といったおおまかな傾向がある. 合掌造りのような切妻造りは, 屋根裏の各層に採光と通風のための窓がとれるので, 他の養蚕民家の形式に比べて, 屋根自体に何らの改造を施さずにすむ利点がある. 桁の上に合掌（叉首）を三角形に組む小屋組は, 日本では一般的な構造形式だが, 養蚕に必要な広大な屋根裏空間を確保するために, このように雄大な合掌造りが生まれたのである. 階上部はすべて養蚕に用いられ, した2階, うえ2階, そら2階の三層とする場合が多いが, 小屋組の最上部にも床を設けたり, 1階部分（居住部）に中2階を設けることもあり, この場合, 全体で6層になる㊿.

江向家は, 五箇山地方の妻入の合掌造りの民家で, 1階の居住部は, いわゆる四間取りの間取り形式だが, 階上部は中段に板を渡して2層とし, 全体で3階建てとしている.

一つの民家形式を決定する要因は, 多数あるだけでなく, 各要因が相互に関係し合っているため, その成立の過程を筋道立てて解き明かすことは難しい. 従って, ここで紹介したいくつかの民家形式も, 気候風土と農業様態の面のみから語りつくせるものではない. しかしながら, 民家が他のいかなる分野の建築より, その二つの面と結びつきが強いことは, 依然として確かなことである. とりわけ, 地方ごとに塗り分けられた多彩な民家に接し, その土地の風土や生活と一つの民家形式との因果に思いをめぐらすことは, 専門の研究者はもとより, 一般の人々がもっとも興味をひかれるところであろう. このような素朴な関心のもとに, 伝統的遺産である民家の重要性を認識していくことが, 保存あるいは次代への継承の大きな力となるはずである.

参考文献

1. 『東北の民家』, 小倉強, 相模書房, 1955年.
2. 『今和次郎集2・民家論』, 今和次郎, ドメス出版, 1971年.
3. 『今和次郎集3・民家採集』, ドメス出版, 1971年.
4. 『民家は生きてきた』, 伊藤ていじ, 美術出版社, 1963年.
5. 『ふるさとのすまい』, 日本建築協会編, 同会刊, 1962年.
6. 『日本民家の研究』, 杉本尚次, ミネルヴァ書房, 1969年.
7. 『滅びゆく民家1, 2』, 川島宙次, 主婦と生活社, 1973年.
8. 『滅びゆく民家3』, 主婦と生活社, 1976年.
9. 『日本の民家・第2巻・農家II』, 宮沢智士編, 学習研究社, 1980年.
10. 『日本建築史基礎資料集成21. 民家』, 太田博太郎他, 中央公論美術出版, 1976年.
11. 『重要文化財伊藤家住宅移築修理工事報告書』, 川崎市編集発行, 1966年.
12. 『重要文化財旧作田家住宅移築修理工事報告書』, 川崎市編集発行, 1971年.
13. 『重要文化財旧工藤家住宅移築修理工事報告書』, 川崎市編集発行, 1972年.
14. 『重要文化財旧江向家住宅移築修理工事報告書』, 川崎市編集発行, 1970年.
15. 『旧広瀬家住宅移築修理工事報告書』, 川崎市編集発行, 1971年.

the space under the roof was remodelled as just described, with a window called the "smoke hole" placed in the front for light and ventilation. The old Hirose House is an example of the older type of Koshu *minka*, first built as a thatched, simple gabled roof but changed at the beginning of the nineteenth century to permit the raising of silk worms by adding a second floor and pushing up the roof. (figs. 38, 39)

Takahappo Style

The unique *takahappo* style of farmhouse adapted to silk worm raising is found in the mountainous Asahi area of Yamagata Prefecture. The roof was originally hipped but as silk worm production spread, the roof was changed to the *kabuto* style to admit light and improve ventilation for the silk worm rooms under the roof, and the happo window was thereby enlarged. Silk worm rooms were placed on the second floor, loft (third floor) and attic loft (a fourth floor). In the roof itself, a window called a *happo* was installed, and in the wall of the gable end was a high window called the "high *happo*," or *takahappo*. As building itself and ceiling of these *minka* were high, it was not so difficult to convert them to a many tiered style. The Shibuya House is an example of a single-story house that was converted to the *takahappo* style. Tamugimata, a village in Yamagata Prefecture, is famed for its *minka;* over half the village burned at the end of the Meiji period, but the *minka* built after that were adapted to the warm-temperature method and many were two-storied. (figs. 41—47)

Gassho Style

Even among all the various kinds of *minka* in Japan, the *gassho* style is particularly impressive and beautiful. Their steep triangular gabled roofs with their distinctive rows of bright paper doors are found among the headwaters of the Shokawa River which flows into Toyama Bay, from the Shokawa and Shirakawa areas in Gifu Prefecture to the Gokayama area of Toyama Prefecture. In general, in Shokawa, entry to hipped-gable style houses is from the long side, in Shirakawa the roofs are simple gables and the entry again on the long side, and in Gokayama the houses are gabled and the entry at the gable end. In gabled roofs like those of the *gassho* style, windows are provided for light and ventilation on each floor under the roof, so there is no need for any other changes to be made in the roof itself. The triangular roof structure above the beams is a common construction in Japan, and the *gassho* style was born from an enlargement of that idea in order to secure the large space under the roof necessary for raising silkworms. The upper floors were all used as worming rooms, and many houses had lower, upper, and loft levels above the main floor; some houses, though, had a loft, or mezzanine, built over part of the living areas of the first floor too, in which cases there were a total of six levels.

In the Emukai House, a gabled *gassho* style *minka* near Gokayama with a four-room plan, boards are laid over the first floor living area and more above that, for a total of three levels. (figs. 48—53)

It is not just the number of factors that have a decisive influence on a style, but the complicated ways in which these factors are related that makes unraveling and explaining them so difficult. Accordingly, the *minka* styles introduced here are more than the products of simple climatic considerations and farming and side work conditions. It is nevertheless certain that the *minka* is more closely tied to these two factors than most other types of architecture. The relationships between the local climate and lifestyles and a particular form of *minka*, especially those that are regionally differentiated, appeals to the professional and all others alike. At the root of this honest admiration is the awareness of their importance as a legacy of tradition, an awareness which should add strength to the preservation movement and the intent to bequeath these to future generations.

THE PRINCIPAL ELEMENTS OF MACHIYA DESIGN

by William R. Tingey

町屋デザイン要素の変遷

ウィリアム・R・ティンギー

「町家」という言葉はしばしば "Town House" という英語に訳される．しかし，"Town House" は特に住居としてだけ機能する建物を意味するために，誤解されることがある．一方，「町家」は一つ屋根の下に「売ること」と「住むこと」を内包する建物に使われる．それゆえ，町家では店の主人が暮らし，そして働く．職住併用という点で職人の家も町家に含めるが，「売ること」と「住むこと」を主目的とするこの種の建築には日本語の「商家」がちょうど当てはまりそうだ．「商家」という言葉は二つの文字の組み合わせで，「商」（しょう，あきない）は売買すること，「家」（か，や，いえ）は住居を意味する．その点でこの言葉はとても明解ではあるが，街の基本的なユニットのひとつだということまでは意味しない．街（都市）は商売ぬきで考えることはできず，専門家はその前提条件として売買をあげる．町家とは異なり，商家

という言葉は「街」には触れない．町家の「町」（まち，ちょう）は街の中の一つの地域，地区を指し，「家」（か，や，いえ）は住居を指す．だから，町家はその意味において「街」，すなわち集まることをも内包するより便利な言葉と言える．この点から本文では，英語の shop よりむしろ町家という単語を全体の標題として用いた．

日本人はかなり広義に町家という言葉を使うが，デパート，明治時代の洋風店舗，地下商店街の店舗などまでは通常含まない．しかし，この論文では目的に合わせて，1）これらがすべて街路や公道に沿って建っていること，2）それらの中で市民との直接売買が行われていること，の2点から，すべて町家に含めて考える．「純粋」な町家と同様，ここで言う町家も日本の風土や都市環境における文化的，社会的変化に対してだけでなく，その環境特有の要素に特

に対応する建築をある程度意味している．

町家の起源

街と町家は多少なりとも互いに依存関係にあるので，町家や商売のための常設建築はおそらく，かなり大きな街が発達するにつれて生まれてきたのであろう．住居・店舗併用と思われる建物が初めて出現したのは平安時代（792〜1185）のことであった．

当時の日本の首都平安京では，市のための土地から離れて，内部の傍に物を売るスペースを持つ住居があった．こうした住居が首都の通りに沿って広がり，最初の町家となった．それは実際，見た目では農家とあまり変わりないけれど，すでに環境の要求に対応し，その基本的構成要素は次第に洗練され，付加されていった．商業及び一般的状況が変わるにつれて他の要素が無視されていったのに対し，こうした要素の

The Word *"machiya"* in Japanese is sometimes translated into English as *town house*. However, this can be misleading as *town house* refers specifically to a type of dwelling and it is only a dwelling. The word *machiya*, however, can be used of architecture where "selling" and "living" activities go on under the same roof. Therefore a *machiya* is where a shop keeper lives and works. It may also refer to the house of a craftsman and so as the primary objects are "selling" and "living" the Japanese word *shōka* (shop) would seem just as appropriate to describe the architecture in question. This word is a combination of two characters 商 *shō* or *akinai* meaning to sell, handle or trade in, and 家 *ka, ya* or *ie* for house. This word is therefore very specific but there is no indication of the fact that the architecture in question is one of the essential units of the collection of buildings called a town. A town (city) would not be a town without trade and the specialist premises where buying and selling take place. The word *shōka* makes no re-

ference to "town" as such, where as *machiya* does. In simple terms (町) *machi* or *chō* refers to a district or section of a town and as with *shōka* (家) *ka, ya* or *ie* equals house. So in fact *machiya* is a rather useful word because it is a collective term which embodies "town" in its meaning and for this reason is used here as an overall heading in preference to the English word shop.

Although the word *machiya* as used by the Japanese has a fairly wide meaning, it would not usually be used to include such things as department stores, western style shops of the Meiji Period, shops in an underground shopping centre or a normal shop. However for the purposes of this article *machiya* is taken to include all of these because, 1) they are all buildings standing at the side of streets or public thoroughfares and 2) they are all buildings in which a form of direct trading with the public takes place. Also, just as much as a "pure" *machiya* does, they all represent an architecture which in some way has reacted

to elements peculiar to the Japanese urban environment in particular, as well as the topography and climate.

The beginning of *machiya*

As both a town and *machiya* are more or less dependant on each other, *machiya*, or buildings of a permanent nature where goods were sold, probably came into existance as sizeable towns developed. The first such buildings, recognizable as being both dwellings and shops emmerged during the Heian period (792 – 1185).

In Heiankyo (Kyoto), at that time the capital of Japan, there were, apart from designated sites where markets were held, dwellings which had part of their interior space set aside for the selling of the goods. These buildings sprangup along the streets of the capital and are the first buildings to be known as *machiya*. They were not really much more than adapted farm houses, but they had already responded to the demands of the environment and the basic elements of which they were composed were gradually refined and added to. Some of

↑奈良県明日香村　Asuka, Nara Prefecture.

↓奈良県今井町　Imai-cho, Nara Prefecture.

①

いくつかは今日の店舗デザインの中にも未だに見られる.

　町家のごく初期の実例は,平安京の屏風絵に見ることができる.通りに沿って町家が互いに隣接して並び,ファサード開口部のアレンジ以外に個性がほとんど,いやまったくと言ってよいほどにない.柱は地中に直接立てられ,その間の壁面は板や網代の類で様々に埋められている.屋根は,外側に固定された木材で押さえられた板で作られている.実際,建物の基本的形態の中には,そこで物が売られたことを示すものが全く見当たらない①.

　床は比較的狭い部分が一段高くなり,板張りにされているのが屏風絵からわかるが,そこはたぶん寝るための場所として使われたのであろ

う.約1/6ほどの床面が高くされ,残りは土間のままとされた.土間のうしろの方で料理が作られ,通りに面した前面の方ではいろいろなものが売られた.

　こうした初期の店舗はかなり開放的で,広い入口から内部へ簡単にはいることができるが,間もなく目的を持った陳列スペースが生まれてきた.窓の外側に固定された板の上に商品を陳列して通行人に見せたのがその最初らしい.この場合,商人は建物の中にいて,通行人とは壁で隔てられている.陳列の形態は商品によって明らかに異なるけれど,商品が確かに陳列されていたという事実は,商人間で間違いなく一種の競争があったことや,「主人」が通行する人すべてに物を売りたいと思っていたことを示し

ている.これはおそらく顧客を引きつける最初の試みであろう.鎌倉,室町時代までに,陳列スペースは発展して町家の内部の配置とつながるようになった.高い床の範囲もかなり増して,床面の半分を越す例も見うけられる.土間は内部のいずれか一方にあるか,あるいは二つの高い床部分の間の廊下のような空間となっている.この二つのタイプのうち,後者は近世までには見られなくなるが,前者はその後の町家の標準的配置となった.

　ファサードも変わった③.一段高い床部分の前面には固定された壁がなく,建物本体からのびた台(揚見世)の上に商品が陳列された.半開放型のファサード以外に「閉鎖型」もあった.唯一の開口は入口で,それも夜にはおそらく戸

those elements can still be seen in shop design today, where as others have been disgarded as trading and general conditions have changed.

These earliest types of *machiya* can be seen in screen paintings of Heiankyo. The streets are lined with *machiya,* one butting onto the next there being little or no individuality in design except that the arrangement of openings on the facade vary some what from one to another. The columns were set directly into the ground and the wall spaces in between were variously filled with weather boarding or a kind of wickerwork. The rooves were made from boards held down by timbers fixed to the outside. Infact a basic building, in the design of which there was little or nothing to indicate that it was a place where things could be bought.

It would appear from the screen

paintings that a relatively small area of the floor was raised and boarded, this probably being used as sleeping area. This would mean that may be as little as 1/6 of the buildings floor area was raised, the remainder being an earth floor or *doma*. Here the cooking would be done in the back part of the building, where as the front of the *doma* facing the street was where any selling would take place.

Although these early shops are fairly open and access to the interior via a wide entrance is easy, it cannot have been long before a purpose built display area developed. First of all this seems to have been a board fixed outside of a window on which goods were displayed to the passing public (figs. 1, 2). In this case the person selling is inside the building and separated from the public by a wall. Obviously the form of the display would

vary according to the goods on sale but the fact that goods were displayed at all surely means that there must have been some kind of competition between traders and also that the 'shop keeper' was hoping to sell to absolutely anybody who might be passing. Also it is probably the first attempt to attract customers. By the Kamakura and Muromachi periods a display area had developed which had become linked to the interior layout of the *machiya.* It would appear that the area of raised floor had increased considerably, in some cases taking up more than half of the area of the building. The *doma* or earth floor was either to one side of the interior or was a corridor like space running between two raised floor areas. Of these two types the latter died out by the late Middle Ages but the former went on to become the standard layout in most subsequent

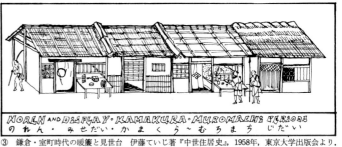

②　　　　　①②　平安時代の町家. *Machiya* of Heian Period.

③　鎌倉・室町時代の暖簾と見世台　伊藤ていじ著『中世住居史』,1958年,東京大学出版会より. *Noren* and display of Kamakura and Muromachi Period.

④　人見梁と船桁，東京．
⑤　船桁造り．洛中風俗図屏風（舟木家本・東京国立博物館蔵）より．
⑥　船桁造り・はね出し町家の鎧師．喜多院蔵・職人尽絵より．
⑦　宿場町奈良井の町家，長野県．
⑧　木曾街道沿いの宿場町妻籠，長野県．
⑨　梲のある町家，妻籠．
⑩　真山家．
⑪　街道筋の断面．2階のはね出しと軒の出がよくわかる．
⑫　町家の屋根伏図．

締まりされたであろう．日中は家紋や店のマークのついた暖簾が開口に吊るされた．暖簾は鎌倉時代末期から室町時代初期の間に使われ始めた．短いものが日覆いとしてよく用いられたが，江戸時代になると店によってはほとんど地面までとどくような長いものを使ったりした．暖簾はそのマークが店を他と区別するのに役立ったばかりでなく，硬いファサードに対し軟かさを与え，内と外を巧妙に仕切った．

入口は二つの柱と冠木（かぶき）とも呼ばれる楣によって組みたてられたが，この種の構法は平安時代にも使われていた．楣はしばしば柱の位置以上に左右に拡がり，鳥居にも似た単純な「門」のようなものを形成する．柱楣形式は日本建築の一般的手法で，初期の町家ではファサードのデザイン要素の一つであった．江戸時代になると，店の正面は例えば店蔵（92，93頁参照）のようにすべて道に対して開放的になり，その開口の梁は欅などの頑丈な木で作られた．この梁は関東地方では人見梁と呼ばれた④．人見はシャッターの役目をする格子窓，蔀がなま

ったものと考えられる．平安から鎌倉時代に至るまで，平安京の町家のファサードの梁からは半蔀が吊られ，その梁が蔀梁と呼ばれた．江戸では今日でさえも「し」を「ひ」と，あるいはその逆に発音する傾向があるので，おそらくその影響によって蔀梁が人見梁に変化していったと考えられる．これは江戸の文化が京都，関西地方の文化を基礎とし，その上に作られたことの好例である．徳川幕府が江戸に設置されると，外くの関西商人が江戸に出店を出した．こうして関西・関東間の知識，言葉，人間，物品の交流が始まった．しかし江戸時代（1603〜1868）には江戸っ子はその個性を失なわず，特に町家のデザインに限って言えば，独特の建築様式を生み出した．それは関西地方特有の厳格な様式に比べると，かなり個性の強いものであった．

一般的に，プライバシーが全くないほどに道が狭く混み合っている時以外，店の正面は広く開放されることが多い．道が狭い時などは格子組のファサードが通りから内部を遮る．しかし日本の気候，特に湿気の多い夏にはできる限り

machiya.

The facade too had changed (fig. 3). Now at the front of the raised floor area there was no fixed wall and wares were displayed on a stand which extended out from the main body of the building.

Other than this type of semi-open facade there was also a "closed" type. The only opening was the entrance which would at night presumably be shuttered. During the day a curtain or *noren* would hang in the opening. This would bear a family crest or shop mark. The use of *noren* started between the end of the Kamakura and the beginning of the Muromachi periods, sometimes a short one was used on the eaves for shade and in the Edo period some shops had a deep one almost down to the ground. The mark on the *noren* must have helped to make one shop distinguishable from another but also added a soft kinetic element to the facade.

Because of the type of construction used even in the Heian period the entrance was framed by two columns and a lintel which is sometimes called a *kabuki.* This member often extended left and right beyond the columns, forming what looked like a simple "gate" which was not unlike the *torii* gate used in shrine architecture. This type of post and lintel arrangement is common in Japanese architecture and on the early *machiya* it was one of the design elements of the facade.

Later on in the Edo period when the whole of a shop front was open to the street, as in a *misekura* for instance, the beam spanning the open space would be a very sturdy timber, usually of zelkova wood. This timber in the Kanto region was known as a *hitomi-bari* or *hitomi* beam (fig. 4). *Hitomi* is thought to be a distorted pronunciation of the word *shitomi,* which was a squared lattice grill used as a shutter. From the Heian period through to the Kamakura period the beam visible on the facade of the Heiankyo *machiya* from which the *hajitomi* or half a *(shitomi)* squared lattice screen was hung, was called a *shitomi-bari* and it was this word which became changed into *hitomi-bari,* possibly because in Edo (Tokyo) even today, "shi" sounds tend to be pronounced "hi" and vice versa.

This is just one simple example of the fact that the culture of Kyoto and the Kansai region was the foundation on which the culture of Edo was built. After the Tokugawa Shogunate was established in Edo, many trading families from the Kansai region set up branch shops in Edo. Thus began the flow of ideas, words, people and goods between Kansai and Kanto. However, during the Edo period (1603 – 1868) the *edo-kko* (equivalent to London's cockney) character developed along its own lines, and particularly as far as *machiya* design was concerned, asserted itself to produce a distinctive architectural style. This was much more flamboyant and overtly

の通風を得るために開放性が必要とされる．店舗の正面が開放的なことは商売の点では有利だが，ファサードの日陰や雨ざらしの陳列商品が問題になるだろう．深い軒は一策だが，室町時代には２階を１階より張り出させる手法が解決策としてしばしば試みられた④⑤⑥．この形態が跳ね出し造りとか船枻（せがい）造りとか呼ばれたものである（船枻という言葉は平安時代の書物に初めて見られ，本来船の建造様式に用いられた．建築形態が船のそれに似ていることから，船枻という名が当てられたと考えられる．しかし建築に船の様式が適用されたかどうかは定かでない）．この２階部分の「箱」のような張り出しは，１階の上部が突き出たという場合もあった．言いかえれば１階建てということだ．この場合建物は２階建てのように見え，それがある象徴としての価値を持ったであろう．この張り出しは，開放的か閉鎖的かにかかわらず，ファサードへの保護となるばかりか，町家の正面に一種の緩衝地帯を作っている．さらに深い軒が付け加えられると，ファサードはより一層

保護され，緩衝地帯という感じがもっとはっきりとしてくる．

跳ね出しや船枻をもっと発展させた形態が木曾路沿いの奈良井や妻籠などの宿場町に見られる⑦⑧⑨．覆い被さった軒や「バルコニー」のような２階により，大雪の地方で通りが通行不能な時でさえ，比較的自由に歩ける歩道を建物の近くに取ることができる．

古い実例では緩衝地帯が建物にはいり込み，「にせ」の２階は単なる倉庫にすぎない（⑩真山家）．時代が新しくなるとファサードにもっと装飾が施され，２階の部屋に一種のにせのバルコニーがつけられる．このバルコニーの出は決して深くはないが，人々は天井の低い２階の部屋を改良して住めるようにした．外部での効果はさらに重要である⑪．奈良井（長野県）のような宿場町では実際の道幅は約７メートル，古い建物の軒までの高さはおよそ４メートルである．道を挟んで向かい合う町家の間の７メートル×４メートルの空間は，突き出た「バルコニー」や深い軒によって侵食され，道幅の約半

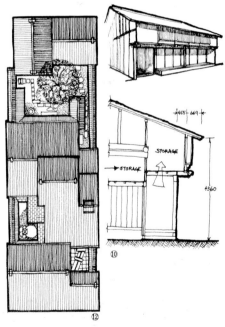

bold in character, compared to the stricter style characteristic of the Kansai region.

Generally speaking the trend was for shop fronts to become more open except perhaps where streets were so narrow and crowded that there was no privacy at all. In which case a lattice work facade would screen the interior from the street. However, the climate in Japan allows or rather demands that buildings are open to gain as much ventilation as possible in the hot humid months of the summer. Also an open shop front has its advantages from a selling point of view but shading of the facade and perhaps goods on display from the sun, wind and rain becomes a problem. Deep eaves would be one way of providing protection but sometime during the Muromachi period, pushing the 1st floor out beyond the ground floor facade seems to have developed as an answer to this problem (figs. 5, 6). This form is called *hanedashi-zukuri* or *segai-zukuri*. (*segai* is a word found first in Heian period texts and probably was used originally to describe a form of boat construction. It is thought that because the architectural form resembles that of the boat, the name *segai* was adopted. However, whether or not the form seen on buildings was adapted from the boat form or developed independantly is not known.) The term *segai* sometimes refers to a type of bracketed balcony seen on farm houses or to a "cosmetic" eave detail.

In the Edo period permission for the use of this was only given to high ranking village headmen. This type of "box" like extention to the 1st floor may in some cases only have been a projection of the upper part of the ground floor. In other words the building may only have had one floor. In this case the building would have appeared to have two stories which may have some status value. However, the overhang produced by the projection as well as giving some protection to the facade, whether open or closed, made a kind of buffer zone at the front of the *machiya*. If deeper eaves were added to this projection even more protection would be afforded and the feeling of a buffer zone would become more pronounced.

Further developments of this *hanedashi* or *segai* form can be seen along the Kiso Highway in such post towns as Narai and Tsumago (figs. 7, 8, 9). The over hanging eaves and "balcony" like 1st floor would also mean that in very snowy regions a relatively clear pathway near the building would remain open even when the road had become impassable.

In older examples the buffer zone extends into the building and the "faked" 1st floor is purely for storage (fig. 10). With more recent examples the facade is more decorative and there is a kind of false balcony to the 1st floor rooms. Although these balconies are not very deep they improve the low 1st floor rooms and make them more habitable.

4. *Hitomibari* and *segai* eaves, Tokyo.
5. Taken from a screen painting, "Scenes of Kyoto", early 17th century.
6. Open shop from with projecting upper section known as *segai-zukuri* or *hanedashi-zukuri*. Early 17th century.
7. *Machiya* of a mountain post town, Narai, Nagano Prefecture.
8. A post town on the Kiso Highway, Tsumago, Nagano Pref.
9. *Machiya* in Tsumago with extended walls forming *udatsu*.
10. Sanayama House.
11. Section of street showing enclosing effect of eaves and projections of 2nd floor.
12. *Machiya* from above.

分が覆われている．このトンネルのような空間は道を保護するようデザインされた建物によって作られ，「活気のある」空間とされていった．空や天気の変化は排除されたが，完全に締め出されたわけではなく，通りに積極的に付加されることによって良い意味での本当の都市空間を形造った．

今日，この通りは暗く静かだが，過去においては重要な交通路として旅人，商人，住人たちで賑った．建物が道に覆い被さることにより，その通りでの様々な生活の情景が強調された．都市生活の光景，音，においは拡散する前に人の目にとまり，俗に言う「浮世」を形成した．

街のプラン，通り，町家のプラン
a．平安京から京都：伝統的町家の敷地
首都平安京は中国の影響を受けて格子状のプランを持ち，最小のブロックユニットは約40丈，121メートル四方である．町家はそのブロックの周辺部に建ち，中央には共有のセミパブリックスペースができた．平安，鎌倉時代の町家は基本的に矩形で幅広く通りと接している．街のグリッドの基本型は京都に未だに見られるが，現在の町家の敷地は細長く，建物が前から後ろまで敷地いっぱいに埋まっている⑫．簡単に言うと，建物は敷地前面が最も私的でなく，奥に行くに従って私的になっていく．例えば，京都御所近くの町家は商店もあるものの，ほとんどが住居で，都市の状況によって形成された．町家の面している道は公道だが，その界隈にはよそ者には不釣り合いな住居向きの雰囲気がある．1本の道は共同体であり，それが集まってより大きな領域の共同体となる．道は一種の「共有空間」で，その近くに住む人々により共用される．通りに面する部屋はその共有地帯から一歩離れたところにあるが，同時にその一部と見ることもできる．共同体にかかわる祭りや葬式といった特別の場合には前面の部屋も利用され，それはあたかも部分的に遮られた通りのニッチのようである．言いかえれば，通りは完全に切り離されたわけではなく，建物の中に浸透することもできるのであった．

こうした町家には日光が差し込み，空間のヒエラルキーによってプライバシーは守られた．しかし，やがて状況や要求の変化に見合うようにプランは変更されていった⑬．とはいえ，新しいプランはどれも日本の木造骨組建築の標準的なグリッドと寸法のシステムを基礎としていたので，デザインやファサードに反映してくる形態とはいつも調和を保っていた．

建築形態のパターンはコミュニティのパターンに応じ，街のプランから町家のファサード，さらにその内部のディテールに至るまでのすべての段階において調和が感じられる．古典的町家が都市環境の圧力にうまく対応し，その本質的な特徴を壊すことなく変化できる理由がここにあろう．

b．江戸時代及びそれ以降：街・道路・町家
江戸時代を通じて，宿場町の主要道路や厳密に区分された城下町の商業地域に町家の特徴とも言うべき細長い敷地が並んだ．東海道の小田原⑭はかつて城下町として栄えたが，江戸時代になると東海道の交通量が増えるにつれて宿場町

But the outside effect is almost more important (fig. 11). In a post-town like Narai (Nagano Prefecture) the width of the road at ground floor level is about 7 meters, and the height to the eaves of most of the older buildings is approximately 4 meters. This 7 x 4 meter space between the *machiya* facing each other across the street, is eaten away by the projecting "balconies" and deep eaves so that almost half the road width is covered. This tunnel like space has been formed by the buildings which have been designed to protect the street and in so doing the street becomes a "live" dynamic space. Nature is excluded but not shut out and therefore adds positively to the street which is then truely an urban space in the best possible meaning of the word.

Nowadays the street is rather still and dark, but in the past the street was part of a major highway and would have bustled with travellers, traders and residents. The overhanging form of the buildings would have enhanced the scenes of life on the street. Sights, sounds and smells of urban life would be held in a little longer for our attention before they drifted away, being only part of the "Floating World."

Town Plan, Street Machiya Plan
The capital Heiankyo was planned along Chinese lines on a grid pattern, the smallest block unit measuring about 40 *jo* or 121 meters square *machiya* stood along the edges of these blocks framing off a common area in the centre. Consequently *machiya* of the Heian and Kamakura periods were basicly rectangular in plan with the long side facing the street. The basic form of the city grid can still be seen in Kyoto (formally Heiankyo), but the *machiya* sites are now long and narrow, and the buildings virtually fill the sites from front to back (fig. 12). Simply speaking the parts of the building at the front of the site are the least private and the rooms become more private the deeper they are in the site.

The *machiya* near Kyoto Gosho (Imperial Palace) for instance, which although not shops are examples of dwellings, incorporating a commercial use, have been moulded by urban conditions. The streets on which they stand are public thoroughfares, but there is a residential air about the streets which makes a stranger feel out of place. One street is a community which in turn is part of a bigger area community. The street is a kind of "common" (in the English village sense of the word), which is shared by those who live beside it. The rooms which face onto the street are just one step removed from that shared area but at the same time they seem part of it. On occasions such as festivals or a funeral which would concern the community, these front rooms are brought into use and it is just as though they are partially screened off street

niches. In other words the street is not completely cut off but allowed to filter through into the building.

In these *machiya* day light punctuates the plan and privacy is protected by the hierarchy of space. Variations of plan (fig. 13) however have developed in time to suit changing conditions and demands, but any new plan has always been based on the standard grid and measurement system of Japanese timber frame architecture. Therefore there is always a harmony of form and design reflected on the facades.

The patterns of architectural form lock in with the patterns of the community and there seems to be harmony at every level, from the town plan to the facades and even right down to the details of the interiors of these *machiya*. This is may be why these classic *machiya* have stood up so well to the pressures of the urban environment, yet have been able to change without their essential character being destroyed.

During the Edo period the long narrow sites so characteristic of *machiya* lined the main streets of the post towns and in the commercial districts of the strictly zoned castle towns. Odawara, (fig. 14) a castle town on the Tokaido (main route between Edo and Kyoto) was important as a castle town at one time but became more important as a post town in the Edo period, as traffic on the Tokaido increased. The *machiya*, (shops, inns, tea shops etc.) lined the Tokaido which

としての重要性が増した．街を縫うように走る東海道に町家（店，旅館，茶屋等）が並んだ．江戸時代後期，1850年には小田原の人口は12,700人であった．支配階級である武士は，僧侶をも含めるとその40％を占め，8％が農民と漁師，14％が職人，そして38％が商人階級であった．商人は東海道や街の主要な通り沿いに細く帯状に犇めきあって生活し，その密度は 400人／ha を越した⑭．

商業地域の裏側にある神社仏閣によって，通り沿いの建物による「壁」が所々破られていた．

小田原のような宿場町は江戸時代を通じて繁栄したが，明治時代になって参勤交代が中止されたり，旅人や品物を運ぶ仕事が鉄道に取って代わられたりすると，衰退を始めた．かつて，宿場町は特に主要路に沿って帯状に発展し，旅館や店舗は神社や大名の泊まる大きな旅館といった焦点の周囲に集まった．街を鉄道が通るようになると，焦点の近くに駅が作られる．そして人々の注目はかつて街の中心であった通りから離れ，駅のまわりが新しい焦点となっていっ

threaded its way through the town. Towards the end of the Edo period in about 1850 the population in Odawara was 12,700. The ruling warrior class, including priests made up 40% of this total, 8% were farmers and fishermen, 14% artisans and 38% were of the mercantile class, who were crowded into the narrow ribbon like zone along the Tokaido, at a density of over 400 people per hectare.

Occasionally the "wall" of buildings along the road was broken by the approach to a temple or shrine which stood behind the commercial zone (fig. 14).

Post towns like Odawara flourished right through the Edo period but especially when *sankin kotai* (the system under which Feudal Lords lived alternately in Edo and their own domains) was suspended at the beginning of the Meiji period and railways began to take over the job of carrying passengers and goods, these towns went into something of a decline. In the past, post towns in particular were ribbon developments on the main highways and inns and shops clustered around a focal point which could be a shrine or the principal inn where a Feudal Lord might stay. When the railway came to such a town, the station was built near that focal point and infact began to take attention away from the road on which the town had originally been centred and created a new focal point around the station. Where this happened, especially since the 2nd World

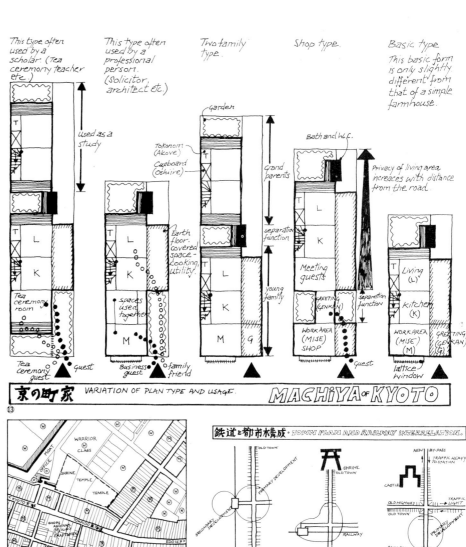

京の町家　VARIATION OF PLAN TYPE AND USAGE.　MACHIYA of KYOTO

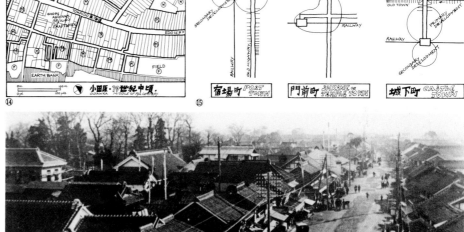

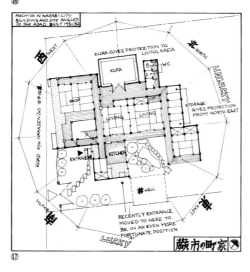

⑬　京の町家．
⑭　19世紀中頃の小田原の街割．
⑮　鉄道と都市構成．
⑯　19世紀末の熊谷の街並，埼玉県．右手の商家は通りに対し斜めに並んでいるが，これはただ，敷地が曲がっているせいであろう．写真：野口泰助．
⑰　蕨市の町家，埼玉県．1931-32年．敷地も建物も道路に対して斜めになっている．

13. *Machiya* in Kyoto.
14. Odawara city, middle of 19th century.
15. Town plan and railway interrelation.
16. Townscape of Kumagaya, Saitama Pref., late 19th century. The shops on the right are angled to the street. This may simply be because the sites are angled.
17. Machiya in Warabi, Saitama Pref., 1931–32. Building and site are angled to the road.

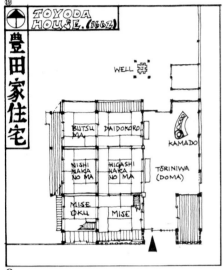

TOYODA HOUSE. (1662)

豊田家住宅

WELL

BUTSU MA　DAIDOKORO

KAMADO

NISHI NAKA NO MA　HIGASHI NAKA NO MA　TORINIWA (DOMA)

MISE OKU　MISE

⑱→⑳　豊田家今井町，奈良県．
㉑　取り外し可能な屋根のついた蔵，町田市，東京．
㉒　えびす造り，桐生，群馬県．
㉓　鬼瓦，出桁，観音開，川越，埼玉県．
㉔　土蔵造りの初期の形態，大沢家，川越．
㉕　防護板を取り付けるための留め金，この例ではむしろ装飾要素となっている．川越．
㉖　京都の白い蔵．
㉗　下から，石造の基礎，海鼠壁，防護板，漆喰壁．土浦，茨城県．

た．特に第２次大戦以降，この種の街では駅の周辺が大きく発展し，店舗，デパートなどの商業施設が古い宿場町の新しい核となっていった⑮．今，かつての街道を歩いてみると，まるで時間の旅をしているような錯覚に陥ることがある．一般的に言って，駅周辺の建物は高く，新しく，そして強烈な活動力を持つ．しかし駅から離れると，道路沿いの店舗，住居は低くなり，雰囲気も寛いだものになる．旧市街や旧道に関連して駅がどこにくるかにより，発展のパターンはいくらか変化する．しかし，結果としてできた「古い町」と「新しい町」の構成に，いかに個性的な環境を作る可能性があろうと，それが発掘されることは稀で，多くの場合伝統的な町家からなる地域は衰退したままであった．

関東地方の宿場町で，その一部が発展とかかわりなく残っているような所では，今でも40年から100年以上も経過した町家が数多く存在する．そのうちいくつかは，直接道路に面してはいるものの，平行に配置されていないことがある⑯．建物が道路に対して角度を持っているの

で，その正面の一方にくぼみができる．こうした建物の向きは明治時代に始まったらしいが，その理由については諸説紛々である．一つの説は官令により鉄砲隊の隠れ場としてくぼみが作られたというものだが，敵兵にとっても同様に有利になるので，この説は疑わしい．店の前に商品を陳列する場所として設けられたという説もあり，それによると特別の時に商品が並べられ，通常は客用に長椅子が置かれたという．他にくぼみに馬をつないだという説もあるが，いずれもこの手法をはっきりとは説明していないように思う．通りに平行であること以上に重要な，例えば家相からみて店の正面，入口などの大切な部分を良い方角に配置するといったことから，思いのほかに得られた結果だと考えるのが正しいのではなかろうか⑰．

耐火と象徴

奈良県今井町には，17世紀から事実上変わることなく残っている共同体とその建物が見られる．今井町は城下町さえ持たない「防御設備」を持

War there has been considerable development around the stations and the shops, department stores and other commercial premises have become a neuculus to alot of these old post towns (fig. 15). Consequently a walk along the route of one of the old highways is like a trip in time. Generally speaking the buildings near the station are high and new, and the activity intense. However, further away from the station the old shops and dwellings along the street are lower and the atmosphere is more relaxed. The pattern of development varies somewhat according to where the station was sited in relation to the old centre or principal street of a town. However any potential to create an environment with a greater character which exists in the resulting "old town", "new town" layout is still largely unrecognized and in many cases the areas consisting mainly of traditional *machiya* have been left to decline.

In the Kanto region there are some Post towns in which certain districts have remained largely untouched by development. Within such areas there are a surprisingly large number of *machiya* which are anything from 40–100 years old. Some of these buildings are not orientated parallel to the road but they still but directly on to it (fig. 16). The building is angled so that a recess is formed at one end of the frontage. This type of orientation seems to have started in the Meiji period but

the reason for doing it is not clear although there are several explanations. One is that under a government ordinance the recess was created to give cover to a soldier using a firearm, but as an enemy would have been able to take just as much advantage of it, this explanation seems rather unlikely. Another is that the space was formed to provide a display area in front of one end of the shop, where on special occasions products would be set out. Ordinarily a bench for customers might occupy the space. Yet another explanation is that the recess was formed so that a horse might be tied-up but both this and the previous explanations do not seem to be strong enough reasons for arranging the buildings in this manner. It is perhaps more likely that, this type of orientation originated out of the desire to bring the more important parts of the building, such as the shop front and entrance to the living area, into a more fortunate quarter of the *Kaso* system compus than it would have been had the building been set parallel to the street (fig. 17. see article in this issue on Orientation from pages 37 to 50).

At Imaicho in Nara Prefecture, we can see a community and its architecture which has remained virtually unchanged since the 17th century. Imaicho is for Japan a rare example of a town with "defenses" which even castle towns lack. The town was constructed around the Buddhist temple Shonenji at the end of

つという，日本にはめずらしい例である．この町は16世紀の終わりに織田信長の弾圧に抵抗する浄土真宗本願寺派の砦として仏教寺院称念寺の周囲に建設された．最後に町は明け渡されたが，住民の強い団結により自治権が認められ，江戸時代の封建制度の数百年を通じて繁栄した．

町はまず5〜7メートル幅の濠で囲まれ，入口としての門は9つあった．道はわずか3〜4メートル幅で東西，南北に走り，戦略のためにいくらか折れ曲がったり，T字路であったりする．町家は直接道に面し，道に囲まれるブロックはほぼ完全に建物で埋められている．中世のこうした密着型の町では火災によって崩壊することが一番多いが，幸運にもこの「木」の町はそれを免れた．ここ今井町には，多少の耐火性を持つ漆喰塗り外壁の木造骨組建築の最古の例が見られる．ディテールこそ違うものの，漆喰仕上げは城郭建築の模倣である．城郭は17世紀のはじめ，今井町がその幼年期にある頃に生まれた幕府の第一の象徴であり，戦略的にも重要な意味を持っていた．今井町の町家は城郭建築

the 16th century as a fortress town in which the Shinshu Buddhist sect resisted the oppression of the local *samurai* Lord. The town finally yielded but because of the strong solidarity of the inhabitants, Imaicho was granted autonomy and prospered through the decades of feudalism in the Edo Period.

The town was originally surrounded by a moat, 5 − 7 meters wide, and was entered by one of nine gates. The streets are only 3 − 4 meters wide and run north − south, east − west with some zigzags and "T" junctions arranged for strategic purposes. The *machiya* face directly onto the streets and now the block spaces between the roads are almost entirely filled in with buildings. Fortunately this "wooden" city has not been severely ravaged by fire which was one of the principal enemies of this type of closely packed town of the Middle Ages. Here on the streets of Imaicho we can see some of the earliest examples of timber framed buildings with plastered exterior surfaces which would at least give some fire protection. This plaster finish, together with other details, mimic elements of castle architecture, the castle being one of the principal symbolic and strategic elements of the Shōgunate which was coming into being about the time Imaicho was in its infancy around the beginning of the 17th century. The *machiya* of Imaicho resist the elements of the natural and urban environment which surrounds them, by borrowing from castle archi-

18, 19, 20. Toyoda House, Imai-cho, Nara Pref.
21. Simple *Kura* shop with detachable roof, Machida-shi, Tokyo.
22. *Ebisu-zukuri*, Kiryu, Gunma Pref.
23. *Onigawara*, *dashigeta* eaves and *kannon-biraki*, Kawagoe, Saitama Pref.
24. Early form of *dozo-zukuri*, Osawa House, Kawagoe, Saitama Pref.
25. Projecting hook from which the weather boarding was hung; this has become a decorative element. Kawagoe, Saitama Pref.
26. White *kura* in Kyoto.
27. Masonry foundations, tiles, weather boarding, and plaster walls. Tsuchiura-shi Ibaragi Pref.

を模倣することにより，周囲の風土，社会や都市環境に対応している．同時に町家は，力と権威にあふれた建築様式を用いることにより生まれるある象徴的な力を利用している．今井町の町家の中で，今西家が1650年に，豊田家が1665年に建てられたことがはっきりしている⑱→⑳．

今井町の町家では漆喰は白くてあまり厚くない（5センチメートル）ので，たぶん強烈な火には耐えられない．この手法は塗屋造りと呼ばれ，漆喰が傷つき易い外壁全面を覆って広がり全体を頑丈にしている．豊田家の東立面には面白いディテールが見られる⑲．屋根梁が壁面から張り出し，漆喰塗りの六角形の突起となっている．格子のついた窓を通して土間下部に光と空気がはいるが，その窓も漆喰が塗られている．窓枠は段々がついていて，一見何気なく配置されながら壁を飾り，完全に漆喰で塗り込められた軒が覆いかぶさっている．軒は壁から約95センチメートル張り出して漆喰塗りの表面を保護するが，もちろんその出は建物のプロポーションとうまく調和している．同様に，城郭建築に

はその大きさに見合った軒の出があるので，特に深い軒は特別の補強を必要とする．その目的で，腕木や出桁がよく用いられた．大きい屋根の垂木は出桁によって支えられるが，その出桁は壁面から等間隔に張り出した腕木により順々に支持された．この手法は，出桁造り，出梁造り，船枻造りなどといろいろに呼ばれる．この船枻という言葉は，しばしば農家に見られる腕木をつけたバルコニーの様式や「化粧」の軒のディテールを指す．江戸時代には，名主以上の者のみに，この軒のディテールを使うことが許可された．町家に使われる場合には，例えば雪の深い地方などでは本来の軒の補強構造としての機能を持つが，主として装飾要素として用いられたらしく，屋根と壁の結合部の贅沢なアクセントとなっている．豊田家の軒は漆喰で完全に覆われて建物を一周し，張り出した垂木や腕木，出桁が全体のデザインに豊かさを与えている．正面の窓の横木も漆喰で塗り込められ，さらに家紋（丸に木の字の定紋）がつけられた．庇の下の1階部分ファサードに漆喰はないが，

別の理由で興味深い．道に面したこのファサードは，公道と建物の半私的店舗部分の間の衝立のような役割がある．ファサードは4つの部分からなり，奥まったところにある入口は真中よりやや右側，そしてその左に二つ，右に一つの部分がある．それぞれの部分のわずかな違いが内部を感じさせる．入口以外の部分には，その奥の状態次第で幅の違う窓すべてに縦格子がかけられている．使用人，奉公人の部屋は入口の右側で，店舗同様，間隔のあいた幅広い桟の格子がかかっている．それに対して店舗の格子はもっと細かい．格子は通りに隣接した部屋にプライバシーを与え，さらに夏のむし暑い日には換気にも役立つ．1階の配置や空間の種類はこのようにファサードに表現される（今井町の町家では格子のファサードが一般的で，そのデザインや配置は無限にあるため単調に陥ることなくデザインの調和を保っている）．実際，1階の格子のついたファサードだけでなく，今井町の建物はデザイン全般にわたってとても似かよっている，これは日本建築，特に伝統的町家の重

tecture. At the same time they utilize some of the symbolic forces implicated by the use of an architectural style which radiates power and authority. This is evident in such buildings as the Imanishi House built in 1650 and the Toyoda House of 1665 (fig. 18).

Here at Imaicho the plaster is white and not very thick (about 4 cm), and infact would probably not stand up to a severe fire. Architecture employing this type of treatment is called *nuriya-zukuri* referring to the spreading of the plaster, which covers all vulnerable external wall surfaces giving a very rich sturdy total effect. If we look at the eastern elevation of the Toyoda House we can see some interesting details (fig. 19). A roof beam has been allowed to jut out beyond the wall surface and has been plastered over forming a hexagonal projection. Simple barred windows through which light and air pass freely to the *doma* below, are also plastered, their ridged frames adding a decorative element to the apparently random composition of this wall, which is "capped-off" by the fully plastered eaves. They project about 95 cm from the wall surface giving some protection to the plastered surface, and the depth of the eaves is of course in keeping with the proportions of the building. Similarly, the scale of castle architecture demands eaves of a depth appropriate to the total design and therefore especially deep eaves may need extra support. This is

often provided with an arrangement of bracket supports and a cross beam. The extended roof rafters are supported by the cross beam which in turn is supported by the bracket arms which project from the wall plain at regular intervals. This arrangement is variously called *dashigeta-zukuri*, *dashibari-zukuri* or *segai-zukuri*.

When applied to Machiya it may have some true support function, say in districts where the snow fall is high, but in the main it seems to be used essentially as a decorative element, making a rich accent at the junction of roof and wall. The eaves on the Toyoda house are completely enveloped in plaster and encircle the building, the projecting rafters, bracket arms and cross beam adding a richness to the total design. The rungs of the windows on the front elevation are also plastered as is the "family crest". However, the ground floor facade under its own canopy roof is unplastered, and its design is interesting for other reasons. This street facade serves as a screen between the public street and the semi-private shop area of the building. The facade has four sections, the recessed entrance being off centre to the right dividing the other sections into two on the left and one on the right. The slightly different treatment of each section tells us something of the internal arrangement of the building. Other than the entrance, each section has a vertical lattice over the window of varying widths, which corresponds to the status of the areas

they screen. The shop hand's or servant's room to the right of the entrance has a lattice of wide rungs and spaces as does the *mise* or shop area. However, the inner room or *miseoku* has a finer lattice. These lattices give some privacy to the rooms adjacent to the street yet at the same time allow good ventilation in the hot humid summer months. (The latticed facades are a common feature of the *machiya* in Imaicho and because the variations of design and arrangement are infinite, a design harmony is achieved without monotony.) The arrangement and type of spaces to be found on the ground floor is thus expressed on the facade.

Infact not only are the ground floor latticed facades very similar but also the overall design of the buildings throughout Imaicho are very similar. This is a good example of *Nusumi* or marrying detail, which is an important design feature of Japanese architecture especially in traditional *machiya* design.

The entrance opens on to the *doma* or earthern floor area (also known as *tōriniwa*) and off this there is the shop hand's and servant's room both on the ground and first floors. The raised floor area extends back from the facade and is divided into three roughly equal areas. In a larger building such as the Toyoda House, there are six defined spaces where as in a smaller dwelling there would only be one row of three rooms. The width of the *tōriniwa* varies according to

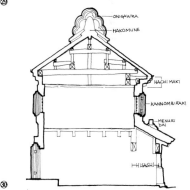

㉘　観音開と目塗台．川越．
㉙　店蔵の敷地．店の背後は蔵で埋まっている．川越．
㉚　店蔵の断面図．
㉛　袖蔵と店蔵，亀屋，川越．
㉜　店蔵の梲，川越．
㉝　1917年頃の日本橋界隈．都市研究会発行『街』第2巻より．

28. *Kannonbiraki* and *menuri-dai*, Kawagoe, Saitama Pref.
29. *Misekura* site. The space behind the shop is filled with kura (store houses). Kawagoe, Saitama Pref..
30. Section of *misekura*, late 19th century.
31. *Sode kura* and *misekura*. Kameya, Kawagoe, Saitama Pref.
32. *Udatsu* on a *misekura*, Kawagoe, Saitama Pref.
33. View of Nihonbashi, Tokyo, about 1917. Note *misekura*.

要なデザイン的特徴である「盗み」の好例である.

土間（通り庭とも言われる）へと入口が取られ，1，2階に使用人の部屋が土間から直接行けるように作られる．一段高い床はファサードから裏側へ向けて広がり，三つのほぼ等しい部分に分けられる．小さな家ではわずか三つの部屋が一列に並んでいるにすぎないが，豊田家のような大きな家では区切られた空間が6つもある．通り庭の幅は商いや有効な空間によって異なるが，場合によっては通りと建物裏の中庭をつなぐ廊下の役目だけしかない．一段高くなった部分の床は，その使い道により板張りであったり，畳が敷かれていたりするが，さらに重要な部屋の床は店や店奥よりわずかに高くなっている．通り庭に隣接したところは居間か仕事場（店の間，中の間，台所）になっている．かまどは通り庭の裏側にあって台所に隣接している．店の間では金の受け渡しが行われるが，商談は店奥で行われる．座敷は特別な場合にだけ使われ，西側の中の間は客用とされた．夜には使用

人の部屋の戸に錠がかけられ，一段高いところにある家族の寝室はすべて通り庭と戸で仕切られ内側から錠がかけられた．通り庭は商いによって醤油，酒，味噌などが置かれたばかりでなく，仕事場としても使われた.

固定された階段がないにもかかわらず豊田家が2階建てだということは隠しようがない．2階は主として倉庫とされる．他の店には，その外観から2階建てではないかと思うものもあるが，実際には倉庫にしかならない低い屋根裏があるだけだ.

今井町の町家は，様式や形態からそれらが育った封建時代をよく表わしていることがわかる．社会の封建的秩序はすべての空間が完結していることだけでなく，部屋の様々な床高や位置関係からも確認される．城郭建築のデザイン要素が象徴的に使われていることは誇示の表われと見ることができる．もっとも誇る相手は城郭の場合と違い敵ではなく，社会全体であるが.

前述のように，今井町の町家は防火のために漆喰が塗られている．この町の如く密に建て込

んでいる所では，各戸間に隙間がほとんどなく，火事は簡単に燃え広がる．今井町ではわずかな耐火性しかない塗屋造り建築以上に，固く結ばれた共同体意識が火から町を守った．しかし，本当の耐火建築として，漆喰と15〜30センチメートル厚の土壁からなる土蔵造りも試みられた．中世には，漆喰塗りの質屋の蔵が木造建築の中にわずかに見られたが，江戸時代までには都市ばかりでなく，地方でもその数を増していった．蔵は財産を保護する建築として，さらに持主の富の象徴として価値があった．蔵の単純な形態はもともと店舗としては使われなかった．倉庫としての蔵は今日も見られ，それには木をはさんで取り外し可能な屋根がついている㉑．近くで火事が起こると屋根は簡単に引き外され，燃え易い材料は漆喰面と直接には接触しなくなる．店舗として使われた蔵は，少し発展してえびす造り㉒と呼ばれたが，これは大小の蔵の組み合わせである．富と商売の神として知られる七福神の一人の名を取って命名されたえびす造りは，瓦屋根と鉢巻きと呼ばれる軒の厚い壁を持って

trades and available space, sometimes only being a connecting corridor from the street to courtyard space at the back of the building. The floors of the rooms on the raised floor area are either boarded or covered with tatami according to their usage and the floors of the more important rooms are slightly higher than the *mise* and *miseoku*. The areas adjacent to the earth floor area or *tōriniwa,* are for the family or work (fig. 20 *mise no ma, naka no ma* and *daidokoro*). Cooking facilities are at the back of the *tōriniwa* adjacent to the *daidokoro*. The *mise no ma,* or shop area is where money would change hands but any business would be carried out in the *miseoku* space. The *zashiki* would only be used for special occasions and the west *naka no ma* would be used by a guest.

At night the servants' doors would be locked and the rooms where the family slept on the raised floor area would all be shuttered off from the *tōriniwa* and locked from the inside. The *tōriniwa* was used as a work area as well as to store such things as barrels of *shoyu* (soya), *sake* or *miso* (bean paste) according to the trade.

The Toyoda House makes no secret of the fact that it is a two-story building although there is no fixed staircase. The 1st floor is mainly for storage, but with other shops we are sometimes lead to believe that there is a first floor judging from the external form but infact there is only a very low attic space used solely for storage.

Styles of Machiya

The *machiya* in Imaicho, both in style and form are very indicative of the feudal times in which they grew up. The feudal order of the society is born out by the various levels and relative positions of the rooms as well as by the way each area is finished. In addition the symbolic use of design elements from castle architecture shows a tendancy towards display, except that here the on-looker is the rest of society and not a prospective enemy.

As previously stated the *machiya* in Imaicho are plastered to give some fire protection. In a densely built-up town such as Imaicho, fire would spread easily from one building to another, there being little or no space at all between individual structures. However, in Imaicho it seems that the close knit community spirit was more protection against fire than the *nuriya-zukuri* architecture which actually only really affords moderate fire proofing. However, *dozō-zukuri*, with plaster and earth walls anything between 15 — 30 cm thick was an attempt to make a truely fire proof architecture. In the Middle Ages the plastered store houses or *kura* of the pawn broker were a rare sight in amongst the forest of wooden buildings, but by the Edo period the number of these *kura* had increased in numbers not only in the towns but in the country side too, being both very practical as protective architecture and as a symbol of the wealth of their owner. The simple form of *kura* or store house was not originally used as a shop, but this store house type is still visible today, even ones with a seperate roof mounted on timbers (fig. 21). If a fire broke out near-by this easily detachable roof would be dragged off meaning that no combustable material would be in direct contact with the plastered surfaces. A slightly more developed form of *kura* used as a shop, is what is called *ebisu-zukuri* (fig. 22), a style where a large and a small *kura* are combined. This style is named appropriately enough after *ebisu-sama,* one of the Seven Gods of Luck, who is known as the God of Wealth and business. The *ebisu-zukuri* form has a tiled roof and a thickened section of wall at the eaves which is called a *hachi-maki*. (Same name as band worn around the head by samurai and Kamikaze pilots.) The matching stepped shutter and window frames *(kannon-biraki),* roof ridge ornaments and the eave treatment seen here in their simple form on the *ebisu-zukuri* stone house/ shop became prominent features of the *dozō* style of shop, or *mise kura,* which flourished along the principal streets of many towns from towards the end of the Edo period up to almost the end of the Meiji period (1868 — 1912).

When fires swept away hundreds of buildings and all that was left were the *kura* in amongst the ashes, the merchants

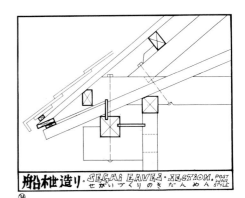

いる．えびす造りの店舗の単純な形態に見られる観音開き，屋根の棟飾り，軒の処理は，江戸時代末期から明治時代（1868～1921）末期頃まで多く町の主要な通り沿いに栄えた土蔵造りの店舗，すなわち店舗の極めて大きな特徴となった．

火事が何百もの建物を一掃したあと，灰の中には蔵だけが残り，貴重な在庫と商いの場所で生計を立てている商人たちは，始めて蔵造りの豊かな可能性を認識したに違いない．12月や1月頃の乾いた季節には，湿気不足から木造建築がとても燃え易くなる．特に江戸では，その頃吹く季節風によってしばしば火事が煽りたてられるので，いっそう蔵が猛烈な炎から商人たちを守ることになった．10万人が命を失ない，広範な地域が焼け落ちた1657年の明暦の大火から5年後の1662年には，江戸にごく初期の店蔵が建てられた．この店は大黒屋と言った．店蔵は平側の方が通りに面しているのが普通だが，大黒屋はえびす造りと同様に妻側が面していたらしい．1720年，幕府により住居についての公式の告知が出されるまで，封建的支配に生活を制限されていた商人たちは，公然と店蔵を建てるという誘惑を抑えていたようだ．公布以後，土蔵造りの店舗が急速に発展し，都市の通りの主要な建築となっていった．

様式は地方によって多少異なるが，大きさは言うに及ばず，かなり派手な材料の使い方や装飾は全体として商人階級にお似合いの象徴と言える．商人は封建制度では一番低い身分とされたが，現実には250年の江戸時代を支配した安定と平和の恩恵を最も受け，金と力のある階級となった．様々な様式にかかわらず，店蔵の形態はいく分堅実である．店舗ということもあって，客がはいりやすいように，通りに対してできる限り開放的に造られている．屋根は箱棟と呼ばれる大きな棟を持つ瓦葺き切妻で，箱棟の両端には鬼瓦がつけられた㉓．軒は出桁造り（船枻造りともいう）か，段々のついた鉢巻きで仕上げられている．壁は多くの貫で結ばれた頑丈な柱で支持されている．貫は柱を通り抜け，竹の網と共に基本的骨組を形成する．その上に土と漆喰の壁が作られるが，店蔵の場合は普通

and shop keepers, who's livelihood depended on their precious stock and a place to sell, must have been the first to realize the full potential of the *kura-zukuri*. It was to become their defence against the raging flames which in the case of Edo in particular would sometimes be whipped up by seasonal winds in the driest time of the year, around December and January, when all the wooden buildings become as dry as tinder due to the lack of humidity. An early example of a *mise kura* was built in Edo in 1662, five years after the Great Meireki fire of 1657, when 100,000 lost their lives and vast quantities of property were destroyed. This shop was known as Daikokuya and like the *ebisu-zukuri* shop it was probably the gable end of the building which faced the street, but it is infact more common for these *mise kura* to have the long side of the building or eaves to the street. Up until 1720 when an official announcement on housing was made by the Bakufu government, it seems as though the merchants and shop-keepers whose way of life was restricted by the feudal government, had resisted the temptation to build *mise kura* openly, but from 1720 the *dozō* style of *misekura* developed rapidly and became the principal urban street architecture of the times.

Styles vary some what through out the country but the fairly flamboyant use of material and decoration not to mention size, seem in totality a fitting symbol of the merchant class, who were officially placed bottom of the feudal ranking system but infact it was the merchants who profited most from the stability and peace which reigned for the 250 years of the Edo period, and so in reality they became a powerful and wealthy class. Although there are various styles, the form of *misekura* is more or less consistent. First and foremost, because they are shops, they are built directly butting onto the street with as large a space as possible open to allow customers easy access. The roof is usually a tiled gable roof with an enlarged ridge called a *hakomune* which is stopped off at the ends by equally large end tiles or *onigawara* (fig. 23). The eaves are most commonly finished in the *dashigeta-zukuri* style, (also known as *segai-zukuri*), or a stepped cornice type *hachimaki*. The walls are supported by stout columns which are connected by many *nuki* or tie rails. These penetrate the columns and form, along with a mesh of bamboo the basic frame work on which the mud and plaster walls are built-up on, which in the case of a *misekura* may not be as thick as those of a normal store house. The final finishing layer of plaster is usually white or black, but sometimes the side or unseen external walls are left with a rough daub finish which is then covered with weather boarding.

Detachable weather boarding is also used to protect the wall surfaces, but this particular type of boarding is only at-

㉞　船枻造りの断面図．
㉟　明治末から大正の頃の船枻造り．藤沢，神奈川県．
㊱　船枻造りの軒，浦和．
㊲　戦前の船枻造り，浦和．

34. Section of *segai* eaves.
35. *Segai* eaves, late Meiji or early Taisho Period. Fujisawa, Kanagawa Pref.
36. *Segai* eaves, Urawa, Saitama Pref.
37. Pre-2nd World War *segai-zukuri machiya*, Urawa, Saitama Pref.

の倉庫ほど厚くはしない．漆喰の最後の仕上げ層は一般に白か黒だが，側面とか見えない外壁はあらい砂摺（すなずり）とされ，さらに横羽目の防護板で覆われた．

取り外し可能な防護板は壁面の保護が目的で，漆喰壁から張り出した留め金㉕の上に固定された一本の横木によって取り付けられただけである．火事が起こると横木が簡単に外され，それによって防護板も取り除くことができる．屋根が外せる場合と同様に燃え易い材料は取り払われて厚い漆喰壁が剥き出しになって，火災に抵抗する．関東地方では黒い仕上げが好まれたが，他の地域では白い漆喰仕上げが普通である㉔．他の地方に比べて関東の店蔵はデザインに重きを置く傾向があるが，これはおそらく単なる地方色であろう．黒い建物は海外にもほとんど無く，それ故関東の店蔵がなぜ黒い漆喰仕上げとされたかは興味深い問題である．店に付属し隣接する倉庫として使われていた普通の蔵は白いものであったろうし，おそらくこれが店蔵の始まりであろう．白い耐火建築は，木造の板壁で

茅葺きか板葺きの屋根の建物の中で見事に目立ったに違いない㉖．周囲が文字通り煙の中に消え去るような火事ののち，蔵の白い壁は火煙で黒く焦げ，その抵抗の様子が人々に深い印象を与えたのであろう．黒くなった壁は「耐火性」の印象から黒い漆喰仕上げを生んだ．他にも，反射を防ぐためとか，武士に対する商人の遠慮から黒く塗られたという見方もある．いずれにせよ，店蔵のディテールの強く，重厚な表現によりその印象はさらに強められた．

壁は軒のところまで漆喰で仕上げられるが，ある地方では，壁の下方が白い漆喰目地で斜めに瓦を張った海鼠壁に仕上げられている㉗．関東では特に，壁の下の部分が厚く，しっかりと盛り上がって「幅木」のようになっている．これは腰巻きと呼ばれて散石の土台の上に立てられ，また，柱や壁の土台が石の基礎の上に置かれる．建物はすべて地上にあるが，大小の石に粘土を加えた基礎が柱位置と壁線の下の地面に埋め込まれた．建物は文字通り地面にしっかりと坐り，地震時には一つの塊として働く．

店蔵は普通二層で，1階は店舗，2階は倉庫や使用人の部屋として使われたが，江戸時代後期になると2階は床の間や違い棚を伴ない，応接間としても使用された．1階は土間部分と，丈夫な畳（琉球畳）が敷かれた高い部分とに分けられる．一段上がったところは帳場（仕切り場）と呼ばれ，客はここで商品の準備ができるまで主人と話をして待ったり，店の者の世話で品物を見たりする．西洋の店舗ではカウンターが客と店員を隔てる線となるが，日本では帳場と土間の高さによる区別以外に障害物はなく，床仕上げによって活動範囲や客と店員との関係が強調される．帳場でも金の受け渡しが行われ，購入記録が台帳に記載される．また，金を入れておく箱（銭箱）も置かれ，そろばんと台帳のための小さな机は帳場格子と呼ばれる低い格子によって仕切られる．帳場の大きさや土間の範囲は商売によって違うが，庇の下は土間であるのが一般的だ．庇は建物本体の外にあって，場合によっては全く壁がない．その時には建物本体の外壁のところに垂直な木製の戸が設けられ

tached by a simple wooden bar locked over the metal hook which projects from the plastered wall (fig. 25). The wooden bar is easily removed when a fire breaks out so that the weather boarding can be removed. Then as in the case of the detachable roof the thick walls are left bare to resist the flames. The white plastered finish (fig. 24) is most common outside of the Kanto region where the black finish seems to have been most strongly favoured. Also the *misekura* in the Kanto region tend to be much heavier in design that those of other regions, which is probably only due to regional tastes. There are very few black buildings in the world and it is interesting to consider how these *misekura* came to be finished in black plaster. The simple *kura* which were first used just as storehouses attached to or adjacent to shops were most likely to have been white as probably were the first *misekura*. These white fire proof buildings must have stood out handsomely amongst the weathered wood and thatch of all the other buildings (fig. 26). However, after a fire when all around them had literally gone up in smoke, the white walls of the *kura* blackened and charred by the flames and smoke must have made a deep impression on those that were alive to see how the *kura* could stand up to a fire. The blackened walls may well have given rise to the black plaster finish, which became part of the "durability to resist fire" image.

Other than this explanation there are two more. One is that the *misekura* were black so as not to be dazzling. The other is that because the *kura* of the *samurai* and upper-classes were white, it was a mark of respect on the part of the merchants not to use the same colour and so black was used and thus any confusion as to the status of the merchants was avoided. The whole effect was further enhanced by the expression of strength and weight of the details utilized in the design of *misekura*.

The walls are plastered right up to the eaves and in some districts part of the lower walls are finished with tiles (fig. 27), set on the diagonal with white plaster jointing. In the Kanto region in particular the lower section of the walls are thicker and form what looks like a sturdy swelling "skirt" to the walls. This is called a *koshimaki*, which is built up on a *chiriishi* base (like a fire stone cement footing) and the columns and wall sill are set up on a base of masonry. There is not part of the actual building which extends below ground level, but foundations of large and small stones plus clay are packed down into the ground under the column positions and the wall line. The building literally sits firmly on the ground and moves more or less as a single unit in an earth-tremor.

A *misekura* is usually a two-story structure with the ground floor being the shop and the first floor is either used for storage, a dormitory for the shop

staff or in post Edo period buildings it is a formal reception area with *tokonoma* and *chigaidana*. The ground floor is divided into an earth floor area, *doma*, and a raised floor section covered with a hardwearing *tatami* matting. This section, called a *chōba* (also known as a *shikiriba*) is where a customer would sit and may be talk with the owner while waiting for their purchases to be prepared or would look at the goods on sale while being attended to buy one of the staff. In a shop in the West the counter is the dividing line between customer and shop staff but in Japan there is no barrier as such, except that the difference between the *chōba* and *doma* in terms of height and floor covering emphasize the zones of activity and the relationship between customer and shop assistant. The *chōba* too was where money changed hands and a record of purchases would be made in a ledger. There would always be a box in which money was deposited (*zenibako*), an abacus and a small table for the ledger screened by a low open work lattice screen called a *choba koshi*. The size of the *chōba* and the area of the *doma* depend on the trade of the shop but the floor under the lean-to roof or *hisashi* is always an earth floor. This *hisashi* part of the building is outside of the main body of the building and is in some cases completely without walls. In such a case the shop would be closed off at the outer wall of the main building by a system of vertical wooden

る．この戸は日中，大きな店でおそらく４～６メートルという間口をすべて開け放した状態に整頓される．もし庇が囲われているとしても，そこには二つの戸袋が間口の片側あるいは両側にあって，中には防火用の引戸が仕舞われている．

　正面の２階部分には，窓と漆喰塗りの観音開きの戸があるが，格子で覆われた前面いっぱいの開口がある．その内側には防火戸，そのまた内側には障子がある．観音開きの戸㉘は通風のため昼間は開放されるが，近所で火事が起こると閉ざされる．戸は左側の「女型」がまず閉じられ，「男型」がそれに続く．戸の蛇腹は閉まった状態での防火が本来の役割だが，開いている時は建物の面白い表情となる．壁と戸の間にはどうしても隙間が残るが，そばに特別に用意された土（荒木田）で目塗りされる．目塗りは庇の上に常設された目塗り台に乗って行われる㉙．目塗りにより倉庫はしっかりと閉鎖され，家族，使用人は店蔵㉚の中に閉じ籠もって内側から防火戸などの目塗りをする．高価な品はすでに車

のついた金庫に入れられ安全のために蔵に運び込まれている．住居はだいたい飾り気のない安っぽい木造で，店蔵と他の蔵の間に位置するが，火事の際には焼け落ちることになる．しかし，商人にとっては蔵の中身が財産であり，住居は鎮火後すぐに建て直されるので心配には及ばない．これに対し，もし蔵の中のものを失なえば商人の生活も崩壊する．

　江戸などの大きな街の街道沿いの敷地はかなり細長く，大きいもので間口は約14～15メートルである．土地が広い時には店蔵がほとんど前面いっぱいに建てられ，残った空間の店蔵の脇に小さな蔵が作られる．この小さな蔵は袖蔵と呼ばれるが，今でも多くの店蔵が使われている埼玉県の川越では妻蔵とも言われる．と言うのは，大きな店蔵の軒が通りに面しているにもかかわらず，妻側がそちらを向いているからである㉛．袖蔵が店蔵の左にくるか右にくるか（あるいは裏か）は通りの位置次第だ．前述の如く，特に関東地方では冬にとても乾いた季節風が吹く．この風は裏日本に大雪をもたらし，さらに

shutters. These would be fixed up during the day leaving the whole of the shop front open, which for a large shop would be a space of perhaps 4 – 6 meters in width. If however the *hisashi* is enclosed there would be two shutter boxes either side were fire proof sliding doors would be kept when not in use.

The first floor front elevation would either have windows and *kannonbiraki* plastered shutter doors, or a large opening running almost the full width of the frontage covered with a lattice screen. On the inside of this there would be sliding fire proof shutters and then inside that, *shōji*, sliding paper screens. The *kannonbiraki* (fig. 28) would usually be left open for ventilation during the day except when a fire broke out near by and then they would be closed. The "female" one on the left being closed first followed by the "male" shutter. The interlocking stepped edges of the shutters which are such an interesting design feature of the building when the shutters are open, take on their true function of keeping fire out when they have been closed. Inevitably a crack remains between the wall and the shutter which would be sealed off with a specially prepared mud kept handy for the job. Sometimes *miso* (Soya bean paste) was used instead. The sealing up of the shutters would be done from a narrow platform which was permanently set up on the *hisashi* roof (fig. 29). With all the shutters sealed up and all the store houses

closed tight, the family and staff would close themselves in the main *misekura* and seal the shutters and fire proof doors from the inside. They would already have moved any valuable items out of the living area, having put them in chests with wheels and rolling them into a *kura* for safety. This would mean that the dwelling which was usually a simple inexpensive wooden structure sandwiched between the *misekura* and other *kura* would burn down. There was no cause to be concerned, as the living area could easily be replaced after the fire had abaited, where as the goods in the *misekura* and storehouses were the wealth of the merchant. If these were lost the merchants livelihood would also be destroyed.

The sites along the main streets of Edo or other large cities were usually fairly long and narrow, the bigger sites having a frontage of about 14 – 15 meters (fig. 30). With larger premises a *misekura* would be built almost filling the frontage and in the remaining space a smaller *kura* would be placed to one side of the main building. This small *kura* is known as a *sodekura* or in Kawagoe, Saitama prefecture, where there are still alot of *misekura* in use, it is called a *tsumagura*. This is because the *tsuma* or gable end of the roof faces the street where as the eaves of the main shop or *misekura* face the street (fig. 31). The placing of the *sodekura* to either the left or right of the *misekura* (or even behind

㊳　明治時代の船枻造り，大宮，埼玉県．
㊴　明治時代の船枻造り．妻壁は漆喰塗になっている．上尾，埼玉県．
㊵　妻壁が漆喰塗の，明治期の船枻造り，１階が蔵になっている．大宮．
㊶　差掛け屋根と主屋根の双方に船枻軒が見られる．煉瓦造の袖蔵に注目．この建物は1923年の大震災にも持ちこたえた．台東区．
㊷　単なる飾りとして使われた船枻軒のパターン，町田市．

38. *Segai-zukuri machiya* of Meiji Period, Omiya, Saitama Pref.
39. *Segai-zukuri machiya* of Meiji Period. Side walls are plastered. Ageo, Saitama Pref.
40. *Segai-zukuri machiya* with plastered side walls, Meiji Period. 1st floor is a storage. Omiya, Saitama Pref.
41. Segai eaves on lean-to roof and the main roof eaves. Note brick built *sodekura* which survived the great 1923 earthquake. Taito-ku, Tokyo.
42. *Segai* eaves used purely for decoration, Machida-shi, Tokyo.

山を越えて関東平野に吹きおろし，雨や雪の前ぶれとなる．そして北または北西から吹いてはしばしば強風となり，ぼやをあっという間に大火にしてしまう．最盛期の江戸はおそらく世界一の「木造都市」であったろうが，そこに12～2月にかけて起きた数多くの大火が，その気候現象による悲惨な結果を立証している．火はすぐに風に乗って広がり，その行く先々を焼き尽くした．火は7～8キロメートルに及び，1000戸以上もの建物を破壊した．

風の向きは予想できるので，店蔵を守るものとして袖蔵を利用することができる．それゆえ関東地方では，袖蔵はほとんど店蔵の北か西に建てられている．つまり冬の風が吹く日には袖蔵が店蔵を守ってくれると期待したわけである．少なくとも関東で，店蔵と風の向きに逆らった袖蔵の配置を見たら，家相の影響と考えられる．家相とは，迷信に従って建物の向きなどを決める方法である．

店蔵の場合は通りから火を受ける危険がほとんどないにもかかわらず，前面が漆喰で塗られ

ている．もっとも通りはだいたいにおいて狭いので，大火はまるで波のように簡単に通りを越えて広がるだろうが．危険のほとんどない場所では前面に漆喰を塗らないことが多い．川越のような街の広い大通りに面した店舗は，通り側からの類焼の危険が減ったこととは無関係に完全な店蔵様式が用いられ，地位の象徴，すなわち富と権威の印となった．そこには，漆喰なしの純粋な木造で，完全な店蔵様式を模倣した建物がいくつか見うけられる．

「耐火建築」にはもう一つ忘れてはならない装置がある．それは梲だ㉜．江戸末期になると，この「火を止める」機能は古くさくなってしまうが，それでも装飾としては用いられていた．

漆喰の建物を作るのは決して簡単な作業でなく，もちろん時間と金がふんだんにかかる．その完成には，漆喰の厚みとディテール次第で1年から4年の歳月がかかる．蛇腹のついた一対の戸を作るという厄介な仕事には，大きさによって70人から100人の人が携っている．1880年に建てられた間口約6メートルの小さな店蔵に

は当時の金で10000円，今で言えば1000万円がかけられた．

土蔵造りはたぶん中世の京都に生まれたが，火災の多い江戸で本当に力強い建築様式に発展した．その様式は貴重な在庫を保護する必要性を満足すると同時に，商人階級の強さと安定にふさわしい象徴であった．

土蔵造り店蔵（文字通り土で造った店や倉庫）の目的は火災から大事な在庫を守ることであったが，基本的な形が装飾されることにより地位と富の象徴となった．関東の店蔵の力強い様式は，この建築様式の最も発展したものであり，20世紀初期まで建てられ続けた．しかし明治時代末期になると，店蔵の「陰気な外観」が時代の変化にそぐわなくなった．店蔵に代わる洋風建築の明るい色の石，暖かい赤の煉瓦といったものが新しい時代のイメージをなし，それとともに通り沿いに眠る「黒い怪物」は次第に洋風建築に取って代わられていった㉝．

日本では大火，地震などの天災がしばしば人命をも奪うが，それは一方で建築様式の変化を

it) depended on the orientation of the street, its previously mentioned, in the Kanto region in paticular, there are very dry seasonal winds which blow in winter. These winds deposit large quantities of snow on the areas facing the Sea of Japan, and then sweep over the mountains and down onto the Kanto plain which is in a rain shadow or rather a snow shadow. Such winds which blow from the north or north-west can get up to gale force at times and would of course whip up a small fire into a raging inferno in seconds. The disasterous results of this climatic phenomena are evidenced by the large number of major fires which occured in the months of December, January and February in Edo (now Tokyo), the city which in its hey day was perhaps the largest "wooden city" in the world. A fire would soon spread down wind consuming all in its path. Such a fire might cover 7 – 8 km destroying upwards of a 1000 buildings on the way.

Because the direction of the wind was so predictable it was possible to use the *sodekura* as added protection for the *misekura*. Therefore, in the Kanto region most of the *sodekura* are placed to the north or west of the *misekura*, in the hope of gaining some extra protection should a fire occur when the winter wind was blowing. In the Kanto region at least, it was very convenient that the siting of the *sodekura* up wind of the *misekura* should also more or less correspond to

beliefs about the layout of buildings related to the *kaso* system, a system by which a building was orientated according to superstitious beliefs.

In the case of a *misekura* the front elevation was also plastered, even though there was less risk of a fire attacking from the street. However, as the streets were often narrow a big fire could easily spread across as a wave of sparks. On less dangerous sites the plaster is sometimes omitted from the front elevation. However, the full *misekura* style seems to have been a status symbol; a sign of wealth and authority because shops on the wide main streets of a town such as Kawagoe are plastered on all elevations regardless of the reduced risk of a fire from the street. Also there are some examples of buildings which mimic the full *misekura* style in just timber without using plaster at all.

There is one more element of this architectural "fire proof machine", which must not be forgotten and that is the *udatsu*. By the end of the Edo period the "fire stop" function of the *udatsu* had become more or less obsolete but it was still used as decoration (figs. 32, 9).

To build one of these plaster buildings was no simple task and was of course very costly in terms of time and money. Completion of such a building could take anywhere between 1 – 4 years depending on the thickness of the plaster and detailing. The exacting work on a pair of the stepped shutter doors would involve

70 – 100 men depending on the size of the doors. A small *misekura* with a frontage of about 6 m built in 1880 cost in those days ¥10,000 which today would represent ¥10,000,000 ($50,000 or £20,000 $1=¥203, £1=¥500).

Dozō-zukuri probably first came into existance in Kyoto in the Middle Ages, but it was in Edo where fires were so numerous that the style developed into a truely bold architectural style, satisfying the need to protect valuable stock and at the same time being a fitting symbol of strength and stability of the merchant class.

The original aim of *dozō-zukuri misekura* (literally, earth built, shop store house) was to protect valuable stocks from fire but the embelishment of the basic form turned it into a symbol of position and wealth. The bold style of the *misekura* in the Kanto region is the most developed of this type of architecture, which was still being built in the early part of the 20th century. However, by the late Meiji period, what was described as the *misekura*'s "gloomy appearance" showed that times had changed. Light coloured store and warm red brick of Western style buildings which had begun to replace *misekura* were part of the image of that new age and so the black monsters which slumbered at the side of the streets were gradually superseded (fig. 33).

In Japan, major fires, earthquakes and other natural disasters cause distress

もたらし，日本人の生活様式をも変えることのできる現象と言うこともできる．1923年の関東大震災では約65000戸以上の建物が崩壊した．また，東京市街だけで土蔵造りの建物の約80％，20000戸以上が壊れ，周辺の地域ではその数はさらに多い．この災害にならって，洋風，特に鉄筋コンクリート造で建てた店の数が増えた．これは，始め耐火上の利点から人気のあった煉瓦，石造建築が，地震時に子供の積木細工のように倒壊したためであった．店蔵も大きな棟と灰色の瓦屋根という自重によりかなりひどい被害を受けた．小田原ではほとんどの建物が崩壊したが，地震が畏怖の念を持って見られるようになってからは，重い瓦の代わりに軽い鉄板が使われた．

しかし，関東大震災以後も本来の日本式町家は建てられている．それは我々がここで船枻造りと呼んでいる手法を用いた町家である．関東地方の町家に船枻造り（出桁造り）が用いられだしたのはたぶん江戸時代後期で，しばしば店蔵のデザイン要素として利用された．店蔵は江戸

末期における江戸など主要な町の街道沿いによく見られたが，漆喰を少し塗った程度か，あるいは完全な木造の町家においては，船枻造りの軒も大きな特徴となったであろう．

今井町の豊田家以前にも同様な船枻は見うけられるが，関東地方では船枻造りがほとんどの町家の装飾要素となり，ファサードに活気と力強さを与えた㉞→㊷．

関東地方に現存する最古の船枻造りの軒を持つ町家は，おそらく1854年から1860年の間に完成したものらしい．この様式は第2次大戦が始まるまで建設され続けた．関東大震災以後の船枻造り町家（船枻軒をもった商店，住居）も多く現存するが，それらは米屋，お茶屋，酒屋などの昔ながらの商売にのみ使われている．

店蔵の横の船枻造り町家は力強いデザインではないものの，とても頑丈そうだ．船枻造りの軒とその出の深さにより強さが微妙に感じられ，店の正面デザインの全体的効果が高められた．軒のディテールと形態の類似性は日本の建物のファサードを何百年にもわたって美しく飾って

⑬

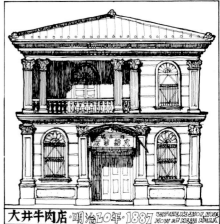
⑭

⑮

⑯

and loss of life, but could also be said to be phenomina which influence change in styles of architecture and can even change the way of life of the Japanese. In 1923 the Great Kanto earthquake destroyed out of a total of about 65000 buildings, upwards of 20000, or roughly 80% of all *dozō-zukuri* buildings in the central part of Tokyo alone and many more in the surrounding areas. In the wake of this disaster shops built in Western architectural styles increased in numbers, particularly re-enforced concrete ones. This was because brick and stone built buildings, which at first had been popular because of their superior fire resistance qualities, tumbled down like so many childrens building blocks when the ground shook. The *misekura* fell heavily too, weighed down by their grand ridge tiles and grey tiled roofs. In Odawara, where almost every building was destroyed, light metal sheeting was used as a roofing material on new buildings instead of heavy tiles, which since the earthquake had come to be regarded with fear.

There was however a truely Japanese style of *machiya* which continued to be built after the Great Kanto earthquake. That was a *machiya* utilizing what we shall call here *segai-zukuri*. The use of *segai-zukuri* (also known as *dashigeta-zukuri*) on *machiya* in the Kanto region seems to have started in the latter part of the Edo period and also was often a component used in *misekura* design.

Although *misekura* was probably the major style of *machiya* towards the end of the Edo period in Edo and on the main streets of other important towns, *segai-zukuri* eaves were the dominent feature of what was probably a much greater number of shops/*machiya* which were either partly plastered, *(nuriya-zukuri)* or entirely timber finished.

We have seen a similar *segai* form before on the Toyoda house in Imaicho, but in the Kanto region *segai-zukuri* eaves developed into a decorative element that gave a vitality and strength to the facade of almost every shop/*machiya*, which stood on the streets of towns large and small (figs. 34—42 are styles of *segai* and styles of shops, also detail).

What is perhaps the oldest existing *machiya* using *segai* eaves in the Kanto region was probably built between 1854 and 1860 (fig. 36), and such buildings continued to be built right up to the beginning of the 2nd World War. However, *segai-zukuri machiya* (shops or dwellings with some commercial purpose which have *segai* eaves) built after the Great Kanto Earthquake, many of which are still standing today, seem only to house traditional businesses such as rice, tea or sake merchants.

Segai-zukuri machiya existed along side of *misekura* and although not as bold in design they are fine sturdy looking pieces of architecture. The total effect of the design of the facade of one of these shops is enhanced by the subtle

⑬ 和洋折衷の店舗，函館．
⑭ 大井牛肉店，神戸．
⑮ 明治20年頃の銀座．写真：喜多川周之．
⑯ 看板建築，台東区．銅板張りのファサードに和風の軒のモチーフが使われている．

43. Mixed Japanese and western style shop, Hakodate, Hokkaido.
44. Butcher's shop at Kobe, 1887.
45. Ginza, late 19th century.
46. *Kanban* architecture, Taito-ku, Tokyo. A Japanese gable motif is used in combination with a sheet copper pattern facade.

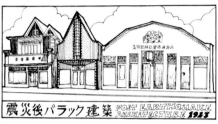

きた．船枻軒のディテールにおける材の組み合わせ，特に軒の下に一列に並ぶ跳ね出した腕木の多さは日本建築の大切な要素である．特に江戸時代以降の町家において，船枻は欠くことのできない要素となり，日本の建築デザインの大きな特徴ともなっていった．

新しい時代

19世紀末，日本が西欧の物や考え方に対しその門戸を開くと，建築も全体として新しい方向へ向かった．店舗はすぐに洋風の装飾を取り付けた．ある店は和洋折衷㊸で，ある店は日本人大工による模倣でというように．しかし，そういう店舗は日本にとって目新しい商売であることが多く，建築的イメージもその商売によった．

英国人Ｊ・コンドル（1852—1920）は1877年に来日し，正式な西洋風の建築教育に大いに貢献した．その結果，日本の建築家もすぐに，店舗やデパートにさえ純洋風のデザインを用いるようになった㊹．しかし政府の援助で，1872年の大火後の銀座再開発計画として初めての洋風

商店街を設計したのは別の英国人Ｔ・Ｊ・ウォルターであった．この計画において日本で初めての車と歩行者の分離，街路樹の導入といった手法が見られた㊺．

19世紀末から，二つのタイプのデザイナーが活躍している．一つは新しく始まった正式な建築教育の産物であり，もう一つは親方から弟子へと知識を伝えられた大工であった．建築家は洋風建築に基づいてデザインしがちだが，日本風の「味つけ」はほとんどしない．一方，大工は洋風の上に日本風を簡単に付け加え，街路に新しい土着的建築を生んだ．それは洋風の最も喜ばれるモチーフを取り込み，日本式の工夫によって和風とうまく組み合わせた「一般大衆」の建築であった．新しい土着様式の一つは看板建築㊻㊼㊽とも呼ばれ，特に1923年の関東大震災以後の東京で広く用いられた．この様式はおそらく切妻の店舗ににせのファサードをつけた時に始まったのだろう．それは一つに新しさを与え，ついで２階を家族にとって役立つものとしたが，内部はだいたい伝統的な日本のデザイ

messages of strength transmitted by the *segai* eaves. The use of this eave detail and forms similar in appeearence have graced the facades of buildings on the streets of Japan for hundreds of years. The interlocking of the members of the *segai* eave detail and especially the rich quality of jutting bracket arms lined-up under the eaves, is an important element of Japanese architecture. Especially on post Edo period *machiya* design *segai* could be said to be an indispensable element and is extremely characteristic of Japan architectural design.

New Vernacular Styles

After Japan had opened her doors wide to things and ideas from the West at the end of the 19th century, architecture as a whole in Japan took on a new direction. Shops soon sprang up sporting the trappings of Western architectural styles: some shops being a mix of Japanese and foreign design styles (fig. 43) and others which were designed by Japanese carpenters mimicing western styles (fig. 44). Such shops tended to house trades new to Japan and so the architectural image went with the businesss.

An Englishman, J. Conder (1852–1920) came to Japan in 1877 and contributed greatly to formal Western architectural training so that Japanese architects were soon making full blooded Western style designs for shops and department stores as well as other types of buildings. However, it was another

Englishman, T.J. Walters who designed and built with sponsorship from the Japanese Government, the first shopping street along Western lines, as a re-development scheme for the Ginza district of Tokyo which had been destroyed by fire in 1872 (fig. 45). In this design for the first time in Japan, we see a separation of wheeled traffic and pedestrians and the introduction of trees on the street.

From the end of the last century there were two types of designers at work. One was the product of the newly instigated formal architectural training, and the other was the carpenter, whose knowledge had always been handed down from master to apprentice. The architects tended to make designs based on western architectural styles and very little Japanese 'flavour' was added. However, the carpenter was quick to add a Japanese touch to selected western styles and a new vernacular architecture of the street was created. This was a 'grass-roots' architecture which assimilated the most acceptable motifs from western design and combined them with home grown inventions to suit Japanese tastes. One of the 'new vernacular' styles, sometimes known as *kamban* (sign board) architecture, really came into its own particularly in Tokyo after the Great 1923 earthquake. This style probably started when a false facade was added to a gabled roof shop, first and foremost to bring it up to date and secondly to

㊼ 大正期の看板建築．隣には最近の一例が並んでいる．土浦．
㊽ 震災後のバラック建築．
㊺ コーヒーショップ，新宿．
㊿ 新宿の地下街．

47. *Kanban* architecture, Tsuchiura, Ibaragi Pref. A Taisho Period shop along side a more recent example.
48. Post earthquake architecture.
49. Coffee shop castle, Shinjuku, Tokyo.
50. Underground shopping arcade, Shinjuku, Tokyo.

ンであったから，皮相な建築にすぎなかった．

大正時代までには，日本の街路に「デザイン の視覚的戦い」が始まり，例えば今井町に見られたような盗みはなくなっていた．1923年の震災直後，東京ではすでに確立していた様式の列の中にもっと軽々しいデザインの町家が加わり，目立つことはもはやタブーではなくなった．昔のように規格化された材料，慣例化したデザインによってすべての建物が一つであった時代には，目立つデザインをするのは容易なことである．しかし今日，特に大きな商店街では，すべての店が目立とうとするので全体が様式をごちゃまぜにしたようになる．店をどうしてどう見せるかを示す計画上の法則は何もない．建築家は店舗の商売に合わせるか，適当に目を引くデザインをするかを自由に選ぶことができる．

前述のように，今日の日本の街，都市は駅の位置に大いに影響を受けており，駅の魅力が特にデパートを引き寄せた．デパートは駅の周辺に集まり，昔のれんにつけた家紋を電気で作り替えたようなネオンサインを設置した．ネオンと高いデパートが，活動と行動の集中する中心地を示すようになった㊼→㊿．

中心地の地価はもちろん高く，交通量も果てしなく大きい．だから，多くの人を運び，同時に地価の高さを相殺するべく，地下商店街㊿が大きな駅から扇形に広がる．しかし多くの場合，地下商店街は商業施設を伴なった便利な通路にすぎない．楽しげにデザインされていても商品のための装置にすぎず，ある雰囲気を持った空間を作る建築的計画とは言えないものが多い．もちろん，物理的，経済的状況がデザインを制限するものの，環境要素をすべて調整する機会のあるこうした「閉鎖的」空間において，一般的に想像力が欠けているのはとても残念なことである．

アーケード同様，地下商店街も天候からいろいろな物を保護する．この種の閉鎖空間は地上にあればさほど制約を受けず，地下にある時に比べて便利である．アーケードも道を覆うことによって作られるが，その道は自然に発展し，すでにそこに存在していた．保護し，閉じた屋根の下，ファサードは好き勝手になって途方もなくなり，その閉鎖空間におけるデザイン相互の関係は強烈なものとなる．

かつては，町家個々のデザインと通りのデザインは一体であった．町家建築は気候やその時代の都市の状態に適切に対応し，同時にその環境を形成していった．通りの建物は都市環境を反映し，同時に環境を創造していた．今日でも条件に変わりはない．今日の日本の都市環境は活動的でかつ激しい．広い意味での町家は適切にそれに応じている．時には質素に，時にはつっぱって，そして時には幻想的な陽気さで．道路を楽しく――途方もないデザインによる興奮――するのは幻想であり，あるいは猥雑とさえ呼ばれるものである．例えばヨーロッパにおいて，建築家が理想を求めたがために，この楽しい雰囲気を失なってしまった例はいくつもある．しかし道路はみんなのものであり，整然としているだけでは物足りない．この点からも，日本の通りや町家は我々に多くを教えてくれるに違いない．

（訳：小堀徹）

make more of the first floor available for family use (figs. 46, 47). This architecture was very much skin deep as the interior was often traditionally Japanese in design.

By the Taisho period (1912–1926) there was the beginnings of a 'visual battle of designs' (fig. 33) on the streets of Japan and the design harmony or *nusumi* of the past, which can be seen in Imaicho for instance, had gone. Immediately after the 1923 earthquake in Tokyo a rather frivolous design of shop/*machiya* (fig. 48) joined the ranks of already established styles and it seems that to be conspicuous was no longer taboo. In the past it would have been all too easy for a design to stand out on streets where, through the use of standardised materials, design conventions and customs, all buildings were as one. However nowadays, particularly on main shopping streets every shop tries to make its mark and consequently there is an exciting mixture of styles all jumbled up together. There are no planning laws which can dictate how a shop looks and so literally anything goes. Designers and architects are free to express in what ever way they think fit, the particular trade of a shop or they can just make a suitably eye-catching design (fig. 49).

As mentioned before the present form of Japanese towns and cities has been strongly influenced by the position of stations and their magnatism draws in particular department stores. They cluster around or near stations and sport neon logos which are rather like electric versions of the family crests seen long ago on the *noren* of shops. The neon and the tall department stores become indicators of centres where activity and movement are most consentrated (fig. 53).

Land at these centres is of course expensive and the numbers of people who pass through such areas can be extremely large. Consequently underground shopping streets (fig. 50) fan out from the larger stations to channel the masses of people and at the same time to offset the high land prices. However, in almost all cases these underground 'arcades' are little more than convenient corridors with shopping facilities thrown in for good measure. Although some of them are pleasantly designed it is often the arrangement of the products and the goods on sale and not an architectural device which gives the space some atmosphere. Of course physical and economic considerations have a restricting effect on the design of these underground 'arcades' but it is a pity that in such 'captive' spaces where there is a chance to control all elements of the environment there is in most cases a sad lack of imagination.

One thing the underground shopping streets do provide is protection from the weather, as do the many arcades in Japan. This type of enclosed space has an advantage over the underground variety being above ground. Also arcades are often formed by covering existing streets which have had time to develop naturally. Under the protective and enclosing roof, designs can be as extravagant as desired and the juxtaposition of designs one against another in this type of enclosed space is always exciting (fig. 51).

In the past the designs of individual *machiya* and the design of a street were as one, and *machiya* architecture reacted appropriately to the conditions of the climate and the urban environment of the times, and of course formed part of that environment. Architecture of the street reflects and at the same time creates the urban environment. Today the situation is the same. The modern Japanese urban environment is dynamic and fierce and the modern *machiya*/ shops have reacted accordingly. Sometimes it is with simplicity, sometimes with gusto and then sometimes light-heartedly with a touch of fantasy. It is the fantasy and what some would call kitsch of some designs which helps to make the streets exciting; an excitement of extravagant design. It is this exciting atmosphere which has been designed out of so many streets in Europe for instance, in the interests of so called good taste. But the street is for everyone and 'good' or 'bad' taste has no meaning. In this respect Japanese streets and *machiya* have much to teach us (figs. 52–66).

SPATIAL COMPOSITION OF THE SHRINE

by Takeo Nakajima

神社空間──その意味と都市における役割

中嶋猛夫

神社とは日本の民族宗教である神道の建物で，神道と神社の関係は，仏教と寺院，キリスト教と教会との関係と同様であるといわれている．しかし神道は宗教というよりも，日本の気候，風土に根ざした，日常生活の心情，価値観といったほうがよいのではないか．それは言いかえれば，「自然，風土尊重」と「現世利益」の二つを骨子とした絶対性なき功利的世界観であり，神社はその観念を共有する共同体の象徴であるともいえる．神社の本来の意味は，人間より上部に位置するもの（カミ）を象徴として結束した集団の意味である．後にカミが擬人化されて住居を社殿とするようになり，主として建物をさすようになった．

神社は複雑な要素をもっているが，それは歴史的変遷によるところが大きい．原始時代，人人は稚拙な技術で自然の産物を食物とし，自然

を畏敬することで信仰心をもち，その象徴として，山・川・木・石を拝んだ．弥生期になると，大規模な灌漑を必要とする稲作が普及した．これは，広い面積の耕地と，大勢の共同作業者を必要とするために，一定の土地と，そこに住む人々（氏族）との結びつきが強くなり，産土神や氏神の概念が生まれた．

6世紀頃になると，天皇家による日本統一が行われ，天皇家の祖先が日本の神々の最高位であるという国家神道（神話）がつくられた．

平安時代には，仏が神という姿になって現われたという神仏混交が一般化し，神道より，仏教がより高次なものとされた．

中世期に入ると，古代社会規準がくずれ，民衆の力が強くなるとともに商工業が発達した．それは今までの農業を基盤とした地縁社会と異なる「座」という同業組合ができ，その共同体

の象徴としての神社ができた．

近世になると，貨幣経済が完成し，都市が発達した．それにより神社は農業とは無縁の都市住民による地縁社会の象徴となり，神に捧げる供物も農産物から現金に代った．

明治になって近代化が行われるとともに，為政者のバックボーンとして国家神道が重視され，神社から仏教色が排除された．

第2次世界大戦の敗戦によって，神社はそれぞれ独立した宗教法人となった．そして，現在の神社には過去にできたいろいろなものが，否定されることなく渾然と存在し続けている．

神社境内の構成

神社をかたちづくる特徴は，その歴史的背景にも述べたように，第一に自然性である．

日本最古の神社の一つといわれる，奈良の大

As Christianity has the church and Buddhism the temple, so the shrine is the building associated with Shinto, Japan's "Way of the Gods." Rather than a religion, Shinto might better be called a feeling or sense of values found in daily life, rooted in Japan's climate and natural conditions. It is a practical view of the world, without any quality of absolutism, built around the two ideas of respect for nature and natural features, and the belief in a divine response to prayer in this world; the shrine is a symbol of the community sharing those views. The original meaning of the shrine is that of a group united under a symbol of something (a god, *kami*) higher than man. Later, the gods were personified and supposed to dwell in the shrine itself, and the word "shrine" *(jinja)* came to indicate the building especially.

The shrine has many complex elements which owe their development largely to the vissicitudes of history. In primitive times, men used unsophisticated techniques to sustain themselves on nature's yield; their respect for nature had a religious feeling and they prayed

to mountains, rivers, trees and stones as symbols of that nature. In the Yayoi period, large scale drainage was necessitated as the practice of rice production spread. This required great land area and vigorous communal workers; particular places and the people who lived there came to be very closely bound, and the concepts of *ubusuna-gami* and *ujigami* were developed. (Roughly, the former refers to the guardian deity of the place where one was born, the latter to that of one's clan — translator's note).

By about the sixth century Japan was unified under an Emperor and the myth was established that the forebears of the Emperor's house were the greatest of all of Japan's gods.

In the Heian period, the teachings of Buddha reached Japan and the image formed of the Buddha was like that of a Shinto god; this image became popularized and Buddhism was considered to occupy a place above Shinto.

In the medieval period, as the standards of the old order crumbled and popular power increased, the merchant and craftsman classes developed. The new

society differed from the former, which had been tied to the land; with the formation of unions, called *za*, among common trades, shrines associated with individual unions came into being.

By modern times, a money-based economy had been established and cities developed. Shrines became symbols of a way of life bound to the land for the citydwellers who had no relations themselves with that way of life, and offerings to the gods changed from farm products to cash.

As modernization progressed in the Meiji era (1868–1911), State Shinto was emphasized as the backbone of the polity and anything reminiscent of Buddhism was expunged from the shrine.

After defeat in the Second World War, the shrines each became independent religious corporations and currently freely continue the traditions of the past with no restrictions.

Spatial Composition of Shrine Grounds

The distinguishing characteristic of shrines, as mentioned in their historical background, is first of all their relation-

① 三輪山. Miwayama.

② 二見ケ浦の夫婦岩. Futami-ga-ura, paired rocks.

③ 那智の滝. Nachi waterfall.

神神社は本殿がなく，背後の三輪山全体が御神体で禁足地となっている．また，和歌山の那智大社は，幅12メートル，高さ133メートルの大滝が御神体である．このように，山・森・川・木・石などが，社殿や鳥居のような諸施設以上に重要である．①→③

神社の境内構成は，「自然地形尊重，景観重視的造形」といえるほど，自然地形を大切にした変化に豊むシークエンスを参拝者に提供する．それはユーラシア大陸全体に見られる宗教空間に，左右対称形などのような「概念的造形」が見られるのと好対照である．

次に日本の大規模な神社境内構成の典型例を示す．

● 伊勢神宮

国家神道の最高神で天皇家の祖先神とされる天照大神を祭る神社である．里に近い外宮と山奥の内宮に分かれ，20年毎に隣地に再建するというめずらしい形式をもつ．神明造りの社殿は高床式の建物で，古代の支配者の住居様式といわれ，東南アジアの民家と類似している．境内は川を結界とした自然林に囲まれ，社殿は南面しているが，参道は複雑に屈曲している．④→⑫

● 厳島神社

宮島とも言われる瀬戸内海の小島の入江に建つ高床式の美しい社殿で，12世紀の宮殿様式である．満潮時には建物全体が海面に浮ぶような状態になる．この神社は海の守り神を祭り，昔

は島全体が禁足地であった．主参道は海路であり，入江の入口には高さ25メートル以上もある朱塗の大鳥居が建っている．この神社の社殿および境内は日本三景の一つになっている．⑬→⑱

● 日光の東照宮

約300年ほど前に徳川家康を祭るためにできたものであるが，関東平野の北端に位置し，古代から信仰の厚い，男体山を中心とする日光の山中にあり，複雑に屈曲した境内参道，結界としての川や橋や鳥居，そして境内に至るまでの数十キロメートルにおよぶ杉並木など，スケールの大きなシークエンスが見られる．⑲→㉖

以上の3例の神社は，過去の各々の時代の為政者によって造られたものである．他に個人や小集団によってつくられた小規模な神社と，ある一定の土地とそこに住む人々の象徴である鎮守社，という三つのタイプに日本の神社は大別される．

東京の鎮守社

全国に10万以上もある神社の大部分は，地縁社会の象徴としての鎮守社である．ここでは特に，村の鎮守社ではなく，日本の代表的都市に生き続ける神社の姿を，東京における鎮守社の調査によってさぐってみる．

● 東京の歴史

東京が本格的な都市になったのは，16世紀末に関東一円の領主となった徳川家康が，当時江戸

ship with Nature.

Said to be one of Japan's oldest shrines, the Omiwa Shrine of Nara reveres not just the *honden*, or main hall, but the whole mountain behind it, Miwasan, which is today a restricted area. The Nachi Great Shrine of Wakayama reveres a large waterfall, a 133 meter cascade of water twelve meters in width. Like these shrines, mountains, forests, rivers, trees, rocks, etc., are of much greater importance than the various built facilities of a shrine such as the main hall or *torii*, gate (figs. 1–3).

The grounds of the shrine itself offer the visitor a rich sequence of changes in the landscape which it reveres, in accordance with its respect for natural forms and built forms emphasizing the scenery. They present a pleasant contrast to the religious spaces seen on the Eurasian continent with their very symmetrical conceptual forms.

Below are typical examples of the spatial arrangements of the grounds of Japan's large-scale shrines.

Ise Jingu: The Ise Shrines celebrate Amaterasu Omikami, the ancestral god of the Emperor's house and the greatest of the gods of State Shinto. It has two parts, the Outer Shrine, near town, and the Inner Shrine, in the mountains, and has the rare tradition of being rebuilt every twenty years on an adjacent site. The shrine buildings are of typical shrine architectural style, *shinmei-zukuri*, a high-floored type used as a residential style by ancient rules and akin to popular housing types of southeast Asia (figs. 4–12).

Itsukushima Jinja: This beautiful high-floored shrine is built in the inlet of a small island, also called Miyajima, in the twelfth-century shrine style. At high tide, the whole building appears to float on the surface of the sea. This shrine celebrates the guardian of the sea; the island itself was once at the foot of a forest. The main approach is by sea, and at the mouth of the inlet stands a great *torii* over 25 meters in height. This shrine with its building and "grounds" is considered one of the three great beauty spots of Japan (figs. 13–19).

Toshogu Shrine, Nikko: Built three hundred years ago by Tokugawa Ieyasu, the shrine is located at the edge of the Kanto Plain, in the mountains of Nikko centering on Nantai-san, a mountain deeply worshipped from earliest ages. The scale is quite large, with a ten kilometer long avenue of tall cedar trees leading to the shrine proper, a winding *sando,* or approach, and the river, bridges, and *torii* of the sanctuary itself (figs. 20–26).

The three examples just cited were all built at the behest of the rulers of the age. There are two other main categories of shrines in Japan: those of a small scale built by individuals or small groups, and tutelary shrines built as a symbol of a particular area and the people who live there.

The Tutelary Shrines of Tokyo

The majority of the over 100,000 shrines in Japan are shrines to tutelary gods and symbols of a society closely related to the land. Nor are they primarily village shrines; the following is the result of a

伊勢神宮 ISE JINGU

④

⑤

⑦

⑧

⑫

④ 鳥居.
⑤ 五十鈴川と宇治橋.
⑥ 板垣南御門から（外宮）.
⑦ 内宮宮地.
⑧ 新用地から本殿を見る.
⑨ 新用地.
⑩ 内宮配置図. 吉田鉄郎著『日本の建築』より.
⑪ 内宮本殿の立面図と平面図.
⑫ 内宮の摂社. ④⑤⑦→⑨⑫の写真：栄美智子.

⑨

4. Torii.
5. Isuzu River and Uji Bridge.
6. Looking from the *Itagaki* south gate to the Outer Shrine.
7. Grounds of the Inner Shrine.
8. The *honden*, main hall, from the site of next rebuilding.
9. Site of next rebuilding.
10. Plan of the Inner Shrine. (From *Nihon no Kenchiku,* by Tetsuro Yoshida)
11. Elevation and plan of the *honden*, main hall, Inner Shrine.
12. Smaller related shrine near the Inner Shrine.

⑥

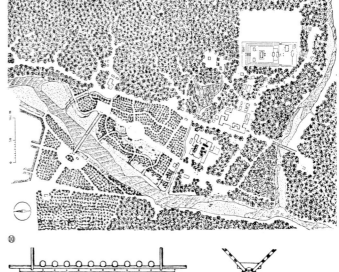

⑩

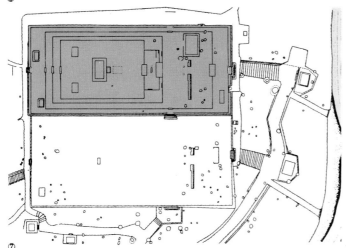

⑦

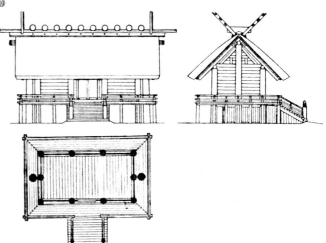

⑪

厳島神社　ITSUKUSHIMA JINJA

⑬　大鳥居を通して見る.
⑭⑮　祓殿.
⑯　回廊を通して本殿方向を見る. ⑭⑯の写真：栄美智子.
⑰　祓殿立面図.
⑱　空から見る.
⑲　配置図. 吉田鉄郎著『日本の建築』より.

13. Looking through the Great *Torii.*
14, 15. *Misogi-den,* pavilion for cleansing the body.
16. Looking toward the *honden* from within the corridor.
17. Elevation of *harae-dono.*
18. View from above.
19. Plan. (From *Nihon no Kenchiku,* by Tetsuro Yoshida)

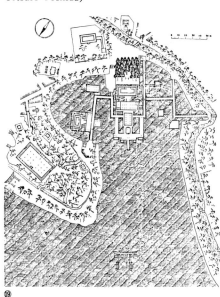

20. Sin-kyo Bridge over Oya River.
21, 22. Shrine Grounds.
23, 24. *Yomei-mon,* gate. 25. Plan.
26. Elevations of the *honden,* main hall, and *honsha,* main shrine precincts.

⑳ 大谷川と神橋.
㉑㉒ 境内.
㉓㉔ 陽明門.
㉕ 配置図.
㉖ 本殿側面図と本社平面図.

107

と呼ばれるこの地に城下町を建設してからである。その都市計画の主要骨子は，東京湾に臨む高台に江戸城と武家屋敷を建て，埋立地の低地に町人住区を置き，自然の河川を利用して外周を囲み防禦とした。現在は1,200万人ほどであるが，17世紀初めには15万人，18世紀中頃には100万人を越え，既に当時のロンドン（85万人）を越して世界一の人口を有していた。

●神社と日常生活
現代人と神社との関わりは日常生活全般に関っている。その一つは，生後30日を祝す宮参り，3歳・5歳・7歳の子供の成長を祝う七五三，結婚式，住居の新築など人生における節目の行事である。もう一つは，季節ごとの年中行事として新年1月の初詣に始まり，2月の節分，夏期の縁日，8月の盆踊り，春秋に行われる祭りなどである。その他，受験，良縁，病気全快，交通安全など諸々の祈願に神社は利用されるが，葬式，および供養は主として仏教寺院で行う。

●氏子組織
鎮守社は，氏子組織とよばれる地縁共同体によって支えられる。神社が鎮守する一定の区域に住む人々を氏子といい，それぞれ近隣社会の単位である町会に所属する。また，各町会から選ばれた氏子総代が，住民代表として鎮守社の運営に参加する。これら小規模で歴史的由緒ある名を持つ町会は，統合されて新住居表示に変えられつつあるが，現在も地縁共同体単位とし

て生きている。

●東京十社
慶応3年（1863年）将軍徳川慶喜は大政奉還し，新たに天皇を頂点とする明治政府が始まり，江戸を東京と改めた。そして首都の安全を祈るために選ばれたのが東京十社であり，これらは当時江戸市民に信仰厚かった神社である。[28]

十社の大部分は徳川将軍の江戸開府以前からの村の鎮守社であったものが，都市化によって町の鎮守社へと変質した。そして鎮守の森が都市に残された貴重なオアシスとなり，祭日にのみ催された芝居，相撲などの興業が大都市の人口にささえられ常設化するなど，神社境内は江戸市民の行楽地の傾向が強くなった。明治になって，西洋的都市公園が新設された時に，社寺の境内が転用された下地がすでに江戸時代に芽生えていた。現在，児童公園を併設している神社も多い。

●十社の境内構成
代表例として挙げた十社に共通する典型的な境内構成を述べると次のようになる。

丘陵部端の眺望の良い高台にあり，全体が樹木で覆われ鎮守の森をなしている。社殿は東か南を向き，前面は各種の附属施設が並ぶ広場となっていて，ほぼ社殿と同方向に石畳の主参道が伸び，入口には石鳥居と社名石が建つ。主参道と直角方向に脇参道があり，石段が附属する。主な施設は，神に奉る踊りを演ずる神楽殿が社

殿に向かって右手にあり，左手には身を浄めるための手水舎がある。神社の運営を行う神主の事務所としての社務所は社殿の右隣りにあり，種々の神を祭る末社が社殿の後背部に散在する。また氏子の町会神輿を収める倉庫が境内周辺部に配置される。参道両脇には石燈籠と厄除けの高麗犬が各々一対ごと建つ。現代的現象として，結婚式場を経営したり，平日に広場を駐車場として使ったりしている神社も多い。[29]

●十社にみる活性度
神社の活性度は，境内構成要素の多さと複雑さにほぼ比例しているといっても良い。それは，神社を構成するすべての施設が，すべて氏子または信奉者の寄附によって設置され，維持されるからである。多くの人々の崇敬を集める神社ほど色々な施設が整えられているようである。そして年間を通じての催事の多さと祭日の露店数が活性度の明確なバロメーターとなっている。

十社の内，特に活性度のある神社の敷地は，13,000平方メートル以上であり，緑地，池などの自然的要素が全面積の1/4以上を占めている。また境内構成要素表に示した項目のうち，20以上を満たす神社は氏子以外の崇敬者が多く，祭日の人出も多い。

しかし，一番重要なのは氏子組織が活力を持ち，地縁社会の象徴として積極的に神社を支えることである。

study of shrines to tutelary gods surviving in the modern city of Tokyo.

History of Tokyo: Tokyo's development as a city began at the end of the sixteenth century when Tokugawa Ieyasu built a castle town called Edo from which to rule the surrounding Kanto Plain. The basic plan of the town was to build the castle and *samurai* residences on the hills facing the bay, with housing for the townspeople on lower reclaimed land, and to use natural river courses to enclose the surrounding area in its defense. Today Tokyo has a population of 12 million, but at the end of the seventeenth century it was 150,000 and by the middle of the eighteenth century it had passed one million, surpassing the population of contemporary London to claim the largest population of any city in the world (fig. 27).

The Shrine and Daily Life: The relationship between people today and shrines pervades their daily life. Typical are ceremonies at decisive points in life, such as the shrine visit roughly 30 days after birth; the "Seven-Five-Three" ceremony at which the healthy development of children of those ages is beseeched; wedding ceremonies; and ceremonies at the beginning of new construction. Then there are seasonal ceremonies throughout the year: the first visit to the shrine at New Years, the end of winter, in February, the summer festival, the Festival of Returning Souls in August, and various festivals in spring and fall. Shrines are also visited to pray for luck in examinations, finding a spouse, prevention of illness or for traffic safety, etc., but funerals and memorial services are usually conducted at Buddhist temples.

The Ujiko System: Shrines to local deities are maintained by groups of residents of the area of the shrine's tutelage, called *ujiko,* who belong to local councils which are units of the *cho,* or neighborhood community. A general *ujiko* representative is selected from each council who participates as a representative of the residents in the management of the tutelary shrine. On this small scale, and although the *cho* are being changed and incorporated in new municipal divisions, these local councils with their historical tradition are still alive today as the communal units of a people tied to the land.

The Ten Shrines of Tokyo

The name Edo was changed to Tokyo in 1863 (third year of the Keio era) when the Shogun Tokugawa Yoshinobu effected a great political change and the Emperor was elevated to the apex of the new Meiji government. Ten of Tokyo's shrines were then chosen to guard the safety of the capitol city, all of them shrines with a great following among the people of Tokyo at that time.

Most of the ten were village tutelary shrines before the institution of the Tokugawa Shogunate and changed character as the city grew to become shrines of the guardian dieties of the *cho,* the local municipal division. The shrine groves became precious oases among the encroaching urbanization, and the holiday performances, *sumo* wrestling matches and special displays of the sacred

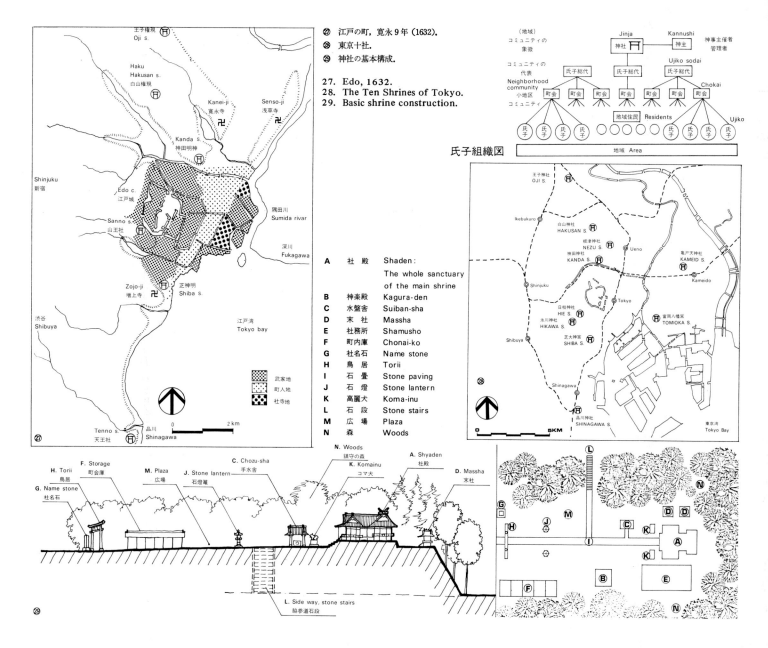

② 江戸の町，寛永9年 (1632).
⑳ 東京十社.
㉙ 神社の基本構成.

27. Edo, 1632.
28. The Ten Shrines of Tokyo.
29. Basic shrine construction.

氏子組織図

			Shaden:
A	社殿		The whole sanctuary of the main shrine
B	神楽殿	Kagura-den
C	水盤舎	Suiban-sha
D	末社	Massha
E	社務所	Shamusho
F	町内庫	Chonai-ko
G	社名石	Name stone
H	鳥居	Torii
I	石畳	Stone paving
J	石燈	Stone lantern
K	高麗犬	Koma-inu
L	石段	Stone stairs
M	広場	Plaza
N	森	Woods

---

palanquin, the *mikoshi,* found support among the population of the great cities and became permanently established, and strengthened the tendency of Edo's populace to use the shrine grounds for pleasant outings. When Western style parks were installed in the Meiji era, the bare ground of the shrines and temple grounds diverted to such use were planted in grass. Today, there are many shrines which sponsor kindergartens on their premises (fig. 28).

Spatial Composition of the Grounds of the Ten Shrines

The following characteristics are common to the Ten Shrines cited above.

The shrines are located on high ground with good views of the surrounding city and amply provided with trees, the grove of the local deity. The *shaden,* main shrine building, faces east or south with an open area before it lined by other shrine buildings. A stone-paved approach, in much the same direction as that faced by the main shrine building, leads from the entrance to the shrine, with the entrance marked by a *torii,* gate, and stone bearing the shrine's name. A side approach with stone steps lies perpendicular to the main approach. Main events such as *kagura,* dance offerings to the deity, are performed in the *kagura-den,* to the left of the main hall, while on the right is the *chozu-sha,* where the worshipper washes hands or otherwise symbolically purifies his body. The *kannushi,* religious official and manager of the shrine, has his office to the right of the main building, and various *massha,* smaller shrines celebrating other gods, are scattered around the grounds behind these buildings. The *ujiko's mikoshi,* or ceremonial palanquin for the god, is kept on the shrine grounds. On both sides of the *sando,* the approach, are stone lanterns and protective talismans of *koma-inu,* or lion dogs, facing each other. Symbolic of our age today, some shrines are used as wedding halls and some rent their open spaces as parking lots during the day (fig. 29).

Activities of the Shrine

The activities of a shrine are in proportion to the number of elements in and complexity of its plan because all of the shrine's facilities come from and are maintained by contributions from the *ujiko* or other worshippers. A shrine can have as many and as rich and diverse facilities as it can attract patrons. The number of events held there throughout the year and the number of stalls at the shrine on festival days are clear barometers of the activity of the shrine.

The more active among the Ten Shrines cover areas of over 13,000 square meters with one fourth of that given over to greenery, ponds, or other natural elements. Also, shrines with over twenty facilities included in the grounds have many worshippers aside from the *ujiko* and attract many people on their festival days.

However, the most important factor for a shrine is the vigor of the *ujiko* council and the positive maintenance of itself as a symbol of a society closely bound to the land.

王子神社　OJI JINJA

所在地：東京都北区王子本町1—1—12

創　建：元享2年（1322）領主の豊島氏が紀州の熊野権現を勧請し、若一王子と称した。それにより王子の地名が起こる。

鎮座地：創建時より現在まで変らず。多摩丘陵の北東端にあり、北及び東の眺望は良い。

境　内：東と北側は崖になっていて、南面する社殿はコンクリート打放しの未完成のままである。鳥居などの諸施設はない。

周　辺：近くを流れる滝野川や、桜で有名な飛鳥山は江戸時代から江戸市民の郊外の行楽地として親しまれ、現在は公園となっている。

例大祭：8月15日。槍祭といい、昔は盛大であったが現在はさびれている。

Address: Oji Hommachi 1-1-12, Kita-ku, Tokyo.
Founding: In 1322 the feudal lord Toyoshima requested the Kumano Gongen of Kishu be moved to Tokyo and called it Jakuichi-Oji. This was the origin of the place name.
Where enshrined: Unchanged from its founding to present; it is located on the northeast edge of the Tama hills with good views to north and east.
Grounds: Bluffs on north and east, the main shrine building is oriented to the south and is of poured concrete and as yet unfinished. It does not have the usual *torii* and other accessories.
Big festival: The yari matsuri, or spear festival, of August 15 was very popular many years ago, but its popularity has recently waned some.
Surroundings: Now a park, it was a favorite spot for suburban outings for citizens of old Edo, with the Takino River and Asuka Mountain famous for its cherry blossoms nearby.

① 江戸時代末期の絵図。　　④ 平日。
② 周辺の現状。　　　　　　⑤ 現在の地図。
③ 祭日。　　　　　　　　　⑥ 境内配置図。
1. Picture map, end of the Edo period.
2. The same area today.
3. A festival day.
4. A usual day.
5. Current map.
6. Plan of the grounds.

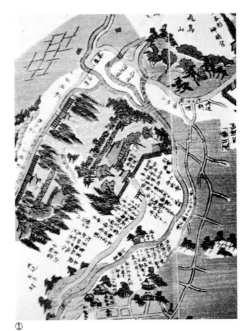

①

②

③

④

⑤

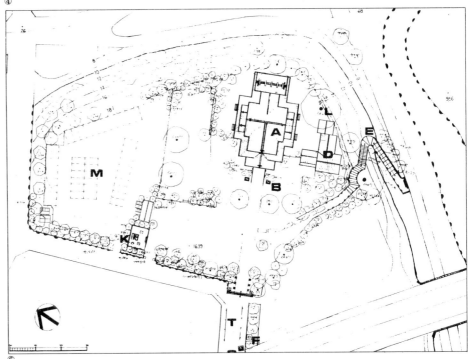

⑥

白山神社 HAKUSAN JINJA

所在地：東京都文京区白山5—31—26

創　建：天暦2年（948）加賀の白山神社を本郷元町に勧請した.

鎮座地：元和2年（1616）巣鴨原に移され，明暦元年（1655）丘陵地南端の現在地に落ちつく.

境　内：南面する社殿は明治期にできたものであるが，南に伸びる参道よりも東へ曲がる参道の方が活性化している. 広場は平日に駐車場となり，社殿背後には児童公園がある.

周　辺：江戸期には郊外にあたり，大名の下屋敷や寺院が多かったが，現在も学校，寺院などが多い. 近くの白山の交叉点は商店街となっている.

例大祭：9月21日. 当日は地元の氏子のみで盛大さはない.

Address: Hakusan 5-31-26, Bunkyo-ku, Tokyo.

Founding: The Hakusan Shrine of Kaga was moved to Hongo Motomachi in 948.

Where enshrined: First built in 1616 on the Sugamo Plain, it was finally settled in 1655 at the southern edge of a range of hills.

Grounds: The main shrine, built in the Meiji period, faces south but the approach winding to the east is more popular than the approach from the south. The plaza is used for a parking lot on work days, and there is a children's park behind the shrine building.

Surroundings: A suburb in the Edo period, it was full of the retreats of feudal lords and temples, and today many schools and temples are found there. The nearby Hakusan intersection is a commercial center.

Big festival: A quiet festival is held on September 21, attended only by the local *ujiko*.

① 江戸時代末期の絵図.
② 周辺の現状.
③ 祭日.
④ 平日.
⑤ 現在の地図.
⑥ 境内配置図.

1. Picture map, end of the Edo period.
2. The same area today.
3. A festival day.
4. A usual day.
5. Current map.
6. Plan of the grounds.

①

②

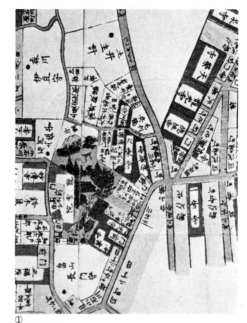

④

③

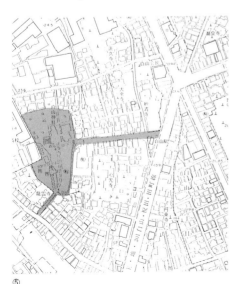

⑤

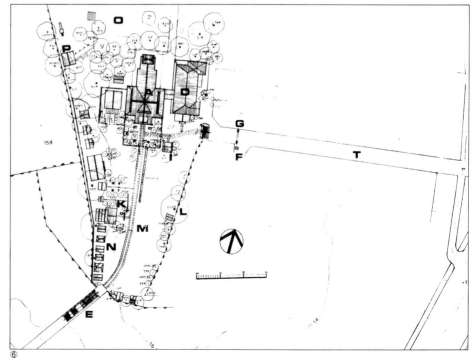

⑥

神田神社　KANDA JINJA

所在地：東京都千代田区外神田２—16—２

創　建：天平２年（730）江戸城近くの芝崎，現在の大手町・将門塚附近.

鎮座地：慶長８年（1603）に駿河台に移され，元和２年（1616）現在地に落ち着いた.

境　内：多摩丘陵の東端にあり，北と東は崖になっている．南々西を向く社殿はコンクリート造で，西側から北側には各種の末社がある．社殿前の広場周辺に，神楽殿，手水舎，楼門などがあり，南の主参道入口には銅製の鳥居が建ち，東の脇参道は石段となっている.

例大祭：天下祭とも言われ，５月15日に日枝神社と隔年ごとに開かれる．江戸の３大祭に数えられ，当日は数10万の人出がある．町会神輿は180基もあり盛大である.

Address: Soto Kanda 2-16-2, Chiyoda-ku, Tokyo.

Founding: The shrine was founded in 730 near the later Edo castle at Shibazaki, the present Ohtemachi area of Tokyo, near Masakado Hill.

Where enshrined: It was moved in 1603 to Surugadai and then in 1616 to its present location.

Grounds: Located at the eastern edge of the Tama Hills, there are sharp hills to the north and east. The *shaden* is of concrete and faces south-southwest; there are various *massha,* other smaller shrines, along its west and north sides. Around the open space in front of the shrine are a *kagura-den, chozu-sha,* cistern, and *romon* or two-storied gate. At the entrance to the main approach are a copper *torii* and the side approach includes stone steps.

Big festival: On May 15, the Tenka Matsuri festival is held in alternate years with the Hie Shrine. Considered one of the three Great Festivals of Tokyo, over 100,000 people turn out for it. The impressive *mikoshi* weighs 180 kilograms (392 pounds).

① 江戸時代末期の絵図.
② 周辺の現状.
③ 祭日.
④ 平日.
⑤ 現在の地図.
⑥ 境内配置図.
⑦ 七五三の宮詣り.
⑧ 社務所.
⑨→⑫ 神田祭.
⑧⑨⑪の写真：廣田治雄.

1. Picture map, end of the Edo period.
2. The same area today.
3. A festival day.
4. A usual day.
5. Current map.
6. Plan of the grounds.
7. 7-5-3 Festival.
8. Office of the shrine.
9-12. Kanda Festival.

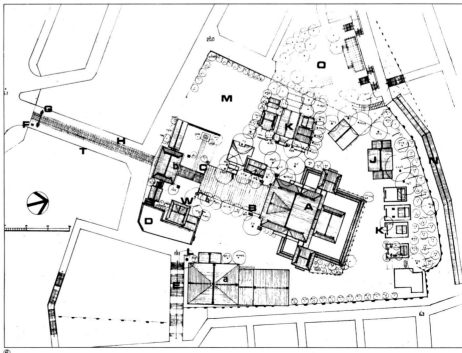

⑦

⑧

⑨

⑩

⑪

⑫

根津神社　NEZU JINJA

所在地：東京都文京区根津1—28—9

創　建：文明年間（15世紀末）領主，太田道灌が社殿
を奉建した.

鎮座地：宝永3年（1706）徳川綱吉が嗣子の生地であ
る現在地に移建した.

境　内：低地に南南東を向いて社殿が建つ. 社殿，中
門，楼門などは江戸時代のもので重要文化財になって
いる. 社殿の西側は崖になっていてツツジが沢山植え
られ，開花時にはツツジ祭が開かれる. 斜面途中には
乙女稲荷社があり信奉者も多く，社殿裏は児童公園に
なっている.

周　辺：神社のある低地は町人住区であるが，高台は
大名屋敷であり，現在大学がある.

例大祭：9月21日. 古い神輿も残っていて，現在も盛
況である.

Address: Nezu 1-28-9, Bunkyo-ku, Tokyo.

Founding: The *shaden,* or shrine building
was built in the latter fifteenth century by
feudal lord Ota Dokan.

Where enshrined: In 1706 moved by Tokugawa
Tsunayoshi to its present location, where the
child who was to be his successor was born.

Grounds: The *shaden* is built on low ground
facing south-southeast. The *shaden,* middle
gate and two-storied gate are of Edo vintage
and now are Important Cultural Properties.
On the west side of the *shaden* is a hill covered
with azaleas which are feted in May when they
bloom. In the middle of the slope is the Otome
Inari shrine with many patrons of its own and
behind the *shaden* is a childrens' park.

Surroundings: The lowland occupied by the
shrine is in a residential area for townspeople;
the highland nearby was a feudal lord's residence and is now the site of Tokyo University.

Big Festival: On September 21, the old *mikoshi*
is paraded through the *cho* district.

① 江戸時代末期の絵図.　　④ 平日.
② 周辺の現状.　　　　　　⑤ 現在の地図.
③ 祭日.　　　　　　　　　⑥ 境内配置図.

1. Picture map, end of the Edo period.
2. The same area today.
3. A festival day.
4. A usual day.
5. Current map.
6. Plan of the grounds.

②

①

③

④

⑤

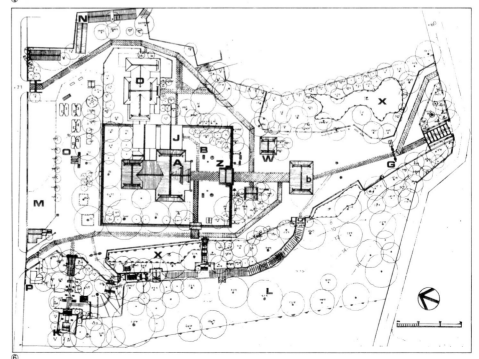

⑥

亀戸天神社
KAMEIDO TENJINSHA

所在地：東京都江東区亀戸3－6－1

創　建：寛文2年（1662）幕府によって開拓された本所地区の鎮守社としてできた．

鎮座地：創建時から変らないが，埋立て地なので地盤は海面下約1メートルである．

境　内：平地で，社殿から参道までほぼ一直線状に並んでいるが，境内の大部分を占める池と藤棚と太鼓橋が有名である．社殿はコンクリート造である．また境内には各種末社や石碑が並んでいる．周囲に公園が少く貴重な休息地となっている．

例大祭：8月25日．沢山の参拝客が集まり盛況である．ここは学問の神として受験生に多大の崇敬を寄せられている．

Address: Kameido 3-6-1, Koto-ku, Tokyo.
Founding: Built by the feudal government in 1662 in its present location as a tutelary shrine.
Where enshrined: Unchanged since its founding but as it stands on reclaimed land, the footings are about one meter below sea level.
Grounds: As it is on flat land, the approach is nearly a straight line to the *shaden,* and most of the site is taken by the famous pond, wisteria trellis and taiko-bashi, or drum bridge. The *shaden* is concrete surrounded by a full complement of shrine buildings and stone monuments. With little other greenery in the neighborhood, the Shrine offers a valuable bit of breathing space.
Big festival: August 25 is the day for many patrons to gather and celebrate. Kameido Tenjin is also known as a shrine of study and attracts many students seeking success in examinations.

① 江戸時代末期の絵図.　　④ 平日.
② 周辺の現状.　　　　　　⑤ 現在の地図.
③ 祭日.　　　　　　　　　⑥ 境内配置図.

1. Picture map, end of the Edo period.
2. The same area today.
3. A festival day.
4. A usual day.
5. Current map.
6. Plan of the grounds.

①

②

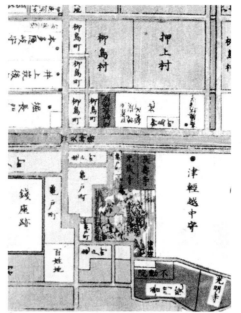

④

③

⑤

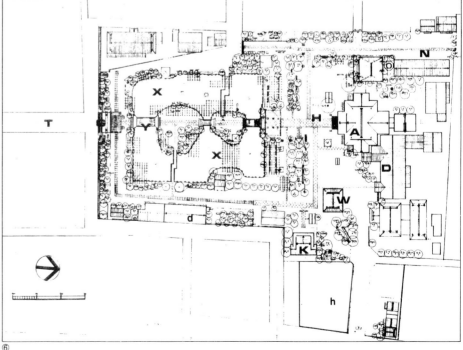

⑥

115

富岡八幡宮
TOMIOKA HACHIMANGU

所在地：東京都江東区富岡1—20—3

創　建：この地域は深川と呼ばれるが，寛永4年（1627）砂州状であった当地一帯を埋め立て永代島をつくり，そこの鎮守社として建てられた．

鎮座地：創建地のまま現在に至る．

境　内：社殿は近年の再建で，ほぼ南面して建ち，参道は一直線状に伸びて途中に手水舎があり入口には石鳥居が建つ．境内全体は樹木におおわれていて，社殿の東・西に各種の末社が並んでいる．西側に深川公園があるが，江戸時代の永代寺跡であり同一の敷地であった．

周　辺：江戸市民の行楽地として繁盛し，現在もその名残りがある．

例大祭：8月15日．3年に一度本祭があるが，その時には数十万人の人出を記録する．この祭も江戸3大祭の一つとされる．

Address: Tomioka 1-20-3, Koto-ku, Tokyo.
Founding: The shrine was built to the deity of Eitai Island, created entirely of reclaimed land, in the sandy waters of the Fukagawa River in 1627.
Where enshrined: Unchanged on its original site.
Grounds: The *shaden* has recently been rebuilt, facing south with the *sando* leading from it in a straight line; a *chozu-sha* or cistern is located along the approach with a stone *torii* at the entrance. The grounds are sheltered by abundant trees and to the east and west are a number of *massha*. Fukagawa Park is to the west on the site of the Edo-period Eitai-ji Temple.
Surroundings: Popular as a place for outings in the Edo-period, it retains the same air today.
Big festival: A large festival is held once every three years on August 15, attracting several hundred thousand people. This festival is also one of Tokyo's three Great Festivals.

① 江戸時代末期の絵図． 　　④ 平日．
② 周辺の現状． 　　　　　　⑤ 現在の地図．
③ 祭日． 　　　　　　　　　⑥ 境内配置図．

1. Picture map, end of the Edo period.
2. The same area today.
3. A festival day.
4. A usual day.
5. Current map.
6. Plan of the grounds.

①

④

②

③

⑤

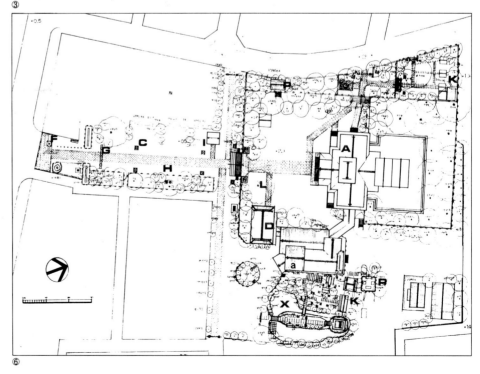

⑥

116

日枝神社　HIE JINJA

所在地：東京都千代田区永田町2—10—5

創　建：文明10年（1478）領主，太田道灌が当時の江戸城内に奉建した．

鎮座地：明暦3年（1657），江戸の大部分を焼失した大火災以後，江戸城の外堀に面する高台に遷座され，現在に至る．

境　内：樹木に覆われた高台の真中に再建された社殿が建つ．正面参道は石段であり屈曲して江戸城へ伸びているが，周辺は官舎が多く活気がない．脇参道は赤坂の繁華街に連絡しているので，現在は主参道にとってかわった．

例大祭：6月15日．天下祭といわれ神田神社と交互に本祭が開かれる．氏子区域は広く，江戸城から，日本橋，銀座の繁華街をも含む．

Address: Nagata-cho 2-10-5, Chiyoda-ku, Tokyo.

Founding: Built in 1478 by Ota Dokan within what was then Edo Castle.

Where enshrined: The shrine was built on high land opposite the Outer Moat of Edo Castle in 1657 after the great fire which destroyed much of Edo.

Grounds: The *shaden* has been rebuilt in the center of the sheltering grove of trees. The formal approach is of stone steps winding toward Edo Castle, but there are many official residences in the vicinity and the area is not active. The side approach connects with a busy Akasaka street and currently functions as the main approach.

Big festival: The Tenka Matsuri is held on June 15 in conjunction with the Kanda Shrine festival. The *ujiko* district is large, reaching from Edo Castle to Nihonbashi and including the busy Ginza area.

① 江戸時代末期の絵図.　　　④ 平日.
② 周辺の現状.　　　　　　　⑤ 現在の地図.
③ 祭日.　　　　　　　　　　⑥ 境内配置図.

1. Picture map, end of the Edo period.
2. The same area today.
3. A festival day.
4. A usual day.
5. Current map.
6. Plan of the grounds.

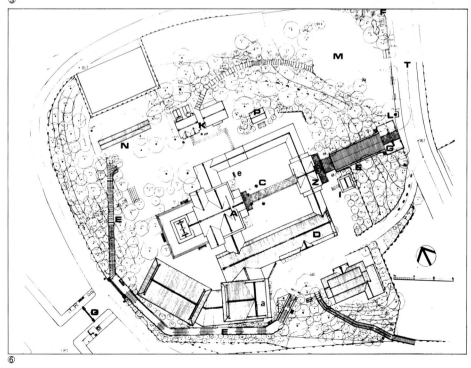

③

⑤

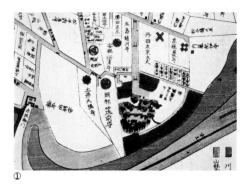

⑥

117

氷川神社　HIKAWA JINJA

所在地：東京都港区赤坂6—10—12

創　建：天暦5年（951）赤坂一ッ木に創紀する．

鎮座地：享保15年（1731）八代将軍吉宗によって赤坂
今井台の現在地に移される．

境　内：樹木に覆われた静かな境内で，南東に面する
権現造り様式の社殿は江戸時代のもので重要文化財に
なっている．主参道よりも北東に伸びる脇参道には石
段もあり活性化している．東側には児童公園もあり周
辺住民の憩いの場となっている．周辺は江戸時代から
閑静な屋敷町である．

例大祭：9月15日．氏子のみで盛況さはないが，地域
に密着した親しさを感じさせる．

Address: Akasaka 6-10-12, Minato-ku, Tokyo.
Founding: Established at Hitotsugi in Akasaka
in 951.
Where enshrined: The shrine was moved in
1731 by the eighth Shogun Tokugawa
Yoshimune to its current location at Imaidai
in Akasaka.
Grounds: The grounds are covered with trees
and very quiet. The *shaden,* facing southeast,
is in the *gongen* style from the Edo period and
is now an Important Cultural Property. The
side approach to the northeast has stone steps
and is more often used than the formal approach. A childrens' park on the east side is
a restful spot for the residents of the neighborhood. It has been a quiet residential area
since the Edo period.
Big festival: On September 15 is a festival held
only for the *ujiko,* but the feeling is one of
great intimacy with the neighborhood.

① 江戸時代末期の絵図．　④ 平日．
② 周辺の現状．　　　　　⑤ 現在の地図．
③ 祭日．　　　　　　　　⑥ 境内配置図．
1. Picture map, end of the Edo period.
2. The same area today.
3. A festival day.
4. A usual day.
5. Current map.
6. Plan of the grounds.

①

②

③

④

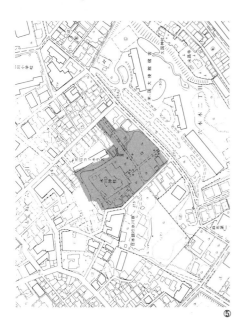

⑤

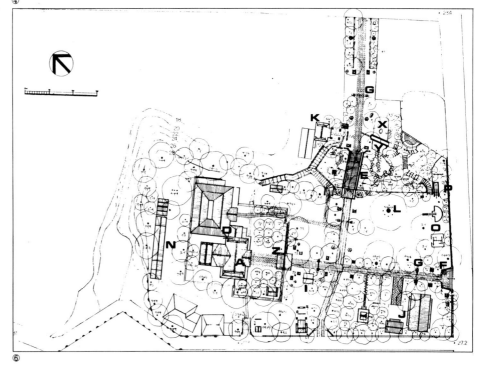

⑥

芝大神宮
SHIBA DAIJINGU

所在地：東京都港区芝大門1—12—7

創　建：寛弘2年(1005)，現在の芝公園の丸山である飯倉山に創建された.

鎮座地：創建地が徳川家の菩提寺である増上寺境内となったために，350年程前の慶長年間に現在地に移された.

境　内：平地であり，江戸時代は広い敷地を有したが現在は非常に狭くなっている. 近年，狭い敷地に人工台地をつくり敷地を2倍にして，上部に社殿を建て下部を駐車場にしている. 参道は門前町が発達して現代的商店街となっているが，祭時には境内的に使われる.

例大祭：9月16日. 昔はダラダラ祭といい何日間も続いて盛況であったが，現在は昔日の面影はない.

Address: Shibadaimon 1-12-7, Minato-ku, Tokyo.

Founding: Established in 1005 on Iikurayama, the Maruyama hill of the current Shiba Park.

Where enshrined: Originally built within the grounds of the Zojo-ji Temple, guardian temple of the Tokugawa family, the shrine was moved to its current site 350 years ago in the Keicho period.

Grounds: The site is flat and in the Edo period was quite generous though now it has become rather small. In recent years a man-made upper level has been added to the narrow site, with the *shaden* on the upper level and a parking lot on the lower. The approach is from *Monzen-machi* and today is a modern commercial street, although at festival times it is used as part of the shrine grounds.

Big festival: On September 16 is the Daradara Festival which at one time lasted for several days and was rather boisterous; today it has lost that quality.

① 江戸時代末期の絵図.　　④ 平日.
② 周辺の現状.　　　　　　⑤ 現在の地図.
③ 祭日.　　　　　　　　　⑥ 境内配置図.

1. Picture map, end of the Edo period.
2. The same area today.
3. A festival day.
4. A usual day.
5. Current map.
6. Plan of the grounds.

①

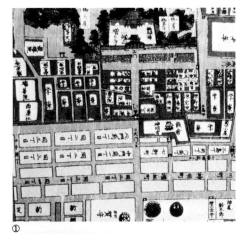

②

③

④

⑤

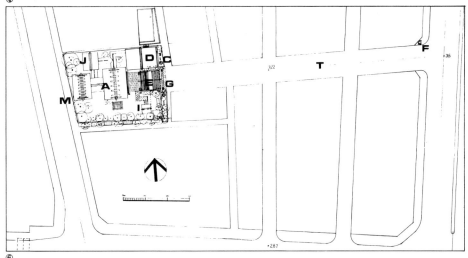

⑥

119

品川神社
SHINAGAWA JINJA

所在地：東京都品川区北品川3—7—15

創　建：700年程前の鎌倉期に品川の鎮守として，州崎大明神または品川大明神と称されていた．

鎮座地：創建時から今日まで，東京湾を見渡せる丘の上にある．江戸時代は天王社と呼ばれていた．

境　内：楕円形の丘の上に東面して再建された社殿が建つ．急勾配の石段が主参道であり，高麗犬や石鳥居は江戸時代のものである．江戸時代に流行した富士山信仰による影響でつくられた浅間神社と小型の富士山等が今も残る．また，児童公園もあり近隣住民に親しまれている．末社の稲荷社も崇敬厚い．

例大祭：6月7日に近い日曜日．三代将軍家光が寄進した神輿が残り，小規模な氏子区域ながら祭日は大盛況である．

Address: Shinagawa 3-7-15, Shinagawa-ku, Tokyo.

Founding: Seven hundred years ago in the Kamakura period this shrine was established for the deity of the Shinagawa River and called Suzaki Daimyojin, or the Shinagawa Daimyojin.

Where enshrined: It has occupied a hill overlooking Tokyo Bay from the Kamakura age to the present. In the Edo period it was called the Tenno-Shrine.

Grounds: The rebuilt *shaden* faces east on top of an oval hill. The approach consists of steep stone stairs, with *koma-inu* lions and a stone *torii* from the Edo period. The Sengen Shrine with its miniature Mt. Fuji, inspired by the Mt. Fuji worship of the Edo period, still remain. There is a children's parks much beloved by neighborhood people. The Inari shrine located there is also well kept.

Big festival: Although the *ujiko* district is small, a well-attended festival is held on a Sunday close to June 7, using a *mikoshi* from the time of the third Shogun Iemitsu.

① 江戸時代末期の絵図．
② 周辺の現状．
③ 祭日．
④ 平日．
⑤ 現在の地図．
⑥ 境内配置図．

1. Picture map, end of the Edo period.
2. The same area today.
3. A festival day.
4. A usual day.
5. Current map.
6. Plan of the grounds.

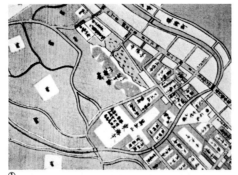

①

②

③

④

⑤

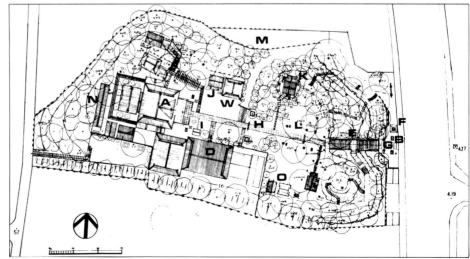

⑥

120

JAPAN—— A PROFILE IN TRANSITION

by Donn E. Stone Jr.

日本にみる変化の様相

ドン・E・ストーン

国民性といわれるものほど，いともたやすく一般通念を裏切るものはない．しかし明らかに独特な性格を示す国があれば，自らそうした国民性を探ろうとする試みは，格別興味をそそるものであり，つきせぬおもしろさがあるものである．日本が，まさにそうした国のひとつである．とはいえ，暗がりで手さぐりをするようなもので，研究には特殊な手法を駆使し，自己の限界を悟るまで続けることが必要である．膨大な情報を前にしたら，細かいことには，目をつぶらなければならない．もし何か特別なことを見つけ出すのが目的ならば，いきなり核心をねらうのではなく，周辺部分から調べてゆくほうが良い．そうすれば全体像が少しずつ，頭の中にできあがってくるだろう．直接見極めようとすれば混乱を招くにすぎない．それはちょうど夜の闇の中で何かを見ようとするようなもので，見当はずれのところに目を凝らすことになりがちである．このことを心に留めて，以下では，時代の異なる二人の人物を通して，物語形式で話

を進めることにより，日本建築を造り使ってきた人々の生活様式に光を当ててみたい．この物語は，神社，民家，町家といった特殊な建築を，それらを生み出した生活の中で採りあげている．

変化に満ちた200年を隔てているにもかかわらず，18世紀の人物である高田郁男と現代人である高田哲也とは，驚くほど共通点が多い．しかし，郁男は彼の階級を代表する典型的日本人とみなして歴史的に一般化してかまわないが，哲也についてはそれができない．哲也は，過渡期の人々の代表であって，彼自身の中で結晶化が進んで，また別の形になっていってしまうからである．日本の本質ともいうべき特徴が，日本建築の中に表現されているのと同様，この過程の中にこそ，大変興味深いものが秘められている．

神社

春の夜道を歩く若い商人高田郁男は，伊勢の大神宮に向う巡礼の途上にあった．彼のいでたち

は，何百という同行の人々と変わるところなく，白の装束に身を包み，笠をかぶり，わらじをはき，杖をついていた．翌日彼は，神宮の前の群衆の中で，神に感謝を捧げ，家族のこれからの幸運を祈った．

ちょうど200年後のこの同じ街道を，こんどは列車に揺られて，もうひとりの高田である哲也が（彼はサラリーマンである），伊勢へ向う現代の巡礼者たちの中にいた．現代では短時間になったものの，昔も今も，旅は心楽しく気ままな気分になれる良い口実であることに変わりない．今朝家を後にしてきた彼らは，徳川時代の高田同様，日々の仕事や抑制から解き放たれて，おいしい料理を口にし，気の合った仲間と冗談を言い合ったりして，にぎやかな雰囲気を楽しんでいる．様々な制約や責任を負わされている彼らにとって，旅行に出かける時間をやりくりするのは決してやさしいことではない．かの伊勢神宮への参拝という口実をもってしても，例外ではない．多くの場合，このような機会は

Nothing defies generalization quite so readily or so properly as the identification of a national personality. But there is a distinct temptation to attempt just such an undertaking when a country appears to provide physical evidence of a unique character and an undying interest in discovering it for themselves. Japan is just such a place. But like trying to see in the dark, the search requires special techniques and the realization of inherent limitations. Detail must be forgotten in the interest of a broad spectrum of information. If some value in particular is the object of study, it is better to play around its edges with investigations and gradually a complete understanding will appear in the mind. Looking at it directly only confuses the issue, much like looking directly at something in night shadows which can only be seen when the eye is consciously focused away from it. With this in mind through the combined personalities of two men from different eras, the following is offered in the form of a narrative as an insight into the lifestyles of the people who produce and use Japanese architecture. Their stories deal with

the life which gives rise to specific architecture – 'jinja', 'minka' and 'machiya'.[1]

Despite two hundred years of enormous change, Takada Ikuo from the late 18th century and Takada Tetsuya a man of modern Japan, have surprisingly much in common. Ikuo, however, may be considered as an historical generalization and as such a prototypical Japanese of his class, Tetsuya on the other hand cannot. He is a representative of a population in transition and as such carries forward within himself the potential for either crystallization or dissipation into another form. The outcome of this process, as the essential Japanese character expresses itself through its architecture, is what holds so much interest.

Jinja

Takada Ikuo a young tradesman walked along a late evening road in spring, a pilgrim on his way to Ise to visit the great Shinto shrine. He was hardly special as there were others with him in his own happy group and they had passed or walked with hundreds more like themselves dressed in white cotton, wide brimmed hat, walking stick and straw

thongs. Tomorrow, he would be standing among the crowd before the shrine to offer thanks and to help ensure continued good fortune for his family in the coming year.

Just 200 years later along this same highway, but now a bed for steel rails, another Takada, Tetsuya (one of the legion of *sarariman*[2]), sat in a railway coach filled with modern pilgrims headed for Ise. The journey was much shorter in modern times, but still just as good an excuse for good humor and self-indulgence as ever. He and his friends had left their homes in the morning and, like his counterpart from the Tokugawa period, had been enjoying a festive atmosphere of good food, friendly company and the lively banter of conversation relieved of day to day business and considered control. Trips were too precious a time to burden them with obligations and responsibilities, and the opportunity and excuse offered by a trip to Ise, the pre-eminent Shinto shrine, was no exception. Too often this chance came only once in a lifetime, even in modern Japan, and so the story must be made of fertile stuff which can grow in importance through

②

③

一生に一度であったし，現代においてもそのくらいのものである．だからこの話も，こうして重ねて語ることによって重要な意味をおびてくるし，内容も豊かなものとなるに違いない．

ふたりとも，夜は伊勢の町に泊まったのだが，よく眠れなかった上に，思いをめぐらすこともできなかった．さらに，彼らは同じ宿に泊まったかもしれない．同じような料理と飲み物を口に運び，同じパターンの音楽や踊りを楽しんだ．また大神宮のような歴史的遺産のまわりでは，あたかも時が釘付けになっているかのようだ．実際に同じでなかったにしても，少なくとも，宿では同様にもてなされ，客たちもそれを望んだであろう．このように巡礼をして楽しむということは決して不遜な行為ではなく，結局のところそれは，そこを訪れる人々の群れによって支えられた生活に，日本人が共に参加するという，あらゆる儀式のうちのひとつなのである．

どんな文化であっても，他の文化をもつ人々に宗教的な体験を伝えることは難しいが，日本の場合は殊に難しい．神道という宗教は，素朴な自然宗教であると同時に，政治と関わりをもち，大神宮（神社神道）とともに想起されるが，日本で最も古くかつ日本独自の宗教体系である．多数の神と伝説が語り継がれているがそこに理論は無い．自然との関連で説明するのがよいだろう．朽ちかけたようなとほうもない桜の老木が，大枝をひろげて花を咲かせていたり，長い乾いた山道の脇にありがたい湧水があると，これらを祀る．日本列島は急峻な山脈と深く彫り込まれた渓谷とから成り，川は海にたどり着く前にわずかな平野を流れる．富士山をはじめ多くの火山が地平線を遮り，これらの山々が生成

された過程を偲ばせる．季節は時を違わずに巡り，しばしば地震にみまわれ，さらにたびたび激しい台風に襲われる．気候の幅が広く，厳しい寒さと豪雪から熱帯のような暑さと湿潤な天候まである．自然の力が土地と人々を形づくってきた．こうした事実を認識することが神道なのである．

最近まで農民だった郁男にとって，自然とのこのような素朴な関連は，彼の宗教的欲求を満たしてあまりあるものであった．しかし伊勢はそれ以上の意味をもっていた．伊勢は天皇と大和民族の始祖である神を祀る．天皇と大和民族が自然界において占めているのと同様な特殊な地位を占めるとされるのが「神社」である．社を訪れ，そこで売っている神聖なお守りを身につけていれば，太陽神天照大神の加護のもとに一家は幸運をもたらされる．天照大神の子孫である天皇は，他の神道の神々の代表として介在し，地方の森や野や道を治めている．神社神道は，日本に仏教が紹介された頃に生まれた．精緻な理論と文字に記された歴史をもつ仏教は，大衆の信仰を集める素朴な神道と，バランスよく混淆されることになった．建築を通して形式を整えたことが，力と影響力を得るのに役立ち，理論的表現の欠除を乗り越えて，仏教を対等のパートナーとして迎えることができた．伊勢およびいくつかの大神社を除けば，神社と寺は，同じ空間を仲良く分け持つことにさえなった．

郁男が巡礼の途に就いた頃は，神社神道は純粋に象徴的な位置にあり，この間，江戸幕府により説き伏せられた天皇は京にあって，名ばかりの権威の体現者に納まっていた．しかし時が経ち，政治の流れが変わり，実質ではないにせ

よ，名目上は明治天皇のもとに権力が戻ってきた．そこで，近年の歴史では神社・神道の重要性が再び高まるわけである．天皇の実権の一翼として，また国家統一の焦点としての伊勢の地位は高まり，神道は日本の国家主義と一致をみることになった．再び政治状況が変化したのは，第二次大戦後，哲也が生まれる少し前であった．そして彼がこの同じ道を歩いている今日，神社は日本の過去によって歪曲されることなく歴史的遺産を継承してゆくための試金石となっている．

哲也はお守りを含めてこの旅行の土産品を買い求めるだろうが，現代人である彼が，このような人工物に宗教的ご利益（りやく）があると信じているわけではない．彼はこれらを家に持ち帰って，家族や友人に分け与える．こうすることによって，彼らは哲也の体験を共同のものとするのである．彼に宗教心が欠けていたとしても，日本人全体の中の一員であるという意識を持っていないはずはない．日本文化は，完全なる参加を要求する文化である．だから彼はいつでも，関わり合う人間たちとの関係を確め，社会における自分の位置を明確にしておかなければならない．こうした絶えざる認識過程を通して，日本文化は支えられ，進められてきたのである．個個人の体験が絶え間ない相互作用を通して，集団としての人格を高め，個人が関与しているいわば出来事に対し，より大きな目的を与える．従って日本人においては，行動様式が重要であり，ものごとへの執着は，参加することによって示されるのである．哲也の場合も，伊勢などの神社への旅行は，集団意識が正当とみなしたことを行っているのである．彼の国がどんな方

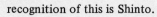

① 銀座に映る現代日本.
② 伊勢神宮外宮.
③ 巡礼姿.
④ 伊勢踊り（広重より）.
⑤ 自然と信仰, 日本海.
⑥ お地蔵さんとお供え物.
⑦ 日光の祭りで「鳥笛」を売る男.

1. Modern Japan in reflection on the Ginza.
2. Ise-Geku Shrine.
3. Pilgrims on the road.
4. Ise-Ondo dancers, from Hiroshige.
5. Man's comment on nature, Japan Sea.
6. Little gods and their offerings.
7. "Bird whistle" man at Nikko.

the re-telling.

Both men stopped for the night in the town of Ise, but neighter slept much nor planned to. They may even have stayed at the same inn, enjoyed much the same kind of food and drink, and listened and watched the same patterns of music and dance that around such historical treasures as great shrines, are locked away from the normal advance of time. If not actually the same, they were, at least, touted as such by the innkeepers and wished to be by the visitors. It was no irreverence to enjoy yourself on these pilgrimages, after all it is a celebration of all that is Japanese to participate in the life which is supported by the crowds who visit there.

The religious experience of any culture is difficult to translate to others and Japan's particularly so. The religion of Shinto, either as a simple nature worship, or with political implications and associated with the great shrines (jinja-Shinto), is the oldest and purest Japanese belief system. Although perpetuating a multiplicity of gods and legends, it does not contain a theology. It is better described as a relationship or association with nature which celebrates the extraordinary — the nearly rotten hulk of a cherry tree bearing one good limb and a cluster of blossoms, or a welcome mountain spring that lies by the side of a long, dry trail. The Japanese archipelago bears steep forested mountain ranges cut deep with racing valleys which flow onto brief plains before being halted by the sea. Mt. Fuji and other volcanoes dominate the horizon, reminders of the processes that made these mountains. The country has a regular progression of seasons, interrupted often with earthquakes, and is frequently host to violent typhoons. The climate ranges from bitter cold and heavy snowfall, to tropically hot and humid conditions. Nature's forces shape the land and people. The

recognition of this is Shinto.

For Ikuo, so recently a farmer, this simple relationship with nature more than satisfied his religious requirements. But Ise meant more than that. Ise celebrated the divine origin of the Emperor and Japan. The jinja recognized the special position that the Emperor and Japan hold in the natural order of things. Visiting the shrines and acquiring the sacred amulets sold there brought good fortune to your house from the sun goddess, Amateraus-ōmi-kami, and her descendant, the Emperor, who intervened on your behalf with the pantheon of lesser Shinto gods that rules the local forests, fields and roads. Jinja-Shinto was born about the time of the introduction of Buddhism in Japan. It arose to balance the marriage of the elaborate theology and written tradition of Buddhism with the less erudite and more primitive Shinto beliefs held by the population. Formalization through architecture lent power and gravity and jinja-Shinto overcame its lack of theological expression, allowing it to welcome Buddhism as an equal partner. With the exception of Ise and the other great shrines, this later even led to an intimate sharing of the same spaces.

At the moment Ikuo made his pilgrimage, jinja-Shinto held a purely symbolic position, since the Emperor in Kyoto during this time was only the titular embodiment of an authority which he had been persuaded to offer to the Tokugawa shogun government in Edo (Tokyo). As time passes, however, politics change and with power later returned nominally, if not actually, to the Emperor Meiji, so in more recent history there was a resurgence in the importance of jinja-Shinto. Ise's position as an arm of the real authority of the Emperor and as a focus for national unity was enhanced and Shinto was identified with Japanese nationalism. The political

situation changed again just before Tetsuya was born after World War II and as he walks along these same paths, the shrine has become just a touchstone to a heritage which succeeds undistorted from Japan's past.

Tetsuya will collect amulets and other gifts from his trip here too, but as a modern man he questions the religious efficacy of these artifacts. Instead he will bear these home to distribute among his family and friends so they may share in his experiences. If he may be lacking in religious fervor, he does not lack in his need to be a part of all that is Japanese, for it is a culture which demands complete participation. Everyday he must re-establish relationships with others that he has contact with and redefine his position in society. It is through this constant identification process that the Japanese culture is supported and promoted by its members. The experiences of each member enhances the collective personality through constant interaction and gives greater purpose to the kind of event an individual participates in. Consequently to be Japanese, a form or pattern of behaviour achieves importance and adherence is indicated by participation. Tetsuya's undertaking of a trip to Ise or another shrine represents his understanding of what the collective consciousness considers as appropriate. Whatever direction his country may take, he is sure that it will remain Japanese as long as he and others like him continue to strengthen the connection to their origins.

Ikuo and Tetsuya, both purified by the sacrifices of the journey, stand together but separate in time, performing a last ritual cleansing on the bank of the Isuzu river where they wash their hands and rinse their mouths in the clear water. Walking the pale gravel pathway through deep groves of towering cedars, ancient beyond comprehension, the dramatic

⑧

⑨

⑩

⑪

⑫

向に向おうと，彼と彼同様の人々が，自らの起源との結びつきを保っている限りは，彼らはやはり日本人なのである．

郁男も哲也も，旅行によって清められ，時を違えてはいるが同じ場所に立ち，五十鈴川の澄んだ水で手を洗い口をすすいで，最後の清めを済ませる．杉の大木が鬱蒼と繁る白い砂利道を歩いて行くと，理解を超えた古代が顔を出し，神社の劇的な様相が時の流れを止めてしまう．霧のかかった森の中を進むにつれて，彼らの他にも，何百万もの足が，ワラジばき，ゲタばき，そして靴をはいた足が，ザクザクと音をたてる．二つの囲みがあって，一方は空地の中央に小さな小屋がある．もう一方には高床の倉のような建物が建っているが，まるで群衆と森の圧力をはね返すかのように高い柵が巡り，本殿は屋根の線だけが見えている．群衆がゆっくりと前進して入口が近づくにつれて，周囲の厳粛さに圧倒されて，にぎやかなおしゃべりも鎮まってくる．気がついてみれば，群衆も前の方は疎になり，二人は小さな社を両脇に控えた本殿の前に立っている．郁男は白装束をまとい，哲也は色の濃い背広に身を包んでいる．彼らは頭を下げ，柏手を打って神の注意を喚起してから，人生が続く限り，見守ってくれるようにと祈りの言葉を静かに唱え，次の人たちと入れ替わる．

民家

二人にとってこの旅は，友だちと一緒に伊勢を旅行するというだけで終るものではなかった．彼らが職を求めて都会へ出る時に後に残してきた人々に会うという目的もあった．友人たちに別れを告げて，故郷へ向う道を進んだ．郁男は，数年ぶりに会う旧友たちを想い浮べながら，徒歩で歩き通した．農家の三男だった彼は，そこで養い得る人数が限られていたため，生家を離れて働き口を見つけなければならないことを，早くから知っていた．運の良いことに，彼は寺子屋で算術の素質を示したので，地方の商人のもとへ奉公に出され，そこで帳面のつけ方と商いの世界の基礎を身につけた．彼の生きている時代は，商業が盛んだった．徐々に崩壊しつつあった幕府を支えるために租税がどんどん重くなっていったにもかかわらず，生活の質は向上し，そのためだれもが今まで以上に多くの品物を求めるようになっていた．郁男は商いの世界の一員となったことを喜ばしく感じており，財産をもらえなかったことをうらみに思うようなことはなかった．それが定められた運命であり，それが彼にできる精一杯のことだった．

彼は最後の峠を越え，故郷の村を眼下に見降ろした．子供の頃住んでいた家の急勾配の茅葺屋根は，去年の秋の穫り入れ後にできた稲の山に似ていた．昔はよく山芋を掘りにここまで登ってきては，振り返って村を見たものだったが，静まりかえった村は神秘的にさえ見えた．時は春で，野は鋤き返され，肥料が施されていた．季節の移り変わりを受けとめてすくすくと育った稲の苗が，あちこちに明るい緑の斑点となって見えていた．2，3週間のうちに，ていねいに引き抜かれ束ねられた苗で田が一杯になり，村人たちが皆田に集まってお祭り騒ぎが始まるだろう．すねまで泥水に浸かった若い女たちが一列に並び，他の村人たちの歌に合わせて，リズミカルに苗を植えながら前進してゆく．どんな農耕社会でもそうであるように，農期の始まりの頃には若さと繁殖力とが重要視される．そしてこれからの数ヶ月というものは，雑草を取り，田の水を保ち，稲を病虫害から守り，稔れば雀を寄せつけないように心を配るなど，目まぐるしく立ち働かなければならない．稲作は最も重要な産業であり，村で産する他のあらゆる作物や労働を合わせたものに匹敵した．租税も小作料も米で納めることになっており，実際，あらゆるものの価値が米を基準に決められていた．にもかかわらず，彼の家族もまた友人たちも，どんぶり一杯の米の飯にすらありつけなかった．彼らの人生は，米を中心にしてその回りを巡っているようなものだった．郁男にしても，給金として実際に米を手にすることはめったになく，自分の収入を米に換算しなければならなかった．将軍や大名，武士はその富を米の石高で計算していたから，当然のことながら，それにそむくことはできなかった．

河床に向かって山を降りると，景色が，音が，臭いが，かろうじて残っている記憶を呼び覚ます．神も仏も一緒に祀られている境内への別れ道を過ぎると，彼の生家がある．三層の丈高い主屋はがっしりしている．明らかに，彼の家族はうまく行っているようで，屋根の葺替えくらいはできそうだ．よく見れば，そろそろ大がかりな葺替えが必要なようで，2，3日のうちに村の衆の手を借りて作業が始まることだろう．そっと扉を開け，敷居を越えて汚れた床に足を踏み込むやいなや大声で叫ぶ彼を迎えたのは，家の一方の端でガサゴソとエサを喰う家畜の音と臭い，そしてもう一方の側にある台所で立ち働く母と兄嫁の笑顔だった．母たちは簡単な挨拶をすませると，彼の旅仕度を解かせ，一段高

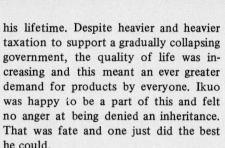

⑧ 七五三の宮詣りを写真に撮る父親.
⑨ 伊勢神宮内宮の五十鈴川.
⑩ 杉木立の中の参道，伊勢神宮外宮.
⑪ 合掌造りの民家，高山.
⑫ 民家のある谷，白川郷.
⑬ 伊雑宮の御田植祭，三重県．写真：田内寛人.
⑭ 民家の屋根にも似た，稲を干すための柵.
⑮ 民家内部.
⑯ いろりのある民家内部．写真：廣田治雄.

8. Father recording participation in the 7-5-3 festival.
9. Isuzu Riverbank where ritual purification takes place at Ise-Naiku.
10. Fog shrouded paths and giant cedars of Ise-Geku.
11. Traditional *gassho-zukuri minka*, Hida Village, Gifu Prefecture.
12. Minka farm valley.
13. Rice planting festival. Spring rice planting was a community event.
14. Traditional rice curing racks with a modern gurdian.
15. *Minka* interior with a cooking stove.
16. *Minka* interior with a fire pit.

presentation of the shrine stills time. The sounds of millions of feet, straw sandal, *geta*[3], or shoe clad, crunch beside them as they enter a misty clearing. Two enclosures, one empty but for a tiny hut at its center, the other filled with towering storehouse-like buildings, their rooflines just showing above the high outer fences, hold back the pressure of crowds and forest. Slowly the masses move forward, the gay chatter silenced by the majestic scale of the surroundings as they near the entrance. The crowd thins in front and the two men find themselves standing before the main hall of the shrine flanked by two smaller buildings. With bowed heads, Ikuo, dressed in ancient garb, and Tetsuya, in his dark business suit, clap their hands to draw the god's attention, quietly recite their prayers, then with one last good look that would have to last a lifetime, they turn away and others take their places.

Minka

For both men this was more than just a trip to Ise with friends, it was also to be a visit home to the families they had left when they each moved to the city in search of work. They bid goodbye to their friends and took to the different highways which would lead them home. Ikuo headed off on foot, alone with his thoughts of youth and old friends which he would see again for the first time in several years. He was the third son in his family and as such knew long ago that he would need to seek his livelihood away from the family farm and holdings which could support only a limited number. Fortunately, Ikuo had shown an aptitude in school for calculations and had apprenticed to a local tradesman in the area where he had learned to do bookkeeping and had grasped the fundamentals of the business world. Commerce was to be on the rise during

his lifetime. Despite heavier and heavier taxation to support a gradually collapsing government, the quality of life was increasing and this meant an ever greater demand for products by everyone. Ikuo was happy to be a part of this and felt no anger at being denied an inheritance. That was fate and one just did the best he could.

As he turned the corner on the final mountain pass he could see his old village below him. The steep thatch roofs of the homes of his childhood looked exactly like the drying racks of rice after harvest in the late fall. He used to come up here at that time to dig for mountain potatoes and looking back at the village then, it looked brooding and mysterious. It was spring now though, and the fields were being turned and prepared with fertilizer. Here and there were light green patches of newly sprouted rice seedlings growing rapidly in the excitement of the weather change. In a few weeks the fields would be flooded, seedlings carefully uprooted, bundled together, and then the whole village in a grand festival would gather in the paddy fields. Young women would stand in a row, shin deep in muddy water and begin to move forward in a line, rhythmically planting the rice seedlings to the chants of the other villagers. As in all agricultural communities, youth and fertility were the main themes here at the beginning of the farmer's year. For the next several months it would be a difficult time of weeding, maintaining water levels and protecting the rice plants from plagues of insects which later gave way to marauding bands of birds. But this was the most important production, for even with all the other crops and piece work done in the village, taxes were collected in rice, rent was paid in rice, in fact all values were determined in rice. Although his family and friends may never see a bowl of cooked rice, it was the hub about which their lives

turned. Even Ikuo who seldom actually received rice as payment in his work, had to recompute his own income against this commodity. The *shogun, daimyo,* (lords), and *samurai* calculated their wealth in rice so naturally it was beyond his ability to disapprove.

As he wound his way down the mountainside to the valley floor, the sights and sounds and smells brought back memories he hardly knew he still held. Before him past the turn off to the village's combination shrine and Buddhist temple lay his family's compound. The tall three story main house looked well kept. Obviously his family was doing well enough to repair the roof with new thatch. Soon, however, it looked like a complete re-roofing would be necessary and then the whole village would arrive to do the job in 2–3 days. He slid the door over carefully and stepping over the sill to the dirt floor inside, he called out and was greeted by the sounds and smells of the family livestock noisily chewing off to one side and a smilling welcome from his mother and his brother's wife who were working in the kitchen at the other side of the house. They quickly greeted him, helped him out of his travelling gear, and then led him to the raised wooden platform that was the floor of the living area. He shed his sandals, stepped up onto the highly polished wood and sat on a straw mat offered by his mother near the fire. He had sat around this square opening many times as he had grown up. As always the fire smouldered, slowly burning the ends off a couple of long branches shoved closer together as they dissolved into coals. He leaned back to watch the blue smoke as it worked its way through the heavy wood drying rack suspended on thick straw ropes above the pit, until it disappeared in the bamboo lattice of the floor above. This was the most memorable part of the house for him.

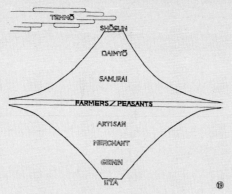

⑰ 布をさらす.
⑱ 茶摘み.
⑲ 徳川時代の階級構造（ブルーノ・タウトをもとに描く）.
⑳ 開発の波の中でかろうじて残っている民家.
㉑ 昔ながらの田植え風景.
㉒ 骨の折れる穫り入れ.
㉓ 稲を切り，集め，束ねる機械.
㉔ 袋詰めされた米.

くなった居間に彼を招き入れた．彼はわらじを脱いで，磨き上げられた板の間に上がり，いろりのそばにいる母が勧めるわら座布団の上に座った．彼はおとなになるまでに何度もその四角いいろりのまわりに座ったものだった．いろりにはいつも火がくすぶっていて，束ねた2本の枝の端をゆっくりと燃やして灰に変えていった．彼は上を向いて青白い煙を見た．煙はいろりの上の火棚（木を格子状に組んで太いわら縄で吊ったもので，いろりからの火の粉を除け，また物を乾燥させるのにも利用された）を抜けて，上階の竹簀の子のすき間に消えていった．彼にとっては，ここが一番なつかしい場所だった．冬の間は，家族も客人も皆このいろりのまわりに集まり，食事をしたり冗談を言い合ったり，勉強したり，手仕事をしたりしたものだった．陽気がよくなっても火は消されることなく，その煙が家の中を漂って，虫害を最小限にくい止め，室内の梁を，田畑で働く日に焼けた農夫の腕や顔のように，黒く色づけるのだった．

彼の父は，耕地の運営を郁男の長兄に委せて隠居していたが，野良にも老人で十分にできる仕事があった．その他にも，わらを綯い，親たちが仕事に出ている間幼い孫たちの面倒をみるなど，仕事はいくらでもあった．郁男の兄たちや妻たち，その子供たちは皆一緒に住んでいた．妹が嫁に行くまではやはりこの家に居たが，今はよその村から来たいとこが，彼女に替わって彼女の仕事をしている．男3人，女4人の成人と5人の子供たちが一緒に住み，皆が何らかの形で仕事を分け合っているが，父はいまだその豊かな経験によって皆の尊敬を集め，現在の地位は責任が軽くなったというものの，彼はむしろ気楽さを楽しんでいるようである．

母もまた，家事の実権を徐々に長男の嫁に譲りつつあった．こうした変化はゆっくりと進み，嫁は後継ぎを含む3人の子を生んでもなお，まだ新来者であった．当時の女性の役割は，家の中に限定されており，従って，姑と嫁の苦闘の末勝ち獲った実権を握った主婦が隠退するまでは，何ら特定の地位に就くことができない．家の中の仕事はたくさんあり，毎日が，料理，掃除，裁縫で明け暮れるのだった．子供を産み育てることも女性の務めだった．一家総出で農作業にかかる季節には，女たちも，決まりきった日常の家事の合い間を見つけては農作業を手伝わなければならなかった．

農家の生活は稲作が中心になってはいたが，それは米が主たる収入源であったということであって，彼らが収穫を食するというわけではなかった．彼ら自身の使用に供するものとしては，麦，ソバ，芋，大根，茶，果物，そして衣類をつくるための綿などが作付けされた．時が経つにつれて，こうした米以外の作物が，税のかからない副収入をもたらすことになり，さらに，上階で養蚕を行うようになると，暮しは楽になったとはいえないものの，飢餓にさらされるほどではなくなった．それでも農業だけで生きのびるのは難しく，農閑期の男たちは近くの町へ，日銭の入る賃仕事を求めて出かけていった．しかし今は，こうした問題も忘れて，郁男の胸の中には，親しみのあるおしゃべりと心のこもった郷土料理があるばかりだった．町での生活や伊勢詣りについて話し，家族が語る村のうわさを聴くにつれて，彼は自ずと旧式な生活様式の中に再び滑り込んでゆくような気がしていた．

夜更けて寝床にゆったりと横になった彼は，家族がつつがなく暮していることに満足する一方で，彼自身は外へ出て自分なりの人生を見つけたことに，より以上の幸福を感じていた．そして彼の親族が，伊勢にいた人々と同じほどたくさんこの地に居て健康に逞しく暮している様は，よそで暮す彼に，より一層の安堵を与えるのだった．明日は壁の修繕をするとかで，彼も手伝う約束をしていたが，その翌日にはもう，妻子や仕事の待つ町へ向かうことになっていた．

徳川時代の商人階級は，重要な役割を担っていたのだが，農民や職人よりも下とみなされていた．当時の階級制度は，たとえてみれば富士山を鏡に映したようなもので，裾野を構成する農民たちが，上へ登るほど人口が少なくなる武士，大名，将軍を支え，天皇は空に浮かぶ雲のような存在だった．農民の下の鏡像は，職人から始まり，商人，そして最後は非人（えた）が先端に位置した．このたとえは本質からいえば非現実的であって，階級闘争の中央に位置していた農民は，上からも下からも締めあげられたというのが真相である．一方の側の商人は経済力を振い，もう一方の将軍，大名，武士は政治力を行使した．明治維新がこうした構造を根底から覆し，利益を目的とした新たな通商を背景とする天皇が復権した．様々な土地再生計画により，また米が通貨基準でなくなったことにより，農民の軛は部分的には多少緩くなったものの，農民を支えたのは物質的豊かさではなくて，いまだに精神的なものであった．ひとりひとりの農民に経済観念が欠けているという痛ましい現実により，日本の農業人口は著しく減少した．列車の中で車輪のきしむ音に耳を傾けている哲

17. Women bleaching *kimono* material.
18. Tea harvesting.
19. Tokugawa class structure — after Bruno Taut.
20. *Minka* survival today is acutting question.
21. Some few still plant in traditional manner.
22. The harvest is still backbreaking work.
23. The machine cuts, gathers, and binds the rice into bundles.
24. The final product bagged and ready.

Winter time, the whole family and any visitors would gather about the fire, eating, joking or doing lessons and hand work. During the warmer weather the fire continued to burn, the smoke sifting through the house keeping the insects to a minimum and darkening the exposed beams in the interior to the color of the sunburned arms and faces of the farmers at work in the fields.

His father had retired and given over the running of the farm to Ikuo's oldest brother, but still there was work enough for an old man to do in the fields. Even if it was just remembering a special method for plaiting rope or entertaining young grandchildren while their parents were busy elsewhere. Both of his older brothers and their wives and children lived at home with the parents. While his sister was unmarried she had been home also, but now her place and work was taken up by a cousin from another village. Altogether there were 3 male adults, 4 females and 5 children living at home, all working and supporting each other on the farm. The oldest brother stood for the family in relationships outside of the home now, but the father still commanded great respect for his experience and genuinely relished his new position of lowered responsibility but enhanced freedom.

Ikuo's mother too, was gradually relinquishing her authority over the household functions to her oldest son's wife. This was occurring much more slowly, however, since the daughter-in-law was still a relative newcomer even though having borne 3 children to the family including the next heir. The role of women at the time was limited to the confines of the home and consequently since there was no special rank perogatives awaiting a retired housewife, giving up a position hard won from a mother-in-law to one's daughter-in-law could be agonizing. There was much to

do in the household, far more than just a full day of food preparation, housecleaning and clothes mending or production. There were the children who had to be raised and educated and this responsibility fell to the women. In between routine household tasks, the women had to find time to help out during the important periods of the growing season when all hands were required.

The farmer's life was centered completely about rice cultivation but it was primarily an income crop for them and not destined for their own consumption. Instead other crops were cultivated for the family's personal use, barley, buckwheat, potatoes, giant radishes, tea and fruit for food, and cotton and hemp for clothing. As time went on these crops became a source of extra family income outside of taxes and with families turning over their upper floors to silk production, their lives although far from feasting were no longer at the edge of famine. Even then it was difficult to survive by just farming, and gradually more and more families released their men during slack growing periods for more lucrative part time work in nearby towns. But for now those problems were far away and it was just friendly conversation and hearty country food Ikuo had in mind. He felt himself slide back into the old patterns of his family life, as he related stories of his life in the city and his recent trip to Ise while listening to all the gossip of the village. Later as he was contentedly lying beneath the *futon*[4], he was happy to have found his family prospering, but even more happy to know he had found a life for himself outside. His roots were in the soil here as much as at Ise, and finding them healthy and strong made him feel even more secure in his life elsewhere. Tomorrow, the dike walls needed repairing and he had promised to help, but the next day he would be back on the road for the return to the

city and his family and job.

During the Tokugawa period merchants and tradesmen classes were looked upon as necessary but ranked well below farmers and artisans. In the classical representation, using a mirror image of Mt. Fuji, the farmers formed a wide base of support which carried the load of ever decreasing populations of *samurai, daimyo,* and *shogun* with the *tenno,* emperor, floating cloudlike in the sky. The mirror image of the mountain below the farmers began with artisans, then tradesmen and merchants, and finally the outcaste *(eta)* at the tip of the reflection. This analogy was essentially unrealistic. The only truth to it was that the farmer was in the middle of a power struggle and being crushed by both sides. The merchants on one side who wielded economic power and the *shogun, daimyo,* and *samurai* on the other who controlled the political power. The Meiji Reformation turned this over completely with the reestablishment of the Emperor backed by young, commerce oriented interests. Through various land reform packages and a change from rice as the monetary standard, the lot of the farmer was partially alleviated, but still his support was primarily philosophical. The painful realities of the uneconomical private farm caused a severe depletion in the farm populations in Japan. When Tetsuya arrived amid the wailing steel on steel and synchronous pneumatics of the electric train, he was graphically aware of the problem. What had once been the strong farming community his family belonged was also caught between the emigration from and sale of farmlands and the inexorable encroachment of the megalopolis.

He reached his family's home through a tunnel that had been bored beneath the old mountain pass before he was born. While he was growing up he and his friends would often walk up the now

也には，問題の所在がよくわかっていた．かつて強固であった農村社会に，彼の一族は属していたが，農地を売り払っての移住とメガロポリスによる非情な浸食との間に捕えられていた．

　古い山道の下にトンネルが開削されたのは哲也が生まれる前だったが，そのトンネルを抜けると，故郷だった．子供の頃友だちと一緒に，今は廃道となった道を登りつめて，谷間を見降ろす所に座ったものだった．春にはそこから，父が古びたトラクターを操るのが見えた．その姿が，大事な行事の始まりを意味し，やがて田に水が引き入れられ，泥水とほこりの中で種籾がかきまわされるのだった．家畜はすべて戦争の時に失なわれてしまい，この機械のかけらが，村にとっては誇りであり頼りであった．とはいえこれは中々扱いにくいしろもので，しかもできることに限度があった．植付けはいまだに人手によって行われていたが，子供たちが大きくなるにつれ，学校から帰った彼らが向かうのは山の古道だった．哲也と友だちはそこで，急速に変化する時代の流れを目のあたりにしたのである．まず最初に，古びた共同のトラクターが姿を消し，個々の農家が所有する，もっと扱いやすい機械が登場し，これはより多くの土を鋤き起した．いくつかの水田が，畔をこわして拡大されていった．小さく分割された田よりも大きい方が仕事がしやすくなったためだ．農業に身を入れたくない者が離農し始め，誰か土地を買える者がいれば売ったり，村に住んでも働き口を他に得て土地を貸したりするようになった．まもなく機械化は田起しから田植え，稲刈りにまで進み，農作業がひとりでできるようになった．こうした機械化は一見幸運をもたらすかにみえたが，実は，他の何もかもの費用が，米の値が上がるよりも速く上昇していった．家族の人数が増えると，農業以外の仕事を捜し始めた．こうして夫が地方の工場に勤め，妻が一日中田畑をかけ回り，農繁期の夜や週末に夫が農作業に携るという状況があたりまえになってきた．

　家を継ぐ責任があるとはいえ，哲也には，農業を続けてゆく展望がひらけなかった．近代的な機械が出回っていることでもあるし，年をとったとはいえ彼の両親が農業を続けてゆくことは困難ではない．そうすれば，土とのつながりは保っていることができる．さらに今日の交通機関を利用すれば，農繁期には故郷に帰って手伝うことも容易である．しかし都会での彼の生活は，自然や季節の移り変わりからはかけ離れていた．彼はいつも，農作業を始めようと田に足を踏み込むたびに生き還るような気がするのだった．まるで自分が大地の一部になったように感じた．大地は強さと生命の源であり，いろいろな物が育ってくるのも大地である．しかしまた，この仕事を毎日続けなければならないとしたら，喜びは薄れることも確かだった．都会の生活を味わってしまうと，そこからもまた離れがたいのである．彼はどちらをも欲しており，両者を手にしていると信じていた．

　故郷の家は数代前からさして変わっていない．100年ほど前に火災に遭ったが，村人たちの助力で再建された．今日でもその時から少しも変わっていない．少し傷んでいるように見えるとしたら茅が古くなったせいである．こうしたたたずまいは，両親がここに住んでいること，そして彼らには屋根の修繕ができないことを示していた．この地域には，この種の農家はもう他に残っていなかった．いくつかは火災で焼けて，代りに何の変哲もない建物が建てられた．一棟は野外博物館に移築され，残るいくつかは住人が転出してしまって崩れるにまかされていた．汲み取り式の便所がまだ使われていたが，もはや糞尿を肥料として使うこともなく，定期的にやってくるバキュームカーにより汚水処理場へ運ばれていた．現代風の飾りといっては何もなかった．電線が庭の外のコンクリート製の電柱と家とをつなぎ，料理用のガスがひかれ，給湯・暖房設備が施されていた．テレビのアンテナが屋根にまたがり，井戸をやめて水道を引いたのは，哲也が高校生の頃だった．室内についていえば，家の片側にある二間続きの部屋に両親が起居しており，障子をたてれば部屋を仕切ることができた．家全体を使うのは，正月や盆に一族が集まった時だけである．そんな時は，さながらお祭り騒ぎのようで，子供たちがかけ回ったり，いろりに火をくべたりするのだった．そうした機会も次第に少なくなっている．彼や彼の弟妹たちが社会的に責任のある年令に達するにつれて，皆が時を同じくして帰ることが難しくなってきているのだ．この地方の高校を出ても農業で身を立ててゆくことができないと悟っていた母は，子供たちに大学の入学試験を受けることを強く勧めた．妹は彼の弟の大学時代の友人と結婚して，南の地方に住んでいる．愛情をもって子供たちを育ててきた母の望みが，一家を離れ離れにする方向に働いたことは，何とも皮肉な話である．

　3人の子供たちに茶を入れている時の母の顔は幸福そうに見えた．そして父はそれにも増して満足気だったが，哲也はまもなくその理由が

25. *Minka* holding against the housing pressure.
26. Evidence of modern accessories stick up everywhere.
27. Disappearing farmland against an approaching backdrop of industry.
28. Housing development outside the city with individual homes.
29. New townhouse outside Tokyo.
30. *Unagi-no-nedoko machiya.*
㉕ ハウジングの波に押される民家.
㉖ 屋根にまたがるアンテナ.
㉗ 工業の進出によって消えてゆく農地.
㉘ 開発の波. 写真：廣田治雄.
㉙ 東京近郊の新興住宅地.
㉚ 「ウナギの寝床」式町家.

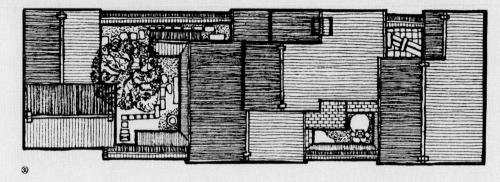

㉚

abandoned old road to the top and sit down at the last turn and look out over their valley. From there in the spring, they could watch their fathers drag out the old rusty hand tractor which was started with great ceremony and led to the fields where it slopped along churning the paddies into a black confusion of soil and water and smoke. All the farm animals had been lost in the war and this piece of machinery was the pride and joy of the community even though its nature was cantankerous and its abilities limited. The planting still had to be done by hand then, but as the children grew older and chose the ancient mountain road as their way to and from school each day, Tetsuya and his friends saw dramatic changes. First came the retirement of the old community tractor and its replacement with newer, more even tempered machines owned by individual families that did more than just stir up the mud. Some rice paddies began to grow as dikes were broken down to make it easier to work one large field instead of several small ones. Less dedicated farming families began to leave when others were able to buy up their land or they simply leased it to others while they worked elsewhere but lived in the community. Soon the machines did everything from field preparation to planting and harvesting and with only one man or woman at the handles. This should have brought about good things, but instead the costs of everything else went up much faster than the price received for rice. In increasing numbers family members began seeking extra work outside of farming. It wasn't unusual for a husband to be employed in a local factory while his wife ran the farm during the day and then find himself in the fields on weekends and evenings throughout the growing season.

Although due to inherit the family property, Tetsuya could see there was

no future for him on the farm. Besides, with the modern equipment, even as his parents grew older they could easily continue farming the land and he would always have that important connection to the soil. Moreover, with today's transportation it was easy for him to return home and help out during planting and harvesting and thereby share in the production. But his life in the city was far away from the pattern of seasons and nature, and he always felt a rejuvenation when he took his first step down into the paddy to begin work. It was almost as if he became a part of the earth which was the source of strength and life for the things that grew there. He was quite sure, however, that if he had to do it everyday the enjoyment would disappear, and after having tasted the city he was equally sure he could never leave it. He wanted both and believed he had them.

The family compound and house had not changed much over several generations. It had burned once about a hundred years earlier, but been rebuilt then with the help of the village. Today it looked the same, a little worn perhaps, the thatch was old and it was obvious that only his parents were living there and could not keep up with the repairs. His home was the last of its kind left in the area. Several had burned and been replaced by less impressive structures. One had been dismantled and re-erected in an open air museum, and some had simply deteriorated after their owners moved out. The dry toilet was still in use, its contents no longer used for fertilizer on the farm, but pumped out regularly by a tank truck and carried to a central sewage plant. There were a few indications of modern accessories. Electric wires now connected the house to a concrete pole outside the yard and there was gas for cooking, hot water and space heating. A T.V. antennae stood astride the ridge of the roof and Tetsuya

was a high school student when they no longer had to pull water from the well but had it piped to a faucet in the kitchen. Inside, his parents were living out of a couple of rooms at one side of the house which they could close off with screens. The only time the entire house was used anymore was when the whole family was together for special holidays. Then it was like one big festival with everyone there, children running about, and the fire pit glowing once again with a hot fire. Those special moments were becoming fewer and fewer as responsibilities made it more difficult for he and his brother and sister to return at the same time. Their mother had realized that they could not succeed living on the farm and although they had gone to a local high school, she had pushed the boys hard so they could take exams to continue at the university. His sister was married to a friend of his brother's from college and lived in southern Japan. It was curious that the ambition of his mother growing out of love for her children helped to push family apart.

But he could see on her face how happy she was to see him as she began to make tea for the three of them. His father seemed rather more content with himself than usual and soon Tetsuya understood why. His father and several other landowners had decided to group their holdings together and sell it to a corporation which was planning to build a housing development. The pressure for living space had begun to reach even this far. Almost half of all the farm land in the valley was soon to be covered by rows and rows of homes. A new station was to be built and a shopping area surrounding it with a chain department store belonging to the railroad. Best of all for him, each of the farmers whose land was a part of the transaction would receive as partial payment a new house

③ 雨に降られる旅人. 東海道五十三次（広重）より.
② 商家の暖簾, 高山.
③ 奥に障子のある商店. 写真：廣田治雄.
④ 商家の並ぶ街路.

31. Travelers caught in a rainshower, from *53 Stages of the Tokaido* by Hiroshige.
32. *Noren* on shop in Takayama, Gifu Pref.
33. Shop interior with *shoji* in background.
34. Old street scene.

解った. 父を含む何人かの地主たちが土地を持ち寄って，住宅開発を計画している会社に売ることになっていたのだ. 宅地開発の動きはこんな遠くにまで及んでいたのである. 農地の半分近くが，遠からず住宅の波に埋まるだろう. 新しい駅が建設されることになっており，その周囲には商店街ができ，鉄道会社系列のデパートが進出することにもなろう. 父にとって都合の良いことは，土地を提供した農家のそれぞれが，代金として自分の土地に新しい家を建ててもらえることだった. そこで，彼の父母は古い家から，新しくてモダンな小さな家へ移ることになるだろう. 隠退するに十分な金はあるし，作物を育てるに十分な土地もまだ残っている. 加えて彼らは，日本のどこへでも旅行できる. いやおそらく海外までも行けるだろう. これは願ってもないチャンスだ. 父が了解している限りでは，良くない点などひとつも無い. 新たに開墾される土地はいつもやせているものだ. 地味を豊かにし，最高の生産性を達成するまでには何年もかかる. しかも，2000年にわたる成果をコンクリートで覆ってしまうという決断は，なみたいていのものではない. 彼らは確かに生きてはいたが，絶えず逆境と誘惑にさらされていた. 作物からの収入はわずかな一方，生きのびるだけにしか役立たない政府の補助金は，かえって彼らの立場を救いようのないものにしていた. 友人も隣人も，彼らのまわりの誰もが，繁栄を満喫していたので，今や放縦にならないように戒めなければならなかった. 自己犠牲の時代は過ぎ去り，代わって，目に見える消費に対する細かな要求が生まれてきた.

哲也はこうしたことを聴かされても驚きはし

なかった. 彼は発展の中での自分の役割を認識していた. 都会にあっては毎日，ラッシュアワーの間自分を締めつけ，仕事ですりつぶす圧力を感じていた. 時が経つにつれて状況が変わるのは避けられないとしても，彼にしてみれば，重要なことの一部に関わることができれば，それで十分だった. そこには他にもまだ働き口はあったし，人はどこかには住まなければならない. 彼だって自分の家を捜しまわるだろう. 都会を離れて郊外に移るとしても，その結果は，片道一時間半に及ぶ通勤ということになる. 彼の場合，両親とともに家を建てて，大きな家に2世帯で住むこともできた. しかしそのような決断は，妻とよく相談してから下した方がよいだろう. いずれにせよ，ここ2，3日は楽しい日が続く. 夜明けとともに起きて，田舎の清浄な空気の中で一日を過ごす. しかも彼をかき立てる都会の騒音や緊張から逃れることができる. ほんの束の間，我を忘れて，土に生きる男のなつかしいリズムの中に，自分の場をみつけることができるのだった.

町家

郁男が，雨の浸みた借り物の蓑と笠を着けて町をとぼとぼ歩いていると，春の雨は一足ごとに激しさを増した.「家は良いなあ」，隣の家の見なれた戸口の前を通り過ぎる時，彼はそう考えた. 彼の家のあたりは，道の両側に間口の狭い商家が並んでいた. 通りに面した店舗の奥が住まいになっており，敷地の形状がひどく細長いことから「ウナギの寝床」と呼ばれる. 郁男が初めて町へやって来た時は茶の問屋に奉公したが，その後小さいながらも自分の店を持った.

今彼は，紺木綿に自分の店の名を白く染め抜いた暖簾を誇らしく見上げるのだった. 暖簾をそっと押し分けて中に入り，濡れた蓑と笠をはずした. 悪天候で客足が少なく商いが忙しくなかったのは，かえってありがたかった. 旅装を解きながら家人を呼ぶと，店と住まいを仕切っている障子を開けて妻が出てきた. 彼女がおじきをすると，背負われた幼な児も彼女と一緒になってかがんだ. 彼女は手早く，夫が濡れた着物を脱ぐのを手伝い，彼が留守中の商いのことをたずねている間も，夫の気分が安らぐように心を配るのだった. 彼がいない間もすべてうまくいっていた. 商売は繁盛している，妻の弟が住み込んで見習いに来ていたが，ちょうど今は配達に出ているところだった.

彼らの生活の中心は店で，そこには茶箱がたくさん並び，知り合いや客に試飲させるために湯の沸いているやかんがあった. 通りから店へは気軽に出入りできたし，逆に天気の良い日には茶箱やイスを外に出しておくこともあった. 彼は，うどん屋と，この地区のとりまとめ役の座を競り合っていたが，郁男は，近隣での地位もあり，いろいろと引き受けていつも快く世話を買ってでていた. 実際，どの店も，程度の差はあれ，このように親しく助け合っていた. 独立独行的な農家とは対照的に，町家の台所には食物を貯蔵しておく場所がほとんど無く，もちろん冷蔵庫も無いので，主婦は食事の仕度の前には毎日のように買物に出なければならなかった. このように絶えずやりとりがあったから，ものごとを取りもつ役目がどうしても重要になり，互いによく通じ合った結束の固い共同体へとまとまっていた.

on their own land. So his father and mother would be moving out of the old and into a more modern and smaller home. There would be money enough for him to retire and still land enough to grow some crops. In addition, his parents would be able to travel and see other parts of Japan and perhaps even the world. It was a great opportunity, but not without its bad side as even his father realized.

A new field is always a poor field. It takes many years of work and fertilizing to bring soil to its most productive level, and it is not an easy decision to cover up the results of two thousand years with a layer of concrete. They were surviving, it was true, but in the face of adversity and temptation. Inflation ate away at their budget, while poor crop prices and increasing government subsidies just for survival made their position unimprovable. All around them their friends and neighbors enjoyed so many luxuries that it was now an embarrassment not to be at least a little self-indulgent. The time for self-sacrifice had passed and in its place had grown a subtle demand for visible consumption.

Tetsuya was not surprised by this announcement, he recognized his own part in its development. Everyday he felt the pressure in the city as it squeezed his during rush hour and wore him down on the job. It was inevitable that situations change with the times and if he could hold on to a part of what was important then that was enough. There were other fields still there to be worked and people have to live somewhere, he could even look at one of the houses for himself. Perhaps it was time they moved out of the city and into the country, after all it was only an hour and a half commute. He could even build with his parents and move into one large house for both families. But that decision, he had better discuss with his wife.

Anyway, the next few days would be enjoyable. Up with the dawn and spend the day out working in the clean country aire without the noise and tension of the city egging him on. Here for a few moments he could forget himself, and just find a place in the old familiar rhythm of men working with the soil.

Machiya

Ikuo plodded along through the town, his rainsoaked borrowed farmer's straw hat and raincoat had been getting heavier with every step in this spring shower. "It is good to be home," he thought, as he passed the familiar doors of his neighbors. His house and the others formed a short commercial street with narrow shops on both sides facing one another. Behind the storefronts were their individual homes extending long and narrow away from the street, sometimes called *unagi-no-nedoko*[5]. When Ikuo had first come to the city he had worked for a tea broker but now owned a small retail shop of his own. He could see with pride the dark colored *noren*[6] hanging in front with the name of his shop emblazoned in white upon it. He lifted it carefully as he quickly ducked inside, relieved that his wet travels were over. Thanks to the poor weather, business was slow and there were no customers. He called out while shaking himself loose of his protective gear and his wife slid aside the screen partition between the shop and their living room. She bowed low in welcome, their tiny son strapped to her back bowing along with her. Then quickly she came forward to help him out of his wet clothes, quietly setting his mind at ease while he pried her with questions about the business. Everything had gone well during his absence. They had been busy and her brother who was learning the trade while living with them was out just now on a delivery.

The center of their life and home was their shop with its displays of boxes and purring kettle of hot water for brewing sample cups for friends and customers. The street slipped into the shop just as easily as the tea boxes and stools merrily spilled into the street on nice days. He was in a pleasant sort of competition with the noodle shop as conversation headquarters for their area and Ikuo welcomed the constant socializing as an indication of his acceptance and position in the neighborhood. In fact, all of the stores to some degree enjoyed this same friendly atmosphere. In contrast to the more self-reliant situation of the farmer, city kitchens held little storage space and no refrigeration, so housewives had to make several daily trips around mealtime to purchase food and supplies from shopkeepers. This constant interaction soon became as important as the procurement of the items themselves and served to tie the community together into a close-knit well informed group.

The family's private life went on behind the *shoji*[7] that formed the back wall of the shop. During busy periods and nice weather these remained open and the customer was presented with a scene of family life out of which the proprietor sprang to offer service. When the weather was cold or the family was eating, the *shoji* were closed, but the customer's entrance was equally as quickly recognized by the noisy appearance of a friendly face. The tradesman's survival was dependent upon his quality of service both for the attraction of clients and his acceptance in the Tokugawa society which considered him at best necessary but non-productive. It was difficult in terms of these pressures, consequently, to see the division between public and private, as Ikuo was so taken up in the merchant life. When compared to the difficulties and impossibilities he could

㉟ マンション.
㊱ 通勤風景. 写真:廣田治雄.
㊲ 古いものは急速に廃れてゆく.
㊳ 洋服を着た若い娘と, 和服姿の祖母.
㊴ 新宿の高層ビル.
㊵ モダンな設備の整った台所.

家庭生活は店の奥の障子の向こう側で繰りひろげられた. 忙しい時や気候の良い時期には障子を開け放ったままだから, 一家の日常が客にまる見えだったし, 客が来るとすぐに奥から主人がとび出してきた. 食事時や寒い季節には障子をたてるが, そうした場合でも客人の来訪は物音ですぐにわかり, 親しげな顔が現われる.

商人が生き残れるかどうかは, 客を引きつけるためのサービスと, 徳川の世に受け入れられるかどうかにかかっている. 生産的ではないにせよそれが一番だ, と彼は考えていた.

従って, 郁男も商人となったからには, こうした状況の中で公私の区別をつけることは困難だった. 農民であれば耐え忍ばなければならなかった困難と比べても, 絶えず増え続ける現金収入, 町での刺激ある生活, 彼自身にも家族にも機会が得られるかもしれない変化のある社会, こうした利点を数え挙げれば, 彼の遭遇しているわずかな問題点を補ってあまりあるものであった. 現在の社会的地位とは裏腹に, 時代のなりゆきは彼ら商人を勇気づける方向にあった. 人々は増々品物やサービスを求め, その結果, 経済力は政治上の立場とは全く一致しなくなっていた.

郁男は少しも力を貯えているとは感じていなかったが, 息子が大きくなった時には, 世の中は彼が巣立ってきた社会とは違っているだろうことは想像できた. 祭りや休日, 季節ごとの客の嗜好も, 彼とその家族にとっては, 先祖を思い出させてくれるものにすぎなくなるだろう. 彼らの生活は増々変わってゆくだろうが, どんなに変わったとしても, 本質的には日本人の固有性を失なうまでには至らないだろう.

何百年後を歩む哲也は, タクシーの扉をポンと開けると, 排気ガスのやや甘い臭いに迎えられた. こうした日常の出来事が日本特有のものであることは, 彼にもわかっていた. 彼のマンションまでの道すがら, 気まぐれで向こう見ずな競争に身を委ねている間に, 彼の生活のペースは加速され, 旅に出る前に脱ぎ捨てていった責任をもう一度身にまとうのだった. 明日はいつもの生活に戻る. 早起きして, 45分間の通勤ラッシュにもまれ, 長く感じる一日の仕事と夕方の会議を終えて, 家にたどり着くと時刻はもう遅い. ある商社の若手課長である彼は, 人生との関わり始めにおいては, 彼の先祖で最初に農業に見切りをつけた者とそう変わるところがなかった. この点までは, 彼らの人生は本質的に同じ伝統に根差しているが, 今の哲也の暮らしは劇的なまでに異なる源泉から抽き出されたものであった. 郁男の状態は, ゆっくりと発展してきたものであり, 仕事は鎖国政策のもとでの圧力に左右されるものだった. しかし徳川幕府による支配が終ると同時に, 日本列島の港は世界に向かって開かれた. 他国との交渉の初期には, 外から入ってくる異国の考え方を注意深く翻訳し練り直すものだが, 日本の場合はむしろ, 人人は, 実践的にも思想的にも経験したことのない発展過程からの産物や考え方にさらされたのである. このように困難にぶつかってガラガラと音をたてているその音が, 電話の向こうで話しかける上役に向かってペコペコおじぎする時の哲也の胸に, 2台のディーゼルの化物が, 歩行者を木造住宅の壁に押しつけて, 狭い道でほえ合っている場面で, 鳴り響いていた.

哲也の住む街の建築やマンションは, 日本の伝統に根差した形態と, 他の文化から選び出された外来の形とを融合させることがいかに難しいかを示している. 街のスカイラインを区切るものは, 鉄とアルミニウムでできた耐震構造の感嘆符で, それは覇気のない, 似たような耐火建築のごたまぜの上にそびえている. かと思うと, コンクリートの谷間を縫ってわけ入った建物と建物の間に, 昔の神社や庭園の入口にあったような古い鳥居や門がひょっこり姿を現わしたりする. 彼の住まいのあるジグラットのようなビルのエレベータを出て, 自分の住戸にたどり着くと, コンクリートと鉄と高度な技術を日本風に使いこなした風変りな空間が待っている. 戸口から中に入ると靴を脱いでスリッパにはきかえ, コンクリートをカーペットやプラスチックで覆った床の上を歩きまわる. 食堂のテーブルに着くと, 日本人向きの大きさに造られた西洋風のイスに座る. 小さな子供たちがはしゃいで彼にまつわり着き, 色々な質問を浴びせたり, カバンの中をあさったりしている. その間妻は, モダンな電気器具やガス器具できらめくばかりに装われた台所で, 茶を入れるための湯を沸かしている. 哲也は子供たちをじらして, カバンを隠すふりをしてすばやくテレビの前のソファにすべり込んだ. そこで遂に, 子供たちはめいめいに紙風船と幸運のお守りというささやかなおみやげを獲得した. まもなくして, 皆がおしゃべりや茶やおみやげに満足した頃, 子供たちはベッドにもぐり込み, 扉が閉ざされ, 明かりが消された. けれども, 汚れのない白壁や艶のある家具が, バルコニーのガラス戸を通して入ってくる都会の夜の明かりを反射するので, 哲也も妻も寝室へ向かうのに支障を感じなかった.

132

35. In modern Tokyo a pile of *manshons*.
36. Crowds of commuters.
37. The old ways are rapidly being discarded.
38. The modern and the traditional, a young girl and her grandmother on the streets of Tokyo.
39. Modern Japan on the rise, Shinjuku.
40. A modern kitchen filled with appliances.

expect as a farmer, the advantages of the ever increasing monetary rewards, the excitement of life in the city and the diversity of opportunities for himself and his family more than compensated for the few problems he encountered. Despite their present social condition, he and other merchants watched with increasing excitement the general change in attitude toward them, as others became more dependent on their goods and services and their resulting economic power demanded a respect incongruent with their political standing.

Ikuo had no sense of coming power, but he did realize that the world his son grew up in would be different from the one he had left. The festivals, holidays and seasonal appetites of his customers would be only calendar reminders for himself and his family of their origins. Their lives had taken a road which would carry them further and further away, but never far enough to break the essential continuity each one felt with their Japanese identity.

Several hundred years later as Tetsuya stepped forward, a cab door popping open and welcoming him through the gray sweet odor of diesel fumes, even he could recognize a particular style that made this commonplace event peculiarly Japanese. Resigning himself to the fitful headlong race through the streets to his city *manshon*[8], the pace of his life began to accelerate, returning him to the responsibilities he had left behind before his trip. Tomorrow, he would be back in the system again with its early wake up, 45 minute commute, long day at work, evening meetings and late return home. The degree of committment to his life as a young junior executive in a trading firm was not much changed from that of his ancestor who first broke the bonds of farming life. Whereas up to this point their lives were grounded in essentially the same traditions, Tetsuya's

now drew sustenance from a dramatically alien source. Ikuo's condition had slowly evolved, determined by pressures at work within guarded beaches. But coincident with the end of the Tokugawa rule, the harbors of insular Japan were thrown open to the world. Rather than the carefully translated and tempered foreign ideas from the outside that had been the mark of early communication with other countries, suddenly the population was showered with ideas and products in the development of which they did not share either practically or ideologically. The crash of this confrontation continues to echo in situations from the humor of Tetsuya's rhythmic bows of respect to his superior while speaking to him over the telephone, to the dangerous passage of two diesel behemoths roaring by one another on a narrow street with pedestrians flattened against wooden house walls.

The architecture of Tetsuya's city and *manshon* graphically displays the uneasy marriage of traditional Japanese configurations and the outworld forms selected from other cultures. The skyline of the city is punctuated by earthquake proof steel and aluminum exclamation points towering above the busy jumble of less ambitious but equally fire proof structures while the twisting concrete that hunts between the buildings finds an old *torii* or gateway leading into an ancient shrine or garden. As Tetsuya steps out the elevator door of the ziggurat like pile that contains his residence, and through his personal entrance, he is greeted by alien patterns translated into Japanese concrete, steel and high technology. Inside the doorway, he removes his shoes and puts on slippers to walk across carpet or plastic covered concrete floors where he sits in Japanese sized western chairs at a dining table. His small children clamor about him, besieging him with all sorts of questions and digging

through his bags while his wife stands watching from the kitchen surrounded by a panoply of gleaming modern gam and electric labor saving devices while urging a kettle of water to boil for *ocha*.[9] Teasing them he pretends to hide his packages while quickly shuffling to the sofa in front of the T.V. where finally each child is dramatically offered little gifts of paper balloons to blow up and Ise good luck charms to wear. As soon as everyone has their fill of stories, tea, and presents, the children are tucked into beds, their door swung shut and the rooms darkened. The clean white walls and shining fixtures of the rooms, however, reflect enough light from the city's night life pulsing through the glass balcony doors for Tetsuya and his wife to see the way to their bedroom.

His wife slides a screen aside, quickly steps out of her slippers, flips a switch, and in the blaze of light steps across a *tatami*[10] floor to the closet for the bedding. Tetsuya closes the screen behind him and begins to peel off his traveling suit, the familier smell and texture of the mats in this the only Japanese style room in their *manshon* reassures him that he really is home. As his wife lays out the *futon*, he puts on an old *yukata*,[11] wrapping the belt low around his hips, ties it and sits watching her. Carefully, he presents his argument about moving out to the countryside to his old village and sharing a residence with his parents. His wife finishes placing the pillows and turns down the top covers. She is not against the idea but recognizes both the economic and health advantages and the loss of a hard fought for autonomy which she has just begun to enjoy. It is a difficult decision which will require many hours of meaningful discussion between themselves and trusted friends.

Tetsuya sits quietly in thought looking about himself at the traditional style of the room, the earth-colored painted

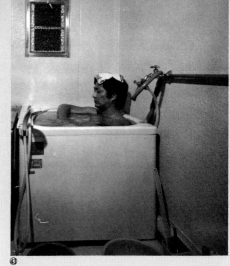

41. Living space interior of manshon.
42. Japanese style *tatami* room in manshon.
43. Man soaking in *ofuro*, relaxing after difficult day of travel or work.

㊶　居間.
㊷　マンションの和室.
㊸　入浴は、仕事や旅の疲れを洗い流してくれる.

妻は襖を開けて、すばやくスリッパを脱ぎ、明かりをつけ、寝具の入っている押入れに向かって、畳の上を軽い足どりで進んだ. 哲也は旅行中着ていたスーツを脱ぎながら、マンションの中の彼らの住まいでは唯一の和室であるこの部屋に入って、なつかしい畳の臭いと感触に出合って初めて、家に帰った実感をかみしめていた. 妻が床をのべている間に彼は浴衣を着、腰に帯をしめ、座って彼女をみつめた. そして、郷里に帰って両親と一緒に住んではどうかという提案を、用心深く切り出した. 妻は掛け布団を折り返し、枕を置き終えていた. 彼女は彼の考えに反対はしない. 経済的にも健康的にも、都合はよいのだ. しかし、自立のための厳しい闘い——彼女は最近ようやく、この闘いをおも

しろいと思い始めていた——に負けるような気がした. この難しい決断を下すには、時間をかけて彼らの間でよく話し合い、信頼のおける友人にも相談する必要があるだろう.

哲也は和室を見まわしながら静かに考えていた. 土壁色に塗ったセメントの壁、窓にとりつけられたプラスチックの障子、小さな床の間には掛け軸がかかり、その下にデジタルの目覚し時計が置かれている. 天井は天然木風の仕上げを施された人工物で、そこからぶら下がっているまばゆい照明器具が、布団の華かな色にさらに生彩を与えている. 彼は、この家から伊勢へ向かい、実家を回って再びここに帰り着いた旅程の長さに、改めて驚いていた. 伊勢神宮にいた時の彼は、何らかの目的を他と共有している

ように感じていた. それが、実家に立ち寄って都会へ帰ってくるまでの間に少しずつ消えていった. 伊勢に着いた時の彼は、まるで本質から離れたものを剥ぎとられたような気分だったが、今の彼は、数日前に戻ってしまい、装飾的付属物に埋もれ、彼が発見したものをもう一度埋め戻しているような気がしていた. 「日本人の生活は非常に複雑になっている」と彼は考えた. 「我々は、時の流れの中で、得るものと同じだけのものを失なっているのかもしれない. けれども、それをなんとかすることはできないことだ」. そこまで考えた哲也は、立ち上がって風呂場へ向かった. 湯に浸かって、まだ残っている旅の緊張をほぐそうというのである.

（訳：M. S.）

cement walls, the plastic *shoji* covered window, the small *tokonoma*[12] with its hanging scroll and the digital alarm clock below it, the natural wood finished metal ceiling and its glaring pendent light which brings the dancing colors of the *futon* to life. He wonders just how long a trip had it been from here to Ise, to his old home, and back again. While at the shrine he had felt a sense of common purpose which had gradually disappeared as he returned through his old home to the city. Just as he had felt a stripping away of non-essentials as he had approached Ise, now he felt as if he had been layering these trappings back on the past few days and reburying what he had discovered. "Life in Japan is so involved," he thought. "We seem to be gaining and losing equally as much as time passes. But then, I suppose it cannot be helped." So with that, Tetsuya stood up and left for the bath to wash and soak out the remaining tension from his journey.

FOOTNOTES

1. *jinja:* Shinto shrine as opposed to *otera* or Buddhist temple.
   minka: A private house, specifically rural and thus generalized to farm houses of Japan.
   machiya: A city tradsman's house.
2. *sarariman:* A salaried worker or white-collar worker refering to the vast numbers of dark suited office personnel in Japan.
3. *geta:* Wooden clogs or sandals with two wooden cross pieces on the sole which raise the wearer several inches above the ground.
4. *futon:* Japanese bedding consisting basically of a thick cotten quilt mattress and comforter usually very colorful. These are layered up depending upon the temperature and placed directly on the mat floor.
5. *unagi-no-nedoko:* Literally, an eel's sleeping place or bed. It refers to the long narrow shape of the houses with a short front on to the street that was typical in the city.
6. *noren:* A short split curtain hanging over a doorway which retards the movement of air and particles between two spaces.
7. *shoji:* A paper screen or sliding door. The pre-eminent symbol of Japanese architecture.
8. *manshon:* From the English mansion, a ferrocement apartment house, the individual units of which are either privately owned or rented.
9. *ocha:* Japanese green tea.
10. *tatami:* The comfortable straw floor mat that serves for walking, sitting and gauging the Japanese interior.
11. *yukata:* An informal summer *kimono* or sleeping and lounging robe.
12. *tokonoma:* The ceremonial recess in a

Japanese room, typically used for significant display.

BIBLIOGRAPHY

Dore, R.P., *City Life in Japan, A Study of a Tokyo Ward,* University of California Press, 1971.

Dunn, Charles J., *Everyday Life in Traditional Japan,* Charles E. Tuttle Co., Tokyo, Japan, 1978.

Engel, Heinrich, *The Japanese House, A Tradition for Contemporary Architecture,* Charles E. Tuttle Co., Tokyo, Japan, 1964.

Fukutake, Tadashi, *Japanese Rural Society,* Cornell University Press, 1972.

Hearn, Lafacadio, *Glimpses of Unfamiliar Japan,* Charles E. Tuttle Co., Tokyo, Japan, 1976.

Nakane, Chie, *Japanese Society,* Penguin Books, Ltd., Middlesex, England, 1977.

Reischauer, Edwin O., *The Japanese,* Charles E. Tuttle Co., Tokyo, Japan, 1978.

Sansom, G.B., *Japan – A Short Cultural History,* Charles E. Tuttle Co., Tokyo, Japan, 1977.

Statler, Oliver, *Japanese Inn,* Harcourt, Brace, Javonovich, Jove Book, New York, 1977.

Taut, Bruno, *Houses and People of Japan,* John Gifford Ltd., London, 1931.

Vogel, Ezra F., *Japan's New Middle Class,* University of California Press, 1971.

TYPOLOGY OF SPACE-CONSTRUCTIONS IN CONTEMPORARY JAPANESE ARCHITECTURE

by Botond Bognar

現代日本建築における空間構成のタイポロジー

ボトンド・ボグナール

西洋建築ではその歴史を通じて，空間概念が常に最も中心的な役割を担っており，近代建築運動においても重要な課題であった．空間は，空虚なもの，無限なものとして考えられ，ものの物理的実体の中にあって，独自の存在であり，かつまた，明確な固定された境界線を周りにもっているものとされた．そのため空間には，「収容するもの」という明確な資質があった．この考え方により，空間は時として科学的でさえあった合理的方法で探究され，幾何学や透視図法の法則にそって扱われた*1．

一方，日本ではこのような空間の概念は，一度も提起されたことはない．そのため，皮肉にも日本の伝統建築においては，空間操作や構成というものは存在しなかった．今日でもそれは

残りもの的で「無視された」資質のように思える．伝統的空間は「普遍的」であり，神道の思想に従えば，自然の中に根ざし，建物によってではなく，土地によって示されるものであった①．いいかえれば，日本が島国であったため，空間は常に限定されたものであり，独自の実在ではなく，丘，岩，木や水などの自然あるいは，環境の現象の中の精神的資質としてみなされていた．すなわち，空間そのものとしてではなく，種々の物的形象や他の「人工的」なものの構成形体の象徴的意味や性格として扱われた．建築もまた自然の中の有機的な一部と考えられ，異なった空間性を意味するものではなかった②．

イサム・ノグチの言葉を借りれば，「それは囲い込むという事実が重要であって，囲い込まれ

た空間ではない*2．

この日本人の直感的理解というより感覚は，近年ハイデッガーの到達した結論ときわめて近いものである．「空間は，位置によってその実存を得るのであって，空間からではない*3．しかしながら，ここにおいても一つだけ両者の間に差異が残る．構成する形態の中に空間の精神が根ざしているために，日本人にとっては，西洋人とは異なり，建物の物理的存続性は不可欠に重要だとは考えられていない．神社，仏閣や宮殿でさえもたびたび移され，時には完全に建替えられることもあった*4．このため，日本の「土地神」はある種の相対性を獲得している．古い信仰の中では，最も知覚しにくい部分例えば，深奥で霧深い山，密生した森，目線が奥まで入

Space conceptions have always played a very important role in Western architecture throughout its history and also became a key point of Modernism. Space was looked upon as something empty or void and infinite, existing independently among the physical entity of objects and/or surrounded by well-defined, fixed boundaries; therefore, it had the definite quality of "containers". Consequently it was always the subject of rational, even scientific approaches and treated along the laws of geometry, perspective etc.*1

This notion of space, on the other hand, has never occurred to the Japanese and so, ironically enough, there was no such thing as spatial operation or construction in the traditional Japanese architecture and, even today, it seems to be only a left-over or "neglected" quality. Traditionally, space was "universal" for them and, in line with the Shinto belief, rooted in Nature and represented by the land rather than buildings (fig. 1). In other words, it was — Japan being an island country — always limited and not a separate entity, but the spiritual quality of natural or environmental phenomena: hills, rocks, trees, water etc. and therefore not dealt with as space per se, but rather as the symbolic character and meaning

of the constituent forms of the various formations and other "artificial" things. Architecture too was regarded as an organic part of Nature and thus did not mean a different spatiality either (fig. 2). "It is the fact of enclosing that is significant, not the space enclosed," as sculptor Isamu Noguchi put it.*2

This instinctive understanding or, better yet, feeling of the Japanese then would bring them very close to the conclusion to which Heidegger arrived recently in saying: "Spaces receive their being from location and not from space.*3" Yet there is one difference remaining between the two. With the spirit of space rooted in the composing forms, the physical or material permanence of the buildings — unlike in the West — was not considered by the Japanese as something indispensably important; shrines, temples and imperial palaces too were often relocated or even completely rebuilt.*4 Therefore the genius loci in Japan gained certain relative character.

Along the ancient belief, the least perceivable locations: remote and misty mountains, thick forests, various small islands of rocks and cliffs impenetrable to the eye and unapproachable physically, or in architecture the dimmest, in-

nermost and hardly visible places were attributed the strongest spirituality expressed by the Japanese word kami.*5 The corresponding spatial interpretation of this concept shows then that space was not homogeneous, but heterogeneous with increasing density around places where it would be the least spatial in the traditional Western sense, that is, where space like in 'black holes' converges to zero. "Thus space was perceived as identical with the events or phenomena occurring in it; that is space was recognized only in its relation to time-flow," writes Isozaki.*6 With this the most ambiguous concepts of oku*7 and ma*8 were born as opposed to the positive and absolute character of center and space respectively (figs. 3, 4).

Having no 'spatial' quality, space was not perceived indeed as a three-dimensional entity, an explanation for the two-dimensional and frontal character of Japanese architectural and urban spaces, a feature which is also represented in their traditional descriptive arts.*9 "What could be termed as spatial logic is practically a hidden trend in the aesthetic evaluation of the 'non existent' pervading the history of Japanese architecture."*10 Therefore, even if we speak about space conception in Japan,

り込むことを拒み物理的にも近寄り難い岩礁や，断涯からなる小島や建築にあっては最も暗く奥まった，ほとんど見ることのできないところに，日本語のカミということばで表わされる最も強い精神性が与えられていた*5. この概念にそった空間解釈においては，空間は均一ではなく，伝統的な西洋での意味においては，最も空間的でない「ブラックホール」のようにそこに向かって収斂するようなところを中心として密度を増す不均一なものであることが理解される．「空間がそのなかで発生する出来事として感知されていた．時間を介してのみ空間はとらえられていたといってもいい」と磯崎新は述べている*6. これによって中心と空間という明確で絶対的な資質に対する全く曖昧な奥*7と間*8の概念が生まれた③④．「空間の資質を持たないため，空間は三次元的実在としては知覚されなかった．これは日本の建築や都市空間の二次元的正面性の理由にもなろう．この性格は伝統的描写手法にも現われている*9．「空間的と呼べるものは，日本建築の歴史に浸透している『不在のもの』の審美的評価においてはほとんど目に見えない傾向である*10．」そのため，たとえ我々が日本で空間概念について語っても，それは西洋の概念とは根本的に異なったものである．

今日の日本における最近の建築は，他のいかなるところのものよりも建設された空間の種々の探究・再定義を提示してくれる．それらに共通するものが一つだけある．即ち空間を科学的にはもとより機械論的・機能論的にも扱うことを拒否していることである．これらは知覚的複雑さを単純な視覚的法則に置き換えた近代主義運動の基本的態度をなしていたものであった．しかしながら，これらの空間の習作は究極的には知覚的でなく，知覚的なるものと観念的なるものの驚くべき混合物である．ここでは知覚的とは，アメリカの皮相的な大衆派のたどる方向とは異なった意味を持ったものである．

このような事柄の理由の一つは，日本に特殊または個有の条件，まさにその伝統的文化環境に依っている．物体や表面，即ち視覚性が事物の一つないしはそれ以下の様相しか示し得ず，その一方で，その裏に隠された様相，即ち「現実」のとらえ難い真の性状は，認識と理解または想像の対象となり，そのために違った解釈が可能であるとするものである．この間の曖昧な概念は，事実日本人のあらゆる行為の中に潜んでおり，必然的に現代の建築空間の中にも見出すことができる．この結果，それらは利用者あるいは体験者に「気楽に行こう」といったほと

this would be radically different from the Western one.

As of today in Japan — more than anywhere else — recent architecture provides us with the most varied approaches and redefinitions of constructed spaces. Among them only one underlying feature is common: the rejection of dealing with spaces in a mechanistic, functional let alone scientific way, a basic attitude of Modernism which replaced perceptual complexity with simple visual rules. However, most of these spatial solutions are not purely perceptual after all, but rather extraordinary mixtures of both conceptual and perceptual and where perceptual would mean something different from what the line the superficiality of the American populists represents.

One of the reasons behind this is exactly the special or unique Japanese conditions, the traditional cultural climate where things and surfaces, that is visuality, reveal only one and probably smaller aspect of the phenomena; while the other underlying aspect, the true but elusive nature of "reality" is subject to our cognition and understanding or imagination and thus open to different interpretations. This very *ambiguous*

concept of *ma*, as a matter of fact, is inherent in practically every deed of the Japanese and inevitably can be traced in the contemporary architectural spaces as well. As a result, they usually do not pretend to offer a "take it easy", almost, effortless cozy complacency to the user or experiencer, a quality which often seems to be difficult for a Westerner, especially for an American, to understand or accept.

The first deliberate departures from the exclusivist theory and practice of Modern architecture started out with the group of Metabolists whose activity marked the architecture of the 60s in Japan. They replaced the previous machine model with a more flexible biological one in which the idea of change was regarded as the most important requirement from architectural spaces.*11 The constant process of change however was supposed to be performed by technological solutions of the highest level. The futuristic and also rather pretentious projects with megastructures and clipped on capsules are widely known today. Individual spatial units were connected to the body of the whole "building" or the city in a way that they were interchangeable, while not disrupting the

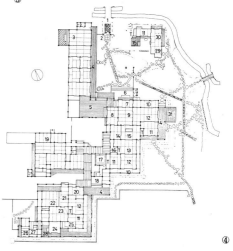

① 日本の景観. 宮島と厳島神社.
② 自然の中の建築. 修学院離宮にある離れ, 京都, 1659年.
③ 日本の住居内部. 桂離宮の松琴亭, 京都, 1620—1645年.
④ 桂離宮と茶席. 月波楼の平面図.

1. Japanese landscape: Miyajima island with the *Itsukushima shrine*.
2. Architecture in nature. Pavilion and bridge (Chitose-bashi) in the garden of the *Shugakuin Imperial Villa*, Kyoto (1659).
3-4. Interior of a Japanese house, the *Katsura Imperial Villa* in Kyoto (1620–1645). 4 — Ground plan of the Villa and one of the tea pavilions, the Gepparo, in the garden.

んど無意識の居心地のよい自己満足を与える素振りを見せないのが普通である．この資質は，西洋人特にアメリカ人には理解し，容認することが困難である．

近代主義運動の排他的理論と実践からの最初の意識的離脱は，1960年代の日本の建築界で活動的に動いたメタボリストのグループである．彼らは，以前の機械論的模型をより柔軟な生物的模型で置き換え，建築空間に対する最重要課題を変化であると考えた*11．しかし絶えざる変化の過程は，最高度の技術の解決に頼っていた．未来派的な，やや見栄をはったメガストラクチュアとクリップオンのカプセルの計画案は，今日広く知られている．個々の空間単位は「建物」全体または都市の構造体に有機体の機能――「生命」――を乱すことなく取替え可能なものとして連結されていた⑤．

しかしこの「組込まれた」可変性を有した新しい空間組織は，依然として機械的であった．それらは，ほとんど宇宙時代的技術水準を要求していた．丹下健三の方法は，情報伝達に明確な優先順位を与えつつ，空間を構造化することを強調するものであった．代表作の東京計画1960，山梨新聞放送センターや大阪万国博'70の

配置計画のように，情報伝達手段が独自に発展するシステムとなり，個々の空間単位は，あたかも二次的なものと言えるほどそれに従属している．これらがこのように二つに厳格に分離したことにより，力強く時にはブルータルでさえある形態が生み出され，構造的システムの圧倒的存在のために建築空間が「食いちぎられていた」⑥⑦．

メタボリストたち一般にも言えることだが，特に菊竹清訓と黒川紀章は，空間のフレキシビリティを増すことと相互の連結により多くの関心を払う．彼らにおいては，異なる機能の空間単位は，カプセル化され，高度の工業化のもとでプレハブ生産され，木葉が枝につくように，受け入れの「幹」に連結というよりは「クリップオン」にされる⑧→⑩．結果として形態は，前者より多彩であり，不完または未完のもの，即ち，時間的要素という古くからの美意識を内に持ったものとなっている．黒川の中銀カプセルタワーの144個の住戸カプセルのアドホック的配列がこれを最もよく示している⑪．

しかしながら，70年代の初めは，エネルギー資源の深刻な欠乏とそれに伴なう世界的な経済・産業の危機をみたのである．その中には当然日本も含まれていた．人々は，徐々にではある

が確実に技術と「機械」の万能に対する信頼を失っていった．構造主義的，メタボリスト的理想と実作はその地歩を失った．今日では，巨大な誇大妄想的都市計画，特に何らかのメガストラクチュアを用いたものを描く権利を与えられていると思う建築家は，ほとんど一人もいないだろう．建築家の自信喪失とともに，以前の理想主義的社会への関心に対して決定的失望をも意味している．一般的にいって，最近の日本建築は内向しはじめており，建築「自身」に内在する表現性，象徴性，意味性を探究し，また今まで無視されていた伝統的・歴史的・文化的遺産に広範に依存しはじめている．この内在化の過程は，何度も紹介されている技術的方法からより複雑で芸術的な方法への移動のみでなく，また日本の建築家が共通の目標を追求するのではなく，個人的な指向や方向によって現状からの脱却を試みているという事実によっても特徴づけられている．この多様性は，とりもなおさず，建築と建築空間のありとあらゆる再定義を意味する．

メタボリズムの人たちの中では，黒川が最初に時代の変化の重要さに気づいた．そのため彼の厳格なカプセル建築は，意図的な変身を遂げた．ソニータワーや国立民族学博物館において

functions or "life" of the total organism (fig. 5).

The new spatial organization with the "built in" changeability was however still mechanical, requiring an almost space age technology. Tange's approach emphasized the need of *structuring* spaces with a clear priority for communication. In his most representative projects like the Plan for Tokyo 1960, the Yamanashi Broadcasting Center or the lay-out for the Osaka Expo '70, the communication channels, for example, became independently developing systems on which the individual spatial units were in turn highly dependent with an almost secondary role. This rigid separation of the two resulted in strong, sometimes even brutal forms wherein architectural spaces were "eaten up" by the overwhelming physical presence of the structural system (figs. 6, 7).

Metabolists in general, but most especially Kikutake and Kurokawa, pay more attention to the increased flexibility of spaces and their connections to each other. With them the different functional space units become *capsulized*, prefabricated on a highly industrialized level, then joined or better yet "clipped" onto the receiving "truck" like leaves on a tree (figs. 8–10). The result in form is

more varied than in the previous case with an inherent touch of the ancient aesthetics of unfinished or incomplete, that is, of time. The ad hoc arrangement of the 144 living studio capsules at Kurokawa's Nakagin Capsule Tower exemplifies this best (fig. 11).

Nevertheless, the beginning of the 70s witnessed serious shortages in energy resources together with the resulting crisis of world economies and industries including, of course, the Japanese as well. People slowly but surely lost their confidence in the omnipotence of technology and the Machine; while the structuralist, metabolist ideology and practice lost ground. Today almost no architect feels entitled to draw up huge megalomaniac city plans and most especially not with some kind of megastructures. With the shaking self-confidence of the architects, this also means a definite disillusionment with the previous idealistic social preoccupations. In general, recent Japanese architecture has started turning inwards, exploiting more the inherent expressive, symbolic and semantic possibilities of architecture "itself" relying extensively also on the traditional, historical and cultural heritage thus far disregarded. This process of *interiorization* is characterized not only by the well-

articulated shift from the technological approaches towards more complex, artistic ones, but also by the fact that Japanese architects, instead of pursuing the same goal, try to find exits from the present situation through their individual and personal directions and methodologies. This multidirectionality means first of all the most varied redefinitions of architecture, architectural spaces.

Among the Metabolists, Kurokawa is the first to realize the significance of the changing times; his rigid capsule architecture itself undergoes a deliberate metamorphosis. As in his Sony Tower Building or the National Ethnological Museum, he retains the capsule idea with some high-tech look in a refined, but "scaled down" manner, yet supplemented by the application of various pop elements, then brings them together or rather juxtaposes them through the introduction of buffer zones: the ambiguous "in-between" spaces and even the many shades of the color grey (figs. 12–14). On the other hand, Tange and Kikutake for example seem to go along with the further elaborations of their original structuralist and metabolist methodologies respectively (fig. 15).

Real change, an extraordinary variety and thus the real excitement in the

⑥

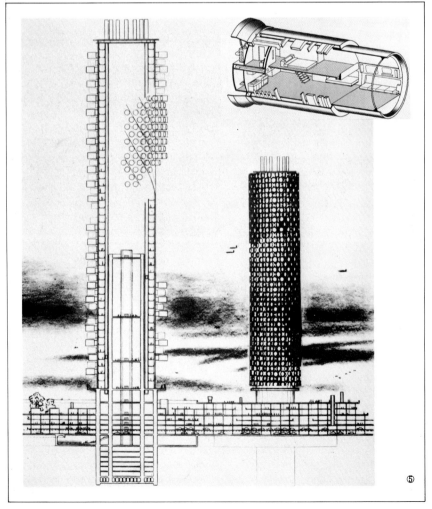

⑤

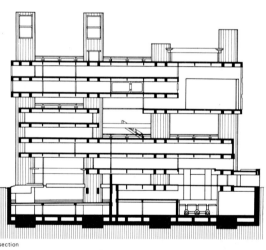

section

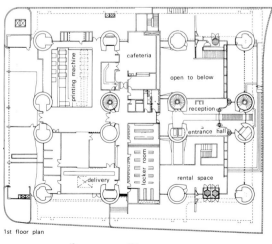

1st floor plan

⑦

| | 10 | 25m |

⑨

⑧

⑩

⑤ 塔状住居の提案.（1958年，設計：菊竹清訓. カプセル単体の断面と詳細).

⑥ 山梨新聞放送センター.（甲府市，1966年，設計：丹下健三).

⑦ 同上. 1階平面図と断面図.

⑧ ホテル東光園.（米子市，1964年，設計：菊竹清訓).

⑨ パシフィックホテル.（茅ケ崎，1966年，設計：菊竹清訓).

⑩ 1970年大阪万国博のお祭広場のスペースフレーム.（設計：丹下健三. これに黒川紀章設計の最初の住居カプセルが取り付けられていた. 1978年に取り壊わし).

5. Proposal for a *Tower-shapped Community* (1958. Kyonori Kikutake). Section and detail of a capsule unit.

6–7. *Yamanashi Press & Broadcasting Center,* Kofu City (1966, 1975, Kenzo Tange). 7 – First floor plan and section.

8. *Hotel Tokoen* in Yonago (1964. K. Kikutake).

9. *Pacific Hotal*, Chigasaki (1966. K. Kikutake).

10. The *Space Frame* of the Festival Plaza in the Expo '70, Osaka (K. Tange) which contained the first experimental residential capsule units (Kisho Kurokawa).

見られるように，カプセルの考え方は洗練され「縮小」されたハイテク風な手法に残されているが，それらを種々のポップ風に補い，さらに中間領域の挿入により結合あるいは並置する．曖昧な「中間体」の空間やねずみ色の色あいの段階などがそれである⑫→⑭．一方で，丹下と菊竹は各々の当初の構造主義的・メタボリズム的方法のさらなる練り上げを続けているように見える⑮．

しかしながら，今日の日本建築の本当の変化，驚くべき多様性とそれゆえに本当の興奮はメタボリズムの修正や改良によってもたらされるのではなく主として若い建築家による「新しい波」の活動によっている．彼らは，基本的に物理的変化の発想を拒否し，そのため「ポスト・メタボリスト」とも呼ばれる．社会の文化的・社会的側面を根本からつくり変えることへの執着に代わって，彼らは社会の多様性，複雑性を受け入れることにより寛容であり，与えられた都市の現状の修正者として人間と建築の新しい関係を通してアイデンティティを取戻し，それによって個人の住環境の微小な改善を遂行しようとしている．これらの関係については，それら空間の特異で象徴的な，多くの場合曖昧な資質を語らなければならない．これらの空間に加えら

れる操作は，奥の概念の再導入や伝統的空間の重層，梱包から歪曲，親近性の排除，解体と再構築することへと拡がる．しかし，何よりも，基本に係わる強固なイメージ——ゲシュタルト——を提示する程，深い意味あいが込められているその手法こそ，例を見ないものである．

これらの操作における最も目立つ道具は，単純な立体を用いた表面の硬い幾何学である．立方体，円柱，正四面体とその変換操作による直交格子と柱と梁の架構などである．これらは，最近の建築の実作のほとんどに見られるものであるが，藤井博巳，安藤忠雄，相田武文，宮脇檀などの若いコンセプチュアルな建築家にあっては，ほとんど唯一の依拠すべき事柄になっている．そのため彼らの建築は，少なくとも一瞥したところでは，以前の近代主義の語彙の或る部分を容易に想起させる．実際，打放しコンクリートの全体にわたる使用という手法は，コルビュジェの建築，ネオ・ブルータリストやメタボリストの建築とさえもあまりに密接に関連づけられているため，皮相的な観察者はすぐに間違った結論へと導かれる．しかしながら，「単純な」形態要素の解釈に依存していることは確かだが，それは建築のエッセンス，特に空間の資質や内部の場の精神に対する根本的に異なっ

Japanese architecture today however comes not from the modified or improved practice of metabolism, but from the activities of the "New Wave", mainly young architects, who basically oppose the idea of physical change, thus are often referred to also as 'post-metabolists'. Instead of the obsession to re-shape and reform the cultural and social aspects of society radically, they are more inclined to accept its plurality and complexity, and as correctors of the given present urban situations, intend to carry out minute improvements in the living conditions of the *individuals* mainly by restoring their *identity* through new relationships between man and architecture. As far as these relationships are concerned, I have to refer to the unique symbolic and often *ambiguous* quality of these spaces with the spatial operations ranging from the re-introduction of *oku*, the traditional space layering, packaging, through distorting, 'defamiliarizing', dismantling until reassembling spaces. But above all, unparalleled is the manner in which they are charged with substantial meanings resulting in elementary and powerful images or *Gestalt*.

One of the most conspicuous instruments in these operations is certainly a hard surfaced *geometry* utilizing the simplest solids: the cube, cylinder, trilateral prism and their transformations the orthogonal grid or the trabeated pergola etc. While this is apparent in most of the recent architectural practices, with some of the young conceptual architects like Hiromi Fujii, Tadao Ando, Takefumi Aida or Mayumi Miyawaki etc., it becomes an almost sole matter of reliance. Their architecture thus would easily remind us of some aspects of the previous modern vocabulary at least during the first time. Indeed the overall use of the unfinished concrete elements is associated so much with Corbusier's, the neo-brutalists and even the metabolists' architecture that its reappearance would easily mislead the superficial experiencer. Nevertheless, while there is certainly a definite dependence on the "simplistic" interpretations of formal elements, this covers — in the true sense of the word — a basically different approach to the essence of architecture, most especially the quality of spaces or better yet of the spirit of places inside. Geometry then serves as a tool for a deliberate aim to re-establish the "genius loci"*[12] through their architecture of mainly small houses which coincides with the strong intention of redefining human existence.*[13] Beyond the mere fact

11. *Nakagin Capsule Tower*, Tokyo (1972. K. Kurokawa).
12. *Sony Tower Building*, Osaka (1976. K. Kurokawa).
13–14. *National Ethnological Museum*, Suita, Osaka (1977. K. Kurokawa). 14 — Interior with the audio-visual information capsules.
15. *Seibu Otsu Shopping Center*, Otsu City (1976. K. Kikutake).
16–17. *Row House* in Sumiyoshi, Osaka (1976. Tadao Ando). 17 — Isometric drawing and floor plans.
18. *PL Institute Kindergarten* in Tondabayashi, Osaka (1973. Takefumi Aida).

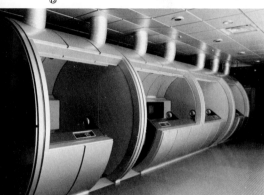

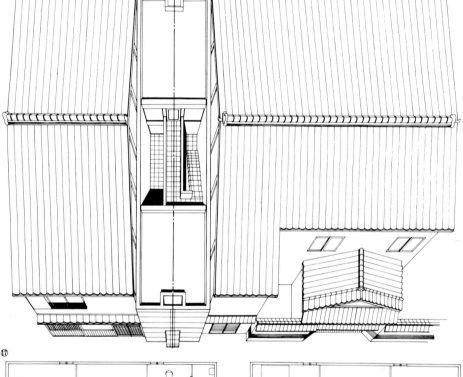

⑪　中銀カプセルタワー．（東京，1972年，設計：黒川紀章）．

⑫　ソニー・タワー．（大阪，1976年，設計：黒山紀章）．

⑬　国立民族学博物館．（吹田市，1977年，設計：黒川紀章）．

⑭　同上，視聴覚情報カプセルと内部．

⑮　西武大津ショッピングセンター．（大津市，1976年，設計：菊竹清訓）．

⑯　住吉の長屋．（大阪，1976年，設計：安藤忠雄）．

⑰　同上，アクソノメトリックと平面図．

⑱　PL学園幼稚園．（富田林，大阪府，1973年，設計：相田武文）．

た手法を文字通りおおっているのである．幾何学は土地神[*12]を再構築する意図的試みのための道具であり，それは人間の存在を再定義しようとする強い意志と彼らの主として小住宅である建築作品を通して合致している[*13]．このような目的という単なる事実以上に，これらの建築家を建築の分野できわだたせるのは，彼の実践における技術の高さである．

これらの建物によってもたらされる最初の印象は，トーチカや防空壕のような，周囲のものすべてに背を向けてしまう強い自衛的性格である．いいかえれば，内部空間と外界の間にはごくわずかの会話も，例えあったとしてもわずかしか存在しない．建築家は依頼された施主または，利用者をますます窮屈にさせ，ときには彼らに敵対する都市環境から隔離し，封じ込める[*14]．個人が物理的のみならず精神的にも自らを再生する条件，相田がいうところの「沈黙」の時を与える[*15]．ここで重要なのは，建物の中に隠された「内なる世界」，「密封されたミクロコスモス」であることは疑いない[16][17]．

相田は，「沈黙」の概念に従って，大阪の近くの幼稚園では，宮庭の「墳墓」として地中に埋め込んでいる[18]．磯崎の初期の「メタボリズム建築」や宮脇の小住宅，銀行の彩色を施され

of such purposes though, the techniques of execution is what distinguishes these architects from the rest of the architectural scene.

The first impression created by these buildings is their strong *defensive* character by which, as bunkers or bomb-shelters, they turn their backs to everything around. In other words, there is very little communication, if at all, between the inside spaces and the outside world. The architect treating his client the owner or user seals him off *hermetically* from the increasingly cramped and sometimes hostile urban environment,[*14] thus providing the conditions, the moments of "silence"[*15] — as Aida says — for the individual to re-create himself physically and spiritually as well. There is no doubt that the emphasis here is on the "inner world", a *"hermetic microcosm"* concealed within the buildings (figs. 16, 17).

Along the notion of 'silence' then Aida builds his kinder-garten near Osaka as an ancient imperial 'burial mound' wherein it disappears under the covering earth (fig. 18). In Isozaki's early "metabolist" works and also in Miyawaki's colored "primary" box-architecture of tiny house and bank buildings, the simple and rigid concrete walls cover unusually dynamic

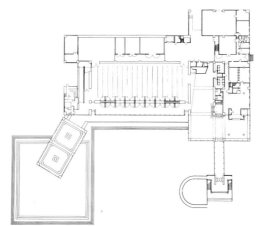

㉓

㉔

た「プライマリー」のボックス建築においては，単純で堅固なコンクリートの壁は異例にダイナミックであり，相田の幼稚園と同様に色彩に富み，気持のよい室内をつつんでいる⑲→㉑．

しかしこの自衛的建築のすべてがこのような「心地よい」，いくらか大衆的空間を内に隠しているわけではない．他の建築家は，実存的建築の考えをさらに進め，ときには極端なまでに押し進めている．彼らにとって，居住者を物理的に守りながら，知覚，認識の通常のステレオタイプと標準的行動様式を提供し続ける建築では，その主目的を達成することができない．このため，建築は使用者の意識の中に入り込み，「空間と人との間の新しい関係」を通して，新しい実存的状況をつくり出すべきである．それでは，この「新しい関係」または自我の永久的再生はどのようになされるのだろうか．

日本のコンセプチュアリストたちは，建築を通して古い通常の意味を消し去り，新しい意味を生じさせようと種々の方法を試みている．この指向性において，デカルト幾何学，特に直交格子の適用を磯崎新が最初に試みた．その試みは，彼の初期の銀行建築の多くに見られ，北九州や群馬の美術館，ハクビきもの学院などで表現をより強める組織立ての道具として使われ，かつ

⑲ 秋田相互銀行盛岡支店．（盛岡市，1970年，設計：宮脇檀）.
⑳ 秋田相互銀行本庄支店．（本庄市，1973年，設計：宮脇檀）.
㉑ 同上，内部.
㉒ 群馬の森美術館 （高崎市，1974年，設計：磯崎新）.
㉓ 同上，建物の概念的下部構造と1階平面図.
㉔ ハクビきもの学院．（東京，1980年，設計：磯崎新）.

19. *Akita Sogo Bank, Morioka Branch Office Building,* Morioka City (1970. Mayumi Miyawaki).
20–21. *Akita Sogo Bank, Honjo Branch Office Building,* Honjo (1973. M. Miyawaki). 21 — Interior detail.
22–23. *Gumma Prefectural Museum of Modern Art,* Takasaki City (1974. Arata Isozaki). 23 — The conceptual substructure of the building.
24. *Hakubi Kimono School,* Tokyo (1980. A. Isozaki).

— and as in Aida's kindergarten — colorful and pleasant interiors (figs. 19–21).

Yet not all of the solid concrete boxes in this defensive architecture conceal such kind of "cozy" and somewhat popular spaces. Other architects go further with the idea of existential architecture pushing it at times to the far extremes. For them an architecture which though protects the habitants physically, but still offers an inner world with the usual stereotypes of perception, cognition and conventional behavioral patterns would not achieve its principal goal. Therefore architecture should enter into the awareness of the user and create *new* existential conditions through "new relations between the space and the person."*16 How then do these 'new relations' or the perpetual renewal of the self come through?

The Japanese conceptualists in one way or another answer this question with their intentions to efface old and conventional meanings and generate new ones with architecture. In so doing it is Arata Isozaki, who turns first to the application of the Cartesian geometry, more precisely the orthogonal grid. In many of his early bank buildings, then more expressedly in the Kitakyushu and Gumma Museums or the Hakubi Kimono

また人工的な無限を下敷にしている．理論的格子は，前例によって自動的に喚起される記憶・視覚性を麻痺させる役割をもち，これらは種々の幻覚・視覚トリック，歪められた現実によって補強されている㉒→㉔．

換言すれば，これはジョナサン・ゲイルがいうところの，建築の「反親密化」である．「このような『知的』な建築の使用者（住人）は，慣れ親しんだものが次々に消し去られていくのを知る．見つからない入口，透視できないガラス，なにも支持しない柱，通常の関連物をはぎとられた壁」*17㉕→㉗．

すべてを圧倒する格子の中の空間の効果に呆然とし，「目がくらみ」，視覚的に「免疫」になった体験者に，磯崎は自分自身を取り戻す新しい方法を提示あるいは示唆する．「磯崎は，合理的であり『無限』としてある格子枠組の建物を多くのインスピレーションを呼ぶ要素で埋めつくす．即ち，注意深く抽象化された引用や暗喩を種々のものから借りてきて，パズルのように取り揃え，各人にその人の知識，能力，経験，記憶の全体の許す限りにその部品をもて遊びまたはそれと格闘させ，そこにその人の見ようとするもの，創造することができるものを構成させる．これは，計画の過程を支配する建築家が

当初，独創的イメージをもっていたとしても，最終的結果にはあらゆる再解釈が許容され，個人的意味合いの付与も可能である」*18㉘→㉚．このマニエリスムによって磯崎は，日本の最近の建築における指向をその翼下に納めており，事実，内外の同時代人に多大な影響を与えつつ，彼らからもまた影響を受けている．

しかしながら，磯崎の建築の根底に内在された考え方を構成する指向性は他の人によっても代表される．彼らは，個々の指向性に焦点を絞るので，個々の指向はさらに丹念に練り上げられ変化する．木島安史を例にとると，彼はつくられた空間の折衷的可能性に興味をもっている．彼の建築では，西洋建築と日本建築の要素をラディカルに並置させることにより，雑種的なものにしてしまう．このような文化的二種人格は，「古典的」な柱が日本の和室の中やゼセッション様式の柱廊の中にあらわれた例や，小さな古い神社の前に列柱に載った小さなローマのエディキュルが増築されたりする例などに見られる．しかし，木島の設計には，幾何学的考察は明らかに欠けている㉛→㉜．

これとは対称的に，藤井はデカルト幾何学を用い，特に，類似，含蓄，接合という異なる操作を基本の立方体に施す．純粋幾何学には，「現

実に対する特定のかかわりあいを有しないので……（藤井の建築では）建築のもつ日常的機能をはぎとる役目を与えられ（それによって）世界を（変革し），……人間の原始状態を（再導入する）*19（傍点筆者）」．このため，彼の小さく単純なコンクリートの建物は，多くの場合，見えざる直交格子によって貫かれ，その切り口が設備や家具まで，可能なかぎりの面に投影された正方形の網目として表わされている．他の例では，立方体の中の立方体，もしくは「箱の中の箱」として想い入れがなされている㉝→㊱．

同様な考え方がより曖昧な形で八木幸二の「1/4方形の家」にみられ，直接的で「鮮明」な形として毛綱モン太の「反住器」の内にみられる．前者においては，2階の二つの寝室のヴォールトのかかった空間は，家の外殻のコンクリートと交差し，貫通し，そのため外でもあり，内でもあるものとなっている．後者においては，三つの立方体が互の中にとり込まれ，「浮いて」おり，宇宙論の段階まで引き上げられた普遍的存在の誕生を意味している㊲→㊴．これらの場合に見られる空間を巻きつけていく手法は興味深いことに，伝統的住居の空間組織にみられる曖昧な中心，「奥」を中心とする空間の重層手法と近似している．この方法によって，日本人に

School, the underlying theoretical grid – an organizing instrument and also the artificial infinite – is assigned a role of paralizing our visuality, memories with the automated mechanism of previous associations promoted also by the numerous illusions and visual tricks, a distorted reality (figs. 22–24). In other words, this is what Jonathan Gale calls the "defamiliarizing" of architecture. "The user of such 'intellectual' architecture is finding less and less that is familiar – entrances that he can't find, glass that he can't see through, columns that don't support anything, walls denuded of their familiar references"*17 (figs. 25–27).

Then so 'blinding' that is visually 'immunizing' the unprepared experiencer by the stupefying effects of spaces within the overwhelming grid, Isozaki offers him, or better yet, hints towards several new ways to get himself together again. "Isozaki packs his buildings, the rational and 'infinite' frameworks with a large amount of inspiring elements, carefully abstracted quotations or metaphors borrowed from various sources like pieces in a puzzle and let everyone play or struggle with them to construct whatever image he would like to see or is able to put together according to his own body of knowledge, intelligence, experiences, memories etc. That is even if there existed an original image from the architect controlling the design process, the final product is open to the most various reinterpretations and private meanings"*18 (figs. 28–30). With his *mannerism* it is Isozaki indeed who spans over most of the recent architectural intentions in Japan influencing greatly his contemporaries yet also being influenced by them from both at home and abroad.

Nevertheless the component directions with the underlying ideas inherent in Isozaki's architecture is likewise represented by others wherein these directions, being focused upon individually, are further elaborated or varied. Yasufumi Kijima for example is interested in the eclectic possibilities of constructed spaces. In his buildings he juxtaposes the elements of Western and Japanese architectures so radically that actually they turn out to be some sort of hybrids. This cultural schizophrenia then results in solutions where "classical" columns appear in the middle of a Japanese *tatami* room or in the corridor of secession style, and where a small Roman edicule on colonnades is built as the extension of a tiny ancient Japanese Shinto shrine. Yet the geometrical considerations are obviously absent in Kijima's designs (figs. 31, 32).

On the contrary, Fujii turns to the Cartesian geometry and especially the different operations – similarity, connotation, junction etc. – of the elementary *cube*. Since pure geometry "has no specific commitment to reality . . . (with Fujii it is given) the ultimate goal of stripping architecture of its mundane functions (in order to transform) the world, that is . . . (to reintroduce) *the primordial condition of man*".*19 (Italics by B. Bognar) Therefore his simple and small concrete buildings often appear as if penetrated by an invisible orthogonal grid with the result of the cuts, the network of squares projected on every possible surface including the installations and furniture as well. In other cases, they are conceived as cube in cube or more precisely 'box in box' (figs. 33–36).

The same idea is seen again, though in a more ambiguous form in Koji Yagi's Quarter-square House and in a direct and "clear" form as "architecture in architecture" in Monta Mozuna's Antidwelling Box. In the first case the vaulted spaces of the two bedroom units on the second floor intersect and interpenetrate the

㉕

㉖

㉗

㉘

㉙

㉚

㉜

㉛

㉕　秀巧社ビル（福岡市，1975年，設計：磯崎新）.

㉖　神岡町役場のガラスブロック壁.（神岡町，1977年，設計：磯崎新）.

㉗　ハクビきもの学院.（東京，1980年，設計：磯崎新）. 鏡面ガラスでつくり出された幻影的な空間.

㉘　同上，2階部分はマリリン・モンローの体の曲線を基に形づくられている.

㉙　同上，超現実主義者のイメージがある1階ロビー.

㉚　秀巧社ビルの階段，そこには視覚的なトリックだけがある.（福岡市，1975年，設計：磯崎新）.

㉛　ホワイト・ハウスの内部詳細.（東京，1973年，設計：木島安史）.

㉜　上無田松尾神社.（熊本県，1975年，設計：木島安史）.

25. Entrance of the *Shukosha Building* in Fukuoka City (1975. A. Isozaki).
26. The glass block walls of the *Kamioka Town Hall* (1977. A. Isozaki).
27–29. *Hakubi Kimono School*, Tokyo (1980. A. Isozaki). 27 — The illusive space created by the mirror glass surfaces. 28 — Part of the second floor is shaped along the curves of Marilyn Monroe's figure. 29 — The surrealist image of the lobby.
30. The stairsteps of the managerial edicule inside the *Shukosha Building* in Fukuoka do not take us anywhere, remaining a visual trick only (1975. A. Isozaki).
31. Interior detail with the columns in the *White House*, Tokyo (1973. Yasufumi Kijima).
32. *Kamimuta Shrine* in Kumamoto (1975. Y. Kijima).

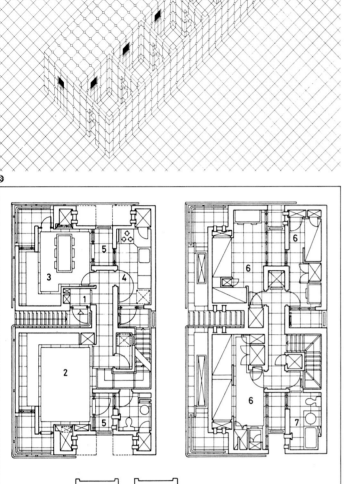

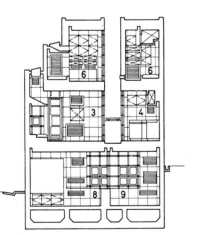

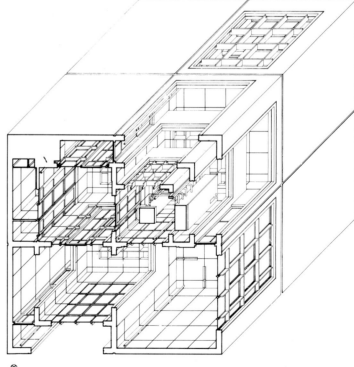

㉝ プロジェクトE-1の無限直交グリッド.（1973年，設計：藤井博巳）.

㉞ 宮島邸の平面・断面図.（東京，1973年，設計：藤井博巳）.

㉟, ㊱ 「ボックス・イン・ボックス」の考え方を示す二つの作品──㉟：マル武人形社屋.（1976年，設計：藤井博巳）. ㊱：等々力邸.（船橋市，1976年，設計：藤井博巳）.

㊲ 藤岡邸.（東京，1978年，設計：八木幸二）.

㊳ 同上，アクソノメトリック.

㊴ 反住器の平面図とアクソノメトリック.（釧路，1971年，

設計：毛綱モン太）.

㊵, ㊶ 「最大の視覚距離」をもつ根本邸のアイソメトリック（1979年，設計：八木幸二）.

33. The infinite orthogonal grid of a small house *Project E-1* (1973. Hiromi Fujii).

34. Floor plans and section of the *Miyajima Residence* in Tokyo (1973. H. Fujii).

35–36. The 'box in box' idea as it appears in two works by Hiromi Fujii. 35 – *Marutake*

Doll Company Building in Konosu (1976). 36 – Plans of the *Todoroki Residence* in Funabashi (1976).

37–38. *Quarter-square House*, Tokyo (1978. Koji Yagi). 38 – Axonometric drawing.

39. Plans and axonometric drawing of the *Anti-dwelling Box* in Kushiro (1971. Monta Mozuna).

40–41. The *House in Tokyo* with "a maximal visual distance" (1979. Koji Yagi). 40 – Isometric drawing.

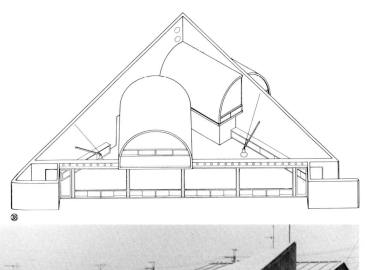
⊗

㊲

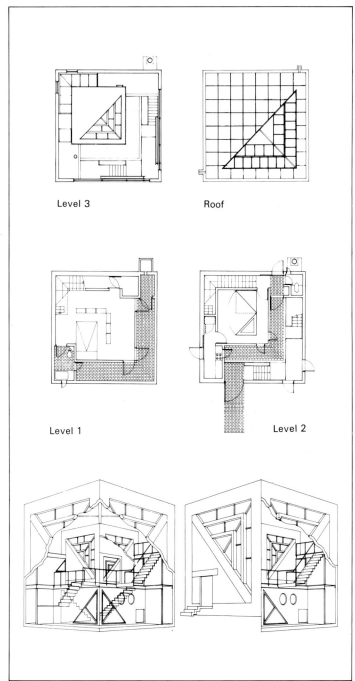

Level 3   Roof

Level 1   Level 2

㊳

㊶

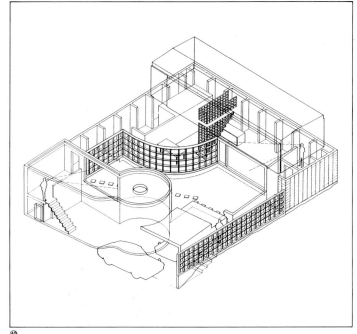
㊵

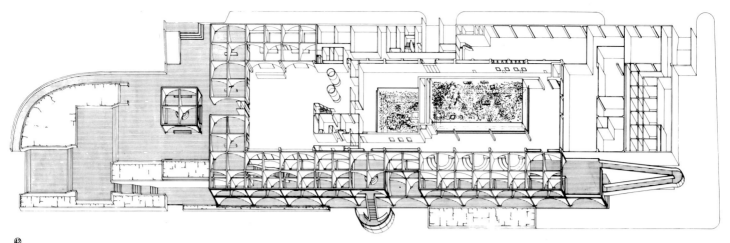

42

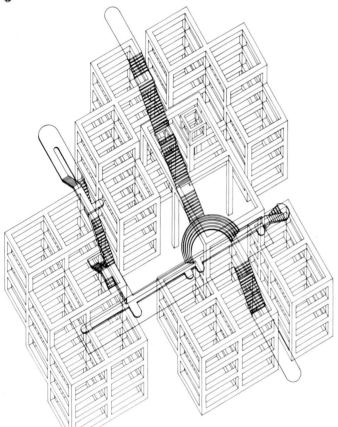

44

43

45

46

㊷　沖縄国際海洋博・海洋生物園.（1975年，設計：槇文彦）.
㊸　代官山集合住宅の入口部分.（東京，1970—76年，設計：槇文彦）.
㊹　岡本邸の構造図.（大阪，1976年，設計：安藤忠雄）.
㊺　福邸.（和歌山市，1980年，設計：安藤忠雄）.
㊻　大西邸.（大阪，1979年，設計：安藤忠雄）.

42. Axonometric drawing of the *National Aquarium* in Okinawa Expo '75 (1975. Fumihiko Maki).
43. Detail of the *Hillside Terrace Apartments*, Tokyo (1970–1976. F. Maki).
44. The structural skeleton of the *Okamoto Housing* in Osaka (1976. Tadao Ando).
45. *Dr. Fuku's Residence*, Wakayama City (1980. T. Ando).
46. *Onishi Residence*, Osaka (1979. T. Ando).

は古くから建物や庭の実際の限られた寸法にかかわらず，奥行と距離の感覚を空間に与えることが可能であった．八木は，「東京の家」で，小さなコートのまわりに種々の景観をつくり出し，その中に「拡がりの感覚を得る」ための斜め方向の最長視線を与えている⑩⑪．

　次に，槇文彦も，重層の手法を彼の「コンテクスチュアル」建築においてかなり意識的に用いている．中でも，沖縄の国立水族館の廻廊や代官山ヒルサイドテラスの住居群で典型的に見られる．代官山では，注意深く「くり抜かれた」形が「外部空間を活性化し，外部空間は最初は，内部空間を発生させ，やがてそれ自身が内部空間となる」＊²¹㉒㉓．

　しかし，槇のコンテクスチュアルな手法は，「密室派」の解釈とはすでに異なっている．彼らでは，内部と外部は鋭く対峙され，安藤が自分の建築についていうところの「景観の異化」に基礎をおいている＊²²．安藤の建築に常にみられる，まぐさ式のパーゴラと確固たるコンクリート壁にとり囲まれ貫通された構造的骨格は，再び最も単純な幾何学的形によって造り出されている㉔→㉖．藤井，伊東豊雄，原広司，相田，八木，ある側面において磯崎も空間を形態として把えるが，安藤は，彼の建物の空間的実存を

ほとんど無限に反復される最少限の要素による構成の組織によって，構造づけている．要素の中では，最近用いられているガラスブロックによる壁面がその曖昧さゆえに特に注目すべきである．このような表面は，内と外の固い境界を保持するが，同時に，伝統的な障子と同様な機能を果たす．それらは，透視を不可能にしつつ昼光を調節して内部に入れ，その効果は，夜には逆転する㊼㊽．槇，石井和紘，土岐新，相田，磯崎さえもがたびたびこれを使用するのは，このためとも思われる㊾．

　藤井は，自身の建築を「精粋」と呼び，それは人間が超越的意味合をもつとされ，人間はそれによって「あきらめて」あるいは最善の場合は自己を変革し，存在に対する新しい感性を経験する運命を負う．このような禅の思想を思わせる認識においては，「意味を読みとりうる主体の目の存在は明白に不在である＊²³」．安藤の建築の場合は状況は多少異なる．ここでも，相当の自己否定を要求されるが，劇的な光と影の導入は，一方で我々の最も深い感覚に訴える．また，ヴォールトや構造的格子のような形態要素は，恐らく無意識的ではあろうが，ローマやルネサンス建築のある古典的解釈の高度に抽象化された歴史的係わり合いをも体現している㊿→

㊿．さらに必ずみられる中庭は，安藤が暮らし仕事を続けている関西地方（大阪，京都とその近郊）の地方的伝統との係わり合いをも示す．

　絶対的ミニマリストの系統では，篠原一男の空間がまた別の方向性をもって現われる．厳格な格子やその他の規則的組織は見当らず，コンクリートで造り出される裸の単純性，純粋に幾何学的形態の中に俳句のような空気のような捉えどころのない資質——これは安藤においてもいくつか詩的エピソードの中に見られるが——が隠されており，実在の「現実性」が虚のものとなり，物質性を喪失して，投影された影となって現われる．その中で突如として，ある要素が自身以外の何物でもなく，絶対的形態となり，その結果ある形而上学的永遠的資質をもつようになる．いくつかの小住宅の中の誇張された，腕木や梁の結合された柱は，実は必要とされる構造上の手法ではなく，祖先回帰の悲劇，または彼がいうところの「野性」の表われである．いずれにせよ，彼の「永遠」の建築では，最も純粋な考え方または課題が基礎をなしており＊²⁴，それは建物の副題として表わされている．例としては，「決断の不断」，「０と１の反復」，「うねりと倒置」，あるいは「機械から野性へ」，「野性と統一」などである㊿→㊿．

exterior concrete shell of the House and thus are both inside and outside of its space; while in the second case the three cubicles are wrapped and "float" inside one another representing the birth of universal existence elevated onto a cosmic level (figs. 37–39). The method of wrapping around spaces in these cases interestingly coincides with the similar *space layering* around the ambiguous innermost "center", the *oku*, in the spatial organization of the tranditional house. With this method the Japanese have always been able to give a feeling of depth and distance to spaces regardless of the actually small dimensions of the buildings and gardens. At the House in Tokyo around a tiny court Yagi creates various vistas including the diagonal maximal visual distance in order to "achieve a sense of expansiveness"[20] (figs. 40, 41).

Fumihiko Maki then employs the technique of layering quite consciously when he composes his 'contextual' buildings. Among others this is obvious at the surrounding arcades of the National Aquarium in Okinawa or at the Hillside Terrace Apartments where the carefully 'hollowed out' forms activate the "exterior spaces, which first serve as the generators of the interior spaces, and become eventually the interior space themselves"[21] (figs. 42, 43).

Maki's contextual approach nevertheless already differs from the interpretations of the "hermeticists" based on the sharp disparity between outside and inside and what Ando in his architecture calls the "catabolism of landscape".[22] With Ando the ubiquitous trabeated pergola and the structural skeleton surrounded and intersected by solid concrete walls are once more created with the use of the simplest geometric forms (figs. 44–46). It is clear though that while Fujii, Ito, Hara, Aida, Yagi and in some aspects Isozaki too conceive space as form, Ando generates the spatial entity of his buildings by structuring it with a system composed of a minimum number of elements, yet repeated almost infinitely. Among them the introduction of the latest one, the glass block wall – because of its ambiguous quality – deserves special attention. Such surfaces retain the protective hard boundaries between exterior and interior, but at the same time function also in a similar way as the traditional paper-covered *shoji* panels filtered daylight, yet rendered the clear visibility through them impossible – an effect which is then repeated in the evening only in a reversed direction (figs. 47, 48). This might be one of the reasons that many contemporary Japanese architects like Maki, Ishii, Toki, Aida and even Isozaki employ it so often. (fig. 49)

Fujii calls his architecture 'quintessential', which is then supposed to carry transcendental meanings for man, who in turn is doomed to 'relinquish' or in the best case, transform himself in order to experience a new feeling of existence. It is obvious that in such kind of cognition, reminiscent of the Zen-buddhist philosophy "the eye of the subject capable of reading the meaning is patently absent."[23] With Ando's architecture the case is somewhat different in the sense that though it too requires significant self-denial, with the introduction of the dramatic light and shade effects, it also appeals to our deepest emotions, while the formal elements – vaults, the structural grid etc. – incorporate probably unintended, highly abstract historical associations with certain classical solutions of the Roman or Renaissance architecture (figs. 50–52). In addition the consistently present inner court – a living space itself – refers to the local tradition of the Kansai Area: Osaka, Kyoto and vicinity, where Ando lives and works.

Along the line of the absolute mini-

47

48

49

50

51

52

53

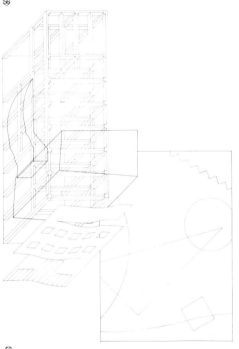

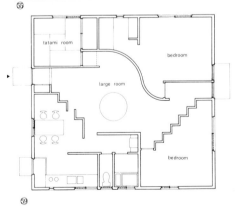

⑰ 石原邸の内部光庭．（大阪，1979年，設計：安藤忠雄）．

⑱ 福邸の内部．（和歌山市，1980年，設計：安藤忠雄）．

⑲ 東金中央クリニックの内部．（東金市，1979年，設計：土岐新）．

⑳，㉑ 安藤の建築における光と影の劇的効果は重要な要素である．⑳—真鍋邸の内部（大阪，1977年）．㉑—大楠邸の内部廊下（東京，1978年）．

㉒ 柱・梁のパーゴラとヴォールト架構は，古典ローマ建築をいささかイメージさせる．領壁の家の内部コート．（芦屋市，1976年，設計：安藤忠雄）．

㉓ 上原通りの住宅．（東京，1976年，設計：篠原一男）．

㉔ 同上，内部．巨大で活気あふれるコンクリートのく体．

㉕ 上原曲り道の住宅の居間．（東京，1978年，設計：篠原一男）．

㉖ 東金中央クリニックの直交構造く体．（東金市，1979年，設計：土岐新）．

㉗ PMTビルの理念図．（名古屋，1978年，設計：伊東豊雄）．

㉘ U邸または中野本町の家の湾曲する内部空間．（東京，1976年，設計：伊東豊雄）．

㉙ 上和田の家．（1976年，設計：伊東豊雄）．

47. *Glass-block House*, Osaka with its inner light court (1978. T. Ando).
48. Interior of the *Dr. Fuku's Residence*, Wakayama (1980. T. Ando).
49. Interior of the *Togane Central Clinic*, Togane (1979, Shin Toki).
50–51. The dramatic light and shade effects are important elements in Ando's architecture. 50 – Interior detail of the *Manabe Residence* in Osaka (1977). 51 – Inner corridor of the *Okusu Residence*, Tokyo (1978).
52. The trabeated pergola and the vaulted structures have a distant reference to the classical Roman architecture. Inner court of the *Ryoheki House* in Ashiya (1976. T. Ando).
53–54. *House in Uehara*, Tokyo (1976. Kazuo Shinohara). 54 – Interior with the huge, robust concrete structure.
55. *House on a Curved Road*, Tokyo (1978. K. Shinohara). The inner space of the living room.
56. The orthogonal structural skeleton of the *Toganei Central Clinic*, Toganei (1979. S. Toki).
57. Idea plan of the *PMT Building* in Nagoya (1978. Toyoo Ito).
58. The curving interior space in the 'U-House' or the *House in Nakano* (1976. T. Ito).
59. *House at Kamiwada* isometric drawing (1976. T. Ito).

151

建築的意味を可能なかぎり0に収斂させ、それを通して人間に自己の存在の新しい局面とも、建築の新しい意味をも創造する可能性を与えようとする指向の観点からみると、篠原、藤井、安藤の建築は大同小異である。この方法により、彼らの建築は確かに、最も内密的、知的またはエリート的であり、また種々の空間解釈の一方の極を代表している。しかし、日本の建築家の大多数にとって、この抽象的系統は出発点として妥当なものであり、彼らは「新しいもの」を定義づける意味でそれに付加していく。即ち、私が磯崎のマニエリスムに*25関して述べたハンプティ・ダンプティをいかにつなぎ直すかを模索しているのである。ことばを変えれば、理論的に組織立てながら構造的でもある3次元の格子が、最近の多くの空間構成において、重要ではあるが隠された役割を果している56。伊東のPMTビルのように、内部のテーマや要素、あるいは外側表面の方が格子そのものより重要であって、それは、磯崎、石井、土岐や伊東の建築の下部構造をしても見出しうる57。

「私の意向は、秩序だったイメージの領域を破壊し、より開かれた、自立的建築を創り出すことだ」と伊東は書いている*26。それは、アルド・ロッシとほとんど同じことばに聞こえる*27。し

かし、手法とその結果は、ヨーロッパのコンテクスチュアリストのものと異なっている。つまり、日本においては、無駄な徒労であるといえよう。都市環境を解体し、抽象化して、伝統的・歴史的ヨーロッパの都市の均一的テクスチュアを保存し、拡張するという指向は持たないのである。移り気な日本の状況においては、新しい要素は必然的に「無秩序の秩序」の一部となる。それが多くの場合、皮相的ファサードとなる意図的指向による場合でも、無視する態度による場合でも同じである。コンセプチュアリストや特に密室的建築家において最もよくみられるところから、反都市的な指向となることが多い。しかし、興味深いことに、多くの建築家の関心は両極にわたっており、その中には、伊東、土岐、最初のポップ建築家竹山実、そしてここでもまた磯崎が含まれる。

伊東は、中野本町の家と、上和田の家において、建築的表面の表現的資質を探究している。即ち、それらは内部空間とともに分解することによって、それから通常の意味を奪い去り、「日本文化に個有のコラージュによる空間のシンタクス」*28を創出する方法で並べ換えるのである58 59。二つの住居においては、このことは、固いコンクリートの境界のある内部で行われるが、

PMTビルでは、美しいうねったアルミの表皮が小さなビルの構造体から遊離する皮相性の方向をとる。同じようなことが磯崎の神岡町役場でも見られる。ここでは、アルミのファサードの一部が虚のファサードとなっている60 61。土岐新や石井和紘のファサード建築には、ルネサンスの微妙な引用が見られ、一方、竹山と磯崎はいくつかの建物に全体をおおうポップ的スーパーグラフィックを施している62→66。

伊東の主要な関心が空間を解体して再構成することなら、相田のは立体で同様なことを試みることだろう。積木の家1と2においては、名の示す通り、基本的建築的形態、特に、屋根や神道神殿の棟持柱のような日本的モチーフを抽出し、それを別の新しい文脈に置き換える。それはちょうど子供が積木を使っていろいろの造形をするのに似ている67 68。このようなおもちゃ的建築は、相田の他の住宅でも、日本古来の起し絵の手法によって空間構成をしていることにみられる。これは、3次元の立体の構成面を連続した一つのパターンに展開する手法である*29 69。

しかしながら相田の「おもちゃ」が「沈黙」を超越した世界にとどまるのに比べて、石井の遊びに満ちた手法は実に楽しげな冗談とでもいえ

---

malists come Kazuo Shinohara's spaces but from another direction again. No strict grid or other regular systems, only the purest geometrical forms, bare simplicity poured in concrete with a concealed ethereal and elusive feature of the *haiku* poems – which in some poetic episodes is also present in Ando's spaces – through which the 'reality' of the entities tend to turn virtual and losing their materiality appear as cast shadows. Then suddenly one element takes an absolute shape, becoming so much nothing else but itself, that as a result gains a metaphysical, eternal quality. The overblown columns with the joining brackets and beams inside several of his small houses for example stand not really for the necessary structural means but for some atavistic tragedies or "savagery" as he himself refers to them. In any case the purest ideas or themes constitute the basis of his "eternal" architecture*24 which also appear as subtitles beside the names of the buildings like: 'Indecision in Decisiveness', 'Repetition of 0 and 1', 'Undulation and Inversion' or 'From Machine to Savegery, Savagery and Unity' etc. (figs. 53–55).

Shinohara's, Fujii's and Ando's approaches are more or less identical from the viewpoint of the intention to make architectural meanings converge to zero as much as possible and in so doing to provide man with possibilities for creating new ones together with new aspects of his existence. This way their architectures prove to be certainly the most esoteric, intellectual or elite and represent one of the extreme poles on the scale of various spatial interpretations. The line of abstract quality however remains a well sensible point of departure for the majority of the Japanese architects who then complement it with the intention of defining the "new" or – as I wrote in relation with Isozaki's mannerism*25 – finding ways how to put Humpty-Dumpty together again. In other words, an organizing theoretical and also structural three-dimensional grid continues to play a significant yet underlying role in numerous recent space compositions (fig. 56). It appears as substructure in Isozaki's, Ishii's, Toki's and Ito's buildings even though the themes and elements within or the surfaces in or in front are more important than the grid itself like in Ito's PMT Building for example (fig. 57).

"My intention is to destroy the realm of ordered imagery and to construct a more open, autonomous architecture,"*26 write Toyoo Ito – which almost sounds as if said by Aldo Rossi.*27 But the method and the consequent result in Japan is different from the one of the European contextualists. Namely, the Japanese do not intend – as it would indeed be a futile endeavor here – to decompose and abstract the urban environment then reconstruct it again to preserve or even extend the identical texture of the traditional, historical European city. In the volatile Japanese conditions, the new element becomes necessarily a part of the 'disordered order' either through a conscious intention which then often results in a superficial facade architecture or through an indifferent attitude which on the other hand often turns out to be a deliberate *anti-urban* approach as it is best seen with the conceptual and particularly with the hermeticist architects. But interestingly enough many architects' concern spans over both of them including Ito, Shin Toki, Minoru Takeyama the first real pop architect and again Isozaki.

Ito in his Houses at Nakano and a Kamiwada exploits the expressive quality of architectural surfaces or more precisely, by *fragmenting* them together with the interior spaces deprives them of conventional meanings and then jux-

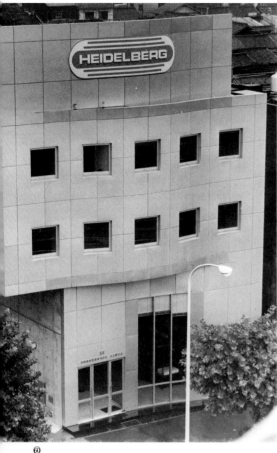

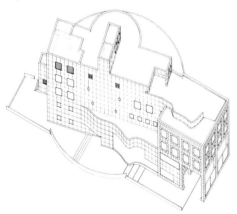

⑥⓪　PMTビル．（名古屋，1978年，設計：伊東豊雄）．
⑥①　神岡町役場の正面．（神岡町，1977年，設計：磯崎新）．
⑥②　三分割構成によるファサード建築．三和ビル．（1977年，設計：土岐新）．
⑥③　土岐邸．（柏市，1978年，設計：土岐新）．
⑥④　児玉邸．（東京，1979年，設計：石井和紘）．
⑥⑤　2番館．（東京，1970年，竹山実）．
⑥⑥　NEG大津工場厚生施設．（大津市，1980年，設計：磯崎新）．

60. *PMT Building*, Nagoya (1978. T. Ito).
61. *Kamioka Town Hall* front elevation (1977. A. Isozaki).
62. Facade architecture with a tripartite arrangement. *Sanwa Building*, Kikuchi (1977. S. Toki).
63. *House with an Independent Facade*, Kashiwa (1978. S. Toki).
64. *Kodama Residence*, Tokyo (1979. Kazuhiro Ishii).
65. *Niban-kan Building*, Tokyo (1970. Minoru Takeyama).
66. *Social Service Building of the Nihon Denki Glass Company*, Otsu City (1980. A. Isozaki).

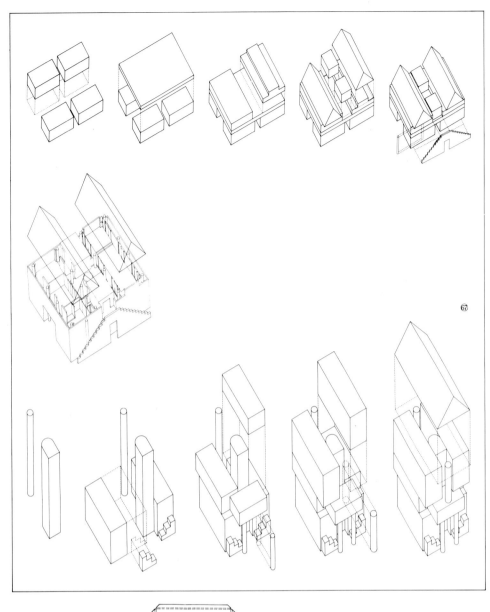

⑥⑦

⑥⑧

⑥⑦　積木の家1および2．空間構成を示す概念図．（設計：相田武文）．

⑥⑧　積木の家2．（横浜，1979年，設計：相田武文）．

⑥⑨　サイコロの家の起し絵図．（1973年，設計：相田武文）．

⑦⓪　54の窓（S診療所＋住居）．（平塚市，1975年，設計：石井和紘）．

⑦①　建部保育園（54の屋根）．（建部町，1977年，設計：石井和紘）．

⑦②　直島町民体育館，波状のコロネードをもつ正面．（直島町，1976年，設計：石井和紘）．

67. *Building Block Buildings 1 and 2* conceptual drawings of the spatial compositions (T. Aida).
68. *Building Block Building 2,* Yokohama (1979. T. Aida).
69. Okoshi-e drawing of the *House like a Die* (1973. T. Aida).
70. *House with 54 Windows,* Hiratsuka (1975. K. Ishii).
71. *Nursery School,* Takebe. The "54 Roofs" (1977. K. Ishii).
72. *Naoshima Gymnasium,* Naoshima with the undulating colonnade in front (1976. K. Ishii).

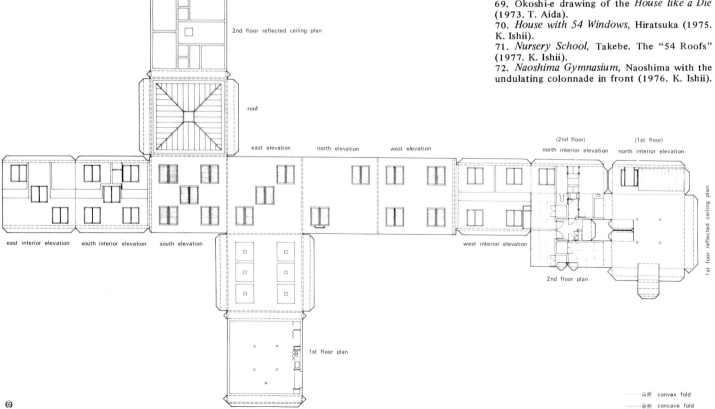

2nd floor reflected ceiling plan

roof

east elevation   north elevation   west elevation

(2nd floor)   (1st floor)
north interior elevation   north interior elevation

east interior elevation   south interior elevation   south elevation

west interior elevation

1st floor reflected ceiling plan

2nd floor plan

1st floor plan

⑥⑨

——— 山折 convex fold
······· 谷折 concave fold

⑦

⑦

⑦

る雰囲気をつくり出し，子供の世界により近い存在である．彼は，ある一つの秩序と一つの建築的要素を選び，その限定された規則のなかで，可能な限りの変化と意味をもて遊ぼうとする．住居と診療所の入った直交格子は，54の違った窓で内も外も色とりどりに埋められ，また同じ大きさの小さな箱のユニットが54の屋根——本当のものも見せかけのもある——を頭にのせて，おとぎ話の中の村のような保育園を造り出す．どちらの例も，歓喜の習作，あるいは音楽的エチュードと見なすことも妥当であろう⑦⑦．この嬉々とした雰囲気は直島中学校体育館のコロネードでは，「本当」の冗談となって，いくつかの柱を本来なら必要な個所から省いている⑫．技術や構造上の解決は，相田や石井の手にかかると，道具にとどまらず，おもちゃにされてしまう．

建築空間の中に安定し秩序を確立しようという強い意向は，ほとんどの人の指向に内在しているが，原広司と毛綱モン太の小さな住宅作品において，その極限を見ることができる．「住居は外界の混乱に対峙して，高度の秩序を発生しうる核をもつべきである」と原は書いている＊30．そのために，最近の彼の作品は徹底的に左右対称に計画されている．倉垣邸では，ややう

taposes them in a way wherein he creates a "syntax of space by collage which is peculiar to Japanese culture"*28 (figs. 58, 59). At the two houses this takes place within the interiors with hard, concrete boundaries but at the PMT Building, it takes the course of *superficiality* with the beautifully undulating aluminum skin departing the tectonic body of the small building. Then almost the same happens at several of Isozaki's buildings like the Kamioka Town Hall, where a part of the aluminum panel clad exterior becomes a false facade (figs. 60, 61). Shin Toki's and Kazuhiro Ishii's facade architecture in addition includes subtle references to Renaissance solutions, while Takeyama and Isozaki paint several of their buildings with overall pop supergraphics (figs. 62–66).

If Ito's main concern is to decompose and reconstruct spaces with surfaces, then Aida's might be the same with solid forms. At the Building Block Buildings 1 and 2, as their names refer, he extracts architectural – most especially Japanese – solutions into basic formal elements like the roof or the ridgepole-supporting pillar *(munamochibashira)* motifs of Shinto shrines and puts them together in a new context similar to the way children build whatever compositions from the

⑬ 倉垣邸. (東京, 1977年, 設計：原広司).

⑭ 同上, 聖所風の内部空間.

⑮, ⑯ 秋田邸. (東京, 1977年, 設計：原広司).

⑰ 建築化された陰陽シンボルをもつ住川邸. (釧路, 1975年,
設計：毛綱モン太).

⑱ 谷口邸. (和歌山, 1976年, 設計：毛綱モン太).

73-74. *Kuragaki House*, Tokyo (1977. Hiroshi
Hara). 74 — The sanctuary-like inner space.
75-76. *Akita House*, Oizumigakuen, Tokyo
(1977. H. Hara).
77. *House with an Architecturalized Ying-
Yang Symbol*, Kushiro (1975. Monta Mozuna).
Plans and isometric drawing.
78. *Constellation House*, Wakayama (1976. M.
Mozuna).

SECOND FLOOR PLAN

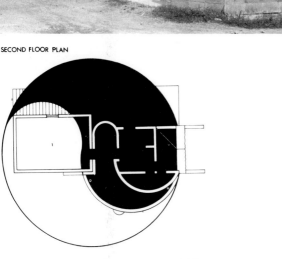

8 VOID
9 TERACE

FIRST FLOOR PLAN

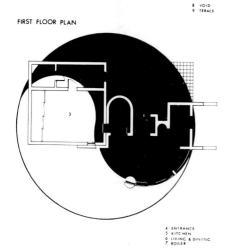

4 ENTRANCE
5 KITCHEN
6 LIVING & DINING
7 BOILER

BASEMENT FLOOR PLAN

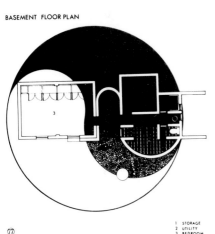

⑦

1 STORAGE
2 UTILITY
3 BEDROOM

⑦

same set of blocks (figs. 67, 68). This toy-like architecture appears again in other houses by Aida where the spatial conception is brought about by the old Japanese *okoshie* method according to which three-dimensional forms are created by laying out all the component surfaces into one joining pattern*[29] (fig. 69).

But while Aida's "toys" remain in the 'silence' of a transcendent world, Ishii's playful manner creates a happy, even joking atmosphere indeed, wherein his buildings are much closer to the world of the little ones. He picks an order and a certain architectural element, then tries to play with as many variations and find as many meanings possible of the theme within the limits of the selected regularity. The orthogonal grid of a small house and clinic is filled with 54 different windows both outside and inside in a colorful cavalcade, then the small box-like units with identical size are capped again with 54 real and false roofs to build a nursery school as some fairy tale village. Both of them could properly be regarded also as joyful exercises or musical etudes (figs. 70, 71). The happy mood turns into a 'real' joke when in the colonnade of the Naoshima Gymnasium he leaves off some of the columns unex-

pectedly, where their presence otherwise would be necessary (fig. 72). Technology and structural solution, in the hands of Aida and Ishii, become not only tools but also mere toys.

The strong endeavor to establish stability and order within architectural spaces, though inherent in practically all of the intentions, nowhere reaches such extremes as in Hiroshi Hara's and Monta Mozuna's tiny private houses. "The dwelling should possess a nucleus capable of generating a high degree of order in opposition to the external disorder," writes Hara*[30] and in order to reach this condition designs his recent buildings meticulously symmetrical. The ordinary and, like in the case of the Kuragaki House, somewhat shabby exterior corresponds with the cramped environment. Within these boundaries then he establishes a central space or better yet a flow of central spaces around which the rest of the house is organized. This space gives the impression of the interior of a highly sculptured cave, yet also serves as the "ordered exterior"; thus it looks as if the house was turned outside in, best exemplified by his own residence but also by the Awazu and Kuragaki Houses. In any case, upon entering these "sanctum-like"*[31] spaces,

⑦⑨

⑧⑩

⑧⑪

⑦⑨　鏡の間―代居邸.（東京近郊，1980年，設計：毛綱モン太）.
⑧⑩　同上，鏡の間の大木造階段.
⑧⑪　同上，鏡に映し出された階段.

79–81. *Mirror Image Hall*, Niiza near Tokyo (1980. M. Mozuna). 80 – The huge wooden stairway in the hall. 81 – Its reflection in the opposite mirror wall.

All photographs taken by the Author Botond Bognar.

らぶれたといってもいいありふれた外観は窮屈な内部と対応している．この限定された空間の中に彼は中心的空間というより，中心的空間の流れを設定して，そのまわりに残りの諸室を組織だてている．この中心空間は彫刻をされた洞窟の印象を与え，また一方では，「秩序ある」外部空間としての役割も与えられている．そのために，住居は裏表が逆転したようにみえる．これは自邸においてもっともよく表わされているが，粟津邸や倉垣邸にも見られる．いずれにせよ，このような「聖域」*31 的空間に入るとき，人は荘厳な宗教儀式の参列者のような感にひたる⑬→⑯．

一方，毛綱の場合は，秩序はコスモロジーの秩序となり，さらに彼自身の風変わりで難解な神秘主義がみられる．それゆえに，彼の作品では，すべてのものは日常的で合理的理由のためでなく，相対する宇宙的力の相互作用の結果として現出するのである．このことは，「建築化された陰陽の家（住川邸）」に直接的に表現されている⑰．このために，篠原，藤井，安藤の空間とは異なり，各々の要素は宇宙にその源を有し，存在理由を外から与えられている．星座の家は大熊座の星の形に従って７つの柱の位置を決めており，鏡の間は，彼の「双子建築」と神

道の信義に基づいて，鏡像のシンメトリーを小さな家に与えている．神道では，鏡は超自然の神の世界への窓と考え，また信仰の対象として祭られていた．「鏡像が宇宙の神秘を解く鍵である」と毛綱は書いている*32．これこそ，この驚くべき空間をもつ住居の裏にある考えを示している．建物の幅いっぱいの巨大な階段が空と星を目指して，反対の二層分の壁いっぱいの鏡に写し出されている．ここでは鏡にあけられた細い縦長の窓を通して，「知覚されない」外界を垣間見せることにより，現実と幻覚はさらに混ぜこぜにされ，この「小さな」空間の曖昧さをさらに強めている⑱→㉑．

まれに見る強い空間効果を得るために，日本の建築家は，とりわけコンセプチュアリスト・ミニマリストの作品によく示されるように，いくつかの機能的・快適性の要件をたびたび意識的に無視する．その一方で，最小限の要素，素材，簡素な形，そして何よりも日本的デザインの絶対的前提条件として存在する最小限の空間とによって，これを表現している．しかしながら，他では障害として受けとられるような，このような限られた状況をこれらの建築家は挑戦すべき課題として受けとめ，のり越え，やがて伝統

的包み込みの手法を通して興味深い作品の基礎に転換している．古来の日本の住宅や庭のように，意外な程の空間的イベント（現象）量と質を同様に多彩でかつ強い意味とともに提示している．

磯崎のマニエリスムであれ，槇のコンテクスチュアリズムであれ，安藤，藤井あるいは篠原の実存的なミニマリズム，伊東の分析的コラージュ，原の形而上学，毛綱の宇宙論，石井のおもちゃ的建築や相田の「沈黙」の建築であれ，これらの空間が我々をとらえるのは，空間の豊かさやあふれるばかりの快適さや，親しみやすい無理のない美しさではなく，触媒として，それは多くの場合意識的に挑発的なものであるが，これらの作品も我々もともに物理的実体以上のものであり，より崇高であると感じさせ信じさせるその力である．このことにおいて，これらは息を呑み目を見張るばかりである．

（訳：日野水　信）

註
1　C.N.シュルツは，著書『実存，空間，建築』において，西洋の空間概念が後のヨーロッパの哲学者より古代ギリシヤの多様で合理的な解釈に，いかに深く長く根ざしているかを適確に述べている．レウキッポスは「空間は物体としての存在はないが実体である」と考えた．プラトンやユークリッドそしてデ

one feels like becoming a participant in some kind of solemn religious ritual (figs. 73–76).

On the other hand, with Mozuna order becomes the order of *cosmology* wrapped also in his idiosyncratic, deep mysticism. Therefore in his architecture everything happens as the result of the interplay between the different opposing cosmic forces — illustrated directly by the House with Architecturalized *Ying-Yang* Symbols — and not for some mundane and rational reasons (fig. 77). Consequently, unlike in Shinohara's, Fujii's and Ando's spaces, here every element obtains its 'raison d'etre' and meaning from outside, being rooted in the skies. The Constellation House for example was designed according to the start formation of the Big Bear with the seven columns of the house, then the Mirror Image Hall along his philosophy of "twin architecture" and the Shinto mythology features a small private house with mirror symmetry. Shinto believed that mirrors were windows to another, a transcendental world of *kami* and as a symbol and an object of worship was placed at times in shrines. Mozuna writes: "The image of the mirror is the key to the secrets of the cosmos."*32 This gives the idea behind the extra-ordinary space of this House where a huge stairway in the total width of the building seeking towards the stars and sky is reflected in the huge mirror covering the entire two storey high wall on the opposite side. Reality and illusion are mixed also by the narrow slot-window cutting through the middle of the mirror vertically with an "unnoticed" glimpse of the outer world, enhancing further the ambiguous quality of the 'tiny' space (figs. 78–81).

To achieve the unusually strong spatial effects, Japanese architects often and obviously disregard several functional or comfort aspects as best protrayed by the architecture of the conceptual minimalist, yet usually rely on a minimum number of elements, materials, austere forms and most especially on a *minimum amount of space,* an existing absolute pre-condition for any Japanese design. However, exactly this — anywhere else a handicap — tightly limited condition is what these architects take as a challenge, cope with it and eventually turn it into the basis of their exciting compositions through the traditional method of *packaging.* Just like the old Japanese houses and gardens, these recent buildings too present an unexpected amount and quality of spatial event (phenomenon) together with the equally varied but strong meanings.

These Japanese spaces — might they be in Isozaki's mannerist, Maki's contextual, Ando's, Fujii's or Shinohara's existential, minimal, Ito's fragmented collage, Hara's metaphysical, Mozuna's cosmological, Ishii's toy-like architecture or in Aida's architecture of 'silence' etc. — impress us definitely not with their spaciousness, overwhelming comfort and a populist, effortless beauty, but with their ability and many times intentionally provocative quality as catalysts, to make us feel and believe that they, and we too, are much more or sublime, something different from what only the physical reality stands for. And in so doing, they are truly breath-taking.

Notes
1. Christian Norberg Schulz in his book *Existence, Space and Architecture* (Praeger Paperbacks, London and New York, 1971) describes very precisely how far and how long Western conception of space was and, in many respects, still is rooted in the different though rational interpretations of the ancient Greek then later other European philosophers. Leucippos for example "considered space a reality, though it has no bodily existence." Plato, Eculides and then Descartes relied on elaborate geometries, as the science of space, even Kant

カルトは，空間の科学として複雑な幾何学に頼り，カントでさえ「空間は物質とは別の独立した人間の認識の範疇と考えた」（同書 9〜10頁）．アインシュタインの相対性理論とともに変化がもたらされた．最近になって空間は物理的実体としてだけでなく，認識の分野においても把えられるようになった．

2　イサム・ノグチに関する章よりの引用（アンドレ・コルドズ著『Living Architecture : Japanese』．

3　アルバード・ホッフシュタッター編『詩・言葉・思想』よりの引用．

4　このような建築物を移築・再建する風習は，現在でも最も神聖とされる伊勢神宮で見られる．20年毎に遷宮が隣り合った敷地を交互に使うことによって行われる．最近では1974年に行われた．

5　神道においては，この世の現象すべてに霊（精神性）があり，日本語では「カミ」と呼ぶ．他に適切な言葉がないので英語のGodと訳した．

6　磯崎新のクーパー・ヒューイット美術館での「日本の時─空間───間」展の中の一節．邦訳は『ジャパン・インテリア』，1979年1月号，61〜74頁参照．

7　奥は，最も内なるもの，最も手の届かないもの，深いまたは奥深いなどの意味がある．このユニークな概念によって，日本人は，庭であれ，建築であれ，都市空間であれ，その実際の狭さとは無関係に空間に奥行きと神秘性を与えることができた．

8　間は直訳すると部屋または空間の意味であるが，間接的に時─空間の次元を示してもいる．この意味合いでは，岩波古語辞典によれば，「連続して存在する物と物との間に当然存在する間隔の意」または「時間に用いれば連続して生起する現象に当然存在する休止の時間間隔」となる．

9　伝統的な日本の版画や絵画においては，パースペクティヴの法則は形においても色においても光と影の効果と同じく，絶えず無視される．

10　1981年中に刊行予定の筆者の著書『日本建築の挑戦』，63頁参照．

11　メタボリズムという言葉は，新陳代謝の過程，生体の変成を意味する．即ち，自然における変化の過程である．

12　C.N.シュルツによる近著『Genius Loci : Towards a Phenomenology of Architecture』の題名でもある．

13　クリス・フォーセットが正しく指摘するように，「日本の家の存在論的状態は『イエ』の『イ』が『生きる』ことを意味するにとどまらず，『居る』ことをも意味するという事実の中に見い出すことができる．それゆえ，家は，人の実存，人の世界内存在と強く結びつけられる」．『G. A. Houses』，No. 4「日本の現代住宅」，1978年，32頁．

14　日本の都市環境の密度は実際想像を絶するものがある．絶え間なく忙しい生活は，住人にスリルと興奮と楽しみを与えるだけでなく，結果として，過大な交通量騒音や空気の汚染は視覚的な極端接近と相まって，住居の最も私的な領域をも侵している．このため，実存が乱されるのである．

15　相田武文は自らの建築を沈黙の建築と呼ぶ──「沈黙」（『日本建築の新しい波』，ニューヨーク，1978年．『新建築』，10・11月号，1977年，1頁）．

16　安藤忠雄「空間と人間の新しい関係」（『新建築』，10・11月号，1977年，44頁）．

17　ジョナサン・ゲイル「安藤忠雄の建築」（Architectural Design，1981年，1頁）．

18　ボトンド・ボグナール「磯崎新にみるマナリズムのタイポロジー，あるいはハンプティダンプティの構成手法」．

19　藤井博巳「実存建築と幾何学の役割」（『日本建築の新しい波』，29頁）．

20　ピーター・バッカナン「冷静さと何げなさ」（Architectural Review，11月号，1980年，311頁）．

21　マイケル・フランクリン=ロスは槙文彦を引き合いに出して述べている（『メタボリズムを越えて：新しい日本の建築』，マグロウヒル出版社，ニューヨーク，1978年，32頁）．

22　安藤忠雄「記憶の系図と他空間の黙示」（『日本建築の新しい波』，20頁）．

23　註19参照．

24　「私は空間によって永遠を刻みたい」と篠原一男は述べている（『新建築』，3月号，1979年，47頁）．

25　註18参照．

26　伊東豊雄「建築のコラージュと皮相」（『日本建築の新しい波』，68，69頁）．

27　アルド・ロッシは「自律の建築」についても述べている（アルド・ロッシ著『都市の建築』，1966年，69年）．

28　註26（69頁）参照．

29　この日本的描法は，子供が紙に書いた面を切り抜いて，折って糊づけしていろいろな立体をつくる方法に似ている．また，日本の空間概念の二次元的資質とも対応している．註8も参照．

30　原広司「反伝統的な建築装置」（『日本建築の新しい波』，39頁）．

31　ケネス・フランプトン「日本の新しい波」（『日本建築の新しい波』，7頁）．

32　毛綱モン太「宇宙建築の理論」（『日本建築の新しい波』，80頁）．

"regarded space as a basic *a priori* category of human understanding different from and independent of matter." (p. 9—10) Change has come with Einstein's theory of relativity and as a result only very recently has space been regarded not only as physical entity but also as the field of perception.

2. Quotation of Noguchi by Andre Corboz in Modern Architecture and Japanese Tradition in Tomoya Masuda, *Living Architecture: Japanese,* Grosset and Dunlap, New York, 1970, p. 3.

3. Martin Heidegger: "Language" in *Poetry, Language, Thought.* Edited by Albert Hofstadter, New York, 1971, p. 154.

4. This custom of rebuilding, relocating architectural pieces is still observed in fact, though only in the case of the most important Ise Shrine, which is reconstructed regularly once in twenty years alternating the two sites beside each other. The last of such reconstruction took place in 1974.

5. In the Shinto mythology every phenomenon in the world has a spirit (spirituality) called *Kami* in Japanese and, for lack of something better, translated as god into English.

6. Arata Isozaki: "Space-Time in Japan — MA" in *MA Space-Time in Japan* catalogue for the exhibition of MAN transforms in the Cooper-Hewitt Museum within the events of the Japan Today Festival sponsored by the Japan Society, Inc., Meridian House International, and the Smithsonian Resident Associate Program, New York, p. 13.

7. *Oku* means the innermost, the least accessible, deep and extending far back. With this unique concept the Japanese have always been able to give a sense of depth and mysterious (ambiguous) quality to their spaces might they be garden, architectural or urban spaces even if they were physically small and shallow.

8. *Ma* has a literary meaning of space or room yet indirectly as the sense of the continuous space-time dimension, has multiple meanings such as "the natural distance between two or more things existing in continuity" or "the natural pause or interval between two or more phenomena occurring continuously" according to the Iwanami's *Dictionary of Ancient Terms.*

9. On traditional Japanese etchings and paintings the rules of perspective both in form and color just as the effects of light and shade are consistently disregarded.

10. Botond Bognar: *The Challenge of Japanese Architecture,* Academy Editions, London, (to be published later in) 1981, p. 63.

11. The word metabolism refers to the metabolic process, the metamorphosis of living organisms, that is, the natural process of change.

12. Also the title of Christian Norberg Schulz's latest book: *Genius Loci: Towards a Phenomenology of Architecture,* Rizzoli International Publications, Inc., New York, 1980.

13. As Chris Fawcett correctly explains: "The ontological status of the Japanese house . . . can be found in the fact that the root 'i' in *'ie'* (house) denotes not only 'to live' but also 'to be' — hence the house is very much bound up with one's existence, with one's being-in-the-world." Chris Fawcett: "Do We Live to Build or Build to Live? . . . Toward an Ontology of the New Japanese House" in *GA (Global Architect) Houses,* No. 4, 1978, p. 32.

14. The density of the Japanese urban settings is indeed beyond imagination where the constantly bustling life not only offers thrill, excitement and pleasure for the citizens, but with the resulting traffic, noise and air pollution plus the close visual proximity also intrudes their innermost privacy of the home, i.e. disturbs their existence.

15. Takefumi Aida calls his works the "architecture of silence." "Silence" in *A New Wave of Japanese Architecture,* IAUS, New York, 1978, p. 14; also in "Silence" in *The Japan Architect,* October—November, 1978, p. 52.

16. Tadao Ando: "New Relations Between the Space and the Person" in *The Japan Architect,* October—November, 1977, p. 44.

17. Jonathan Gale: "Tadao Ando's Architecture" an article to be published in *Architectural Design* later this year. The manuscript is at my disposal, p. 1.

18. Botond Bognar: "Typology of Arata Isozaki's Mannerism or How to Put Humpty-Dumpty Together Again." Manuscript of an essay to be published later, p. 16.

19. Hiromi Fujii: "Existential Architecture and the Role of Geometry" in *A New Wave of Japanese Architecture,* p. 29.

20. Peter Buchanan: "The Cool and the Casual" in *Architectural Review,* November 1980, p. 311.

21. Michael Franklin-Ross quotes Fumihiko Maki in *Beyond Metabolism: The New Japanese Architecture,* Architectural Record, McGraw-Hill Publication, New York, 1978, p. 32.

22. Tadao Ando: "The Genealogy of Memories and the Revelation of Another Scape" in *A New Wave of Japanese Architecture,* p. 20.

23. See Note 19.

24. "I want to carve out eternity in spaces", as he writes in Kazuo Shinohara: "The Savage Machine as an Exercise" in *The Japan Architect,* March 1979, p. 47.

25. See Note 18.

26. Toyoo Ito: "Collage and Superficiality in Architecture" in *A New Wave of Japanese Architecture,* pp. 68—69.

27. Aldo Rossi also talks about an "autonomous architecture" in his book *L'Architectura della Citta* (The Architecture of the City) 1966, 1969.

28. See Note 26. p. 69.

29. This traditional Japanese drawing method is similar again to the way children make different geometrical solids by cutting the connecting surfaces out of paper, then fold and glue them together, and also corresponds to the "two dimensional" quality of their space conceptions. See also Note 8.

30. Hiroshi Hara: "Anti-Traditional Architectural Contrivance" in *A New Wave of Japanese Architecture,* p. 39.

31. Kenneth Frampton: "The Japanese New Wave" in *A New Wave of Japanese Architecture,* p. 7.

32. Monta Mozuna: "Theory of the Cosmic Architecture" in *A New Wave of Japanese Architecture,* p. 80.

FURTHER READING

参考文献

A Guide to Japanese Architecture, Japan Architect.

Ashihara, Yoshinobu. *Exterior Design in Architecture,* Van Nostrand Reinhold Co., New York, 1970.

Beardsley, R.K., Hall, J.W., Ward, R.E. *Village Japan,* University of Chicago Press, 1959.

Benedict, Ruth. *The Chrysanthemum and the Sword,* Charles E. Tuttle Co. Inc., Tokyo, 1973.

Blaser, Werner. *Temple and Tea-House in Japan,* New York, 1957.

Borson, Richard M. ed. *Studies in Japanese Folklore,* Kennikat Press, 1963.

Conder, Josiah. *Landscape Gardening in Japan,* Kelly & Walsh, Tokyo, 1893.

Critchlow, Keith. "NIIKE: The Siting of a Japanese Rural House", in *Shelter, Sign and Symbol* by Oliver, Paul (ed.), The Overlook Press, Woodstock, New York, 1977.

Drexler, Arthur. *The Architecurre of Japan,* The Museum of Modern Art, New York, 1955.

Engel, David E. *Japanese Gardens for Today,* Rutland & Tokyo, 1959.

Engel, Heinrich. "The Japanese House", *A Tradition for Contemporary Architecture,* Charles Tuttle Co., Ruthland, Vermont, Tokyo, 1964.

Erskine, William Hugh. *Japanese Festival and Calendar Lore,* Kyo-bun kwan, Tokyo, 1933.

Frank, B. *Kata-imi et Kata-tagae: Etude sur les Interdits de direction a'l epoque Heian,* IN Bulletin de la Maison Franco-Japonaise, NS, Vol. 5, Nos. 2-4, Tokyo, 1958, (Kata-imi and Kata-tagae: A Study of Directional Prohibitions in the Heian Period, tr. into English: Nitschke, Gunter).

Fukuyama, Toshio. "Heian Temples: Byodo-in and Chuson-ji," Vol. 9 of the *Heibonsha Survey of Japanese Art,* Weatherhill/Heibonsha, New York, Tokyo, 1976.

Furuta, Shokin. "The Philosophy of the Chashitsu", in *Japan Architect,* 1964, in eight installments.

Gropius, Walter. *Scope of Total Architecture,* New York, 1953.

Grinnell Cleaver, Charles. *Japanese and Americans: Cultural Parallels and Paradoxes,* Charles E. Tuttle Co., Tokyo, 1978.

Gulick, Sidney L. *Evolution of the Japanese,* London, 1903.

Harada, Jiro. *Japanese Gardens,* Charles T. Branford Comp., Boston, 1956.

Haussy, Martine et Arisawa Makoto. Le "Sakuteiki" Illustre ou la *Composition des Jardins Japonais,* Ichiyosha, Osaka, 1978.

Hayakawa, Masao. "The Garden Art of Japan", Vol. 28 of the *Heibonsha Survey of Japanese Art,* Weatherhill/Heibonsha, Tokyo, New York, 1972.

Heibonsha Survey of Japanese Art, Weatherhill/Heibonsha, Tokyo, New York, 1976.

Hirai, Kiyosi. *Feudal Architecture of Japan,* Weatherhill/Heibonsha, Tokyo 1973.

Hoover Thomas. *Zen Culture,* Vintage Books Ed., 1977.

Horiguchi, Sutemi. *Tradition of Japanese Gardens,* KBS, Tokyo, 1962.

Humphreys, Christmas. *Buddhism,* London, 1954.

Itoh, Teiji and Futagawa, Yukio. *The Essential Japanese House,* John Weatherhill, Inc., Tokyo, 1962.

Itoh, Teiji. *The Elegant Japanese House*—Trad. Sukiya Architecture, Walker/Weatherhill, New York, 1969.

Itoh, Teiji. *The Japanese Garden*—An Approach to Nature, Yale Univ. Press, New Haven, 1972.

Itoh, Teiji. *Traditional Domestic Architecture of Japan,* Weatherhill/Heibonsha, Tokyo, New York, 1972.

Itoh, Teiji. *Space and Illusion in the Jap. Garden,* Weatherhill, New York, 1973.

Itoh, Teiji. *Kura-Design and Tradition of the Japanese Storehouse,* Kodansha International, Tokyo, 1973.

Itoh, Teiji and Futagawa, Yukio. *The Classic Tradition in Japanese Architecture,* Tokyo.

Japan Architect. "Nature, Space and Japanese Architectural Style," in June 1964.

Japan Architect. "Villages and Festivals" — Design Survey Series No. 1 to 6, in January to June 1973.

Japanese Architecture: Guide to East Japan.

Japanese Architecture: Guide to West Japan.
Japanese Architects Association, Publication Bureau of Asahi Shinbun, Tokyo.

Kirby, John B. Jr. *From Castle to Teahouse: Japanese Architecture of the Momoyama Period.*

Kubo, Tadashi. "Saku-tei-ki", *An Oldest Note of Secrets on Japanese Gardens,* Bulletin of Osaka Prefectural University, Series B, Vo. 6, 1956.

Kuck, Loraine E. *The Art of Japanese Gardens,* John Day Company, New York 1940.

Morse, Edward S. *Japanese Homes and their Surroundings,* Dover Publications, 1961; C.E. Tuttle Co., Tokyo, 1976.

Mirei, Shigemori. *Gardens of Japan,* Nissha Printing Co., Ltd., Kyoto, 1949.

Mirei, Shigemori. *Artistic Gardens of Japan,* 3 Volumes, Riko Tosho, Tokyo, 1957.

Naito, Akira. *Katsura, a princely retreat,* Kodansha International, 1977.

Nakane, Chie. *Japanese Society,* University of California Press, 1973.

Nishihara, Kiyoyuki. *Japanese Houses: Patterns for Living,* Trans. by R.L. Gage, Japan Publications Ltd., Tokyo, 1968.

Nishiyama, Uzo. "Japanese Houses", in *Japan Architect.*

Nitschke, Gunter. "Prozess-Planung, erlaeutert am Beispiel eines Japanischen Fischerdorfes", in *Baumeister* No. 8, August, 1967.

Nitschke, Gunter. "Sand-Rock-Water", A Typology of Japanese Gardens, in *Kyoto Monthly Guide,* December, 1969.

Nitschke, Gunter. "Shime: Binding/Unbinding", *AD* 12, 1974.

Nitschke, Gunter. "Ma, The Japanese Sense of Place" *AD.*

Ota, Hirotaro. *Japanese Architecture and Gardens,* Kokusai Bunka Shinkokai, Tokyo, 1966.

Okawa, Naomi. *Edo Architecture: Katsura and Nikko,* Weatherhill/Heibonsha, Tokyo, 1975.

Paine and Soper. *The Art and Architecture of Japan.*

Ramberg, Walter Dodd. Some Aspects of Japanese Architecture", in *Perspecta* The Yale Architectural Journal.

Rudofsky, Bernard. *The Kimono Mind,* C.E. Tuttle Co. Inc., Tokyo, 1973.

Saito, Katsuo and Wada, Sadaji. *Magic of Trees & Stones* — Secrets of Japanese Gardening, Japan Publications Trading Company, Tokyo, 1964.

Saito, Katsuo. *Designing Japanese Gardens,* Gihodo Co., Tokyo, 1961.

Seike, Kiyosi. *The Art of Japanese Joinery,* Weatherhill/Tankosha, 1977.

Seike, Kiyosi. *A Japanese Touch for your Garden,* Kodansha International, Tokyo, 1980.

Shigemori, Mirei. *Measured Drawings of Japanese Gardens.*

Shimoyama, Shigemaru (tr.). *Sakuteiki* — The Book of Garden, Town & City Planners, Inc., Tokyo, 1976.

Shinohara, Kazuo. *Kazuo Shinohara 16 Houses & Architectural Theory,* Bijutsu Shuppansha, Tokyo, 1971.

Suzuki, Daisetus T. *Zen and Japanese Culture,* Routleage and Kegon Pavi, London, 1959, Princeton University Press, 1973.

Tamura, Tsuyoshi. *The Art of Landscape Garden in Japan,* KBS, Tokyo, 1953.

Tange, Kenzo and Kawazoe, Noboru. *Ise, Prototype of Japanese Architecture,* The M.I.T. Press, Cambridge, 1965.

Taut, Bruno. *Houses and People of Japan,* Sanseido Co., Tokyo, 1937, 1958.

Thiel, Philip. *The Problem of Sequential Connectedness in the Urban Environment,* Urban Planning/Development Series, No. 1, University of Washington.

Thiel, Philip. *Visual Awareness and Design,* University of Washington Press, Seattle, 1981.

Yoshida, Tetsuro. *Gardens of Japan,* Praeger, New York, 1957.

Yoshida, Tetsuro. *The Japanese House and Garden,* Praeger, New York, 1969.

Watanabe, Yasutada. *Shinto Art: Ise and Izumo Shrines,* Weatherhill/Heibonsha, Tokyo, 1974.

LOCATION MAP
所在地地図

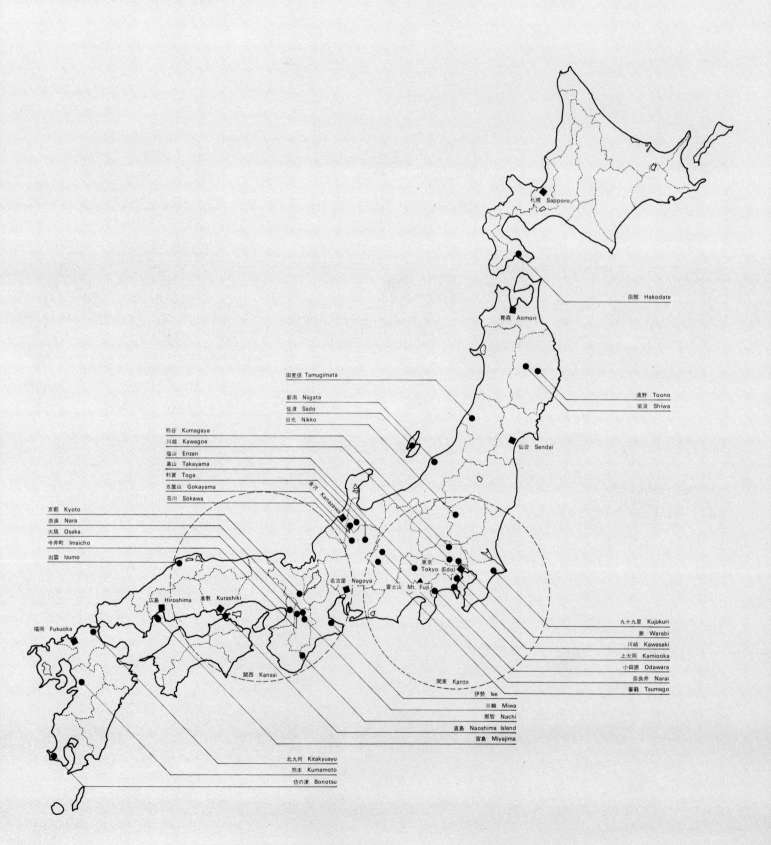

札幌 Sapporo

函館 Hakodate

青森 Aomori

田麦俣 Tamugimata

新潟 Niigata
佐渡 Sado
日光 Nikko

遠野 Toono
紫波 Shiwa

熊谷 Kumagaya
川越 Kawagoe
塩山 Enzan
高山 Takayama
利賀 Toga
五箇山 Gokayama
荘川 Sōkawa

仙台 Sendai

金沢 Kanazawa

京都 Kyoto
奈良 Nara
大阪 Osaka
今井町 Imaicho
出雲 Izumo

東京 Tokyo (Edo)

名古屋 Nagoya

富士山 Mt. Fuji

広島 Hiroshima
倉敷 Kurashiki

九十九里 Kujūkuri
蕨 Warabi
川崎 Kawasaki
上大岡 Kamiooka
小田原 Odawara
奈良井 Narai
妻籠 Tsumago

福岡 Fukuoka

関西 Kansai

関東 Kanto

伊勢 Ise
三輪 Miwa
那智 Nachi
直島 Naoshima Island
宮島 Miyajima

北九州 Kitakyusyu
熊本 Kumamoto
坊の津 Bonotsu